Whistling in the Dark

Whistling

in the Dark

Memory and Culture in Wartime London

Jean R. Freedman

THE UNIVERSITY PRESS OF KENTUCKY

Publication of this volume was made possible in part
by a grant from the National Endowment for the Humanities.

Scholarly publisher for the Commonwealth,
serving Bellarmine College, Berea College, Centre
College of Kentucky, Eastern Kentucky University,
The Filson Club Historical Society, Georgetown College,
Kentucky Historical Society, Kentucky State University,
Morehead State University, Murray State University,
Northern Kentucky University, Transylvania University,
University of Kentucky, University of Louisville,
and Western Kentucky University.

Editorial and Sales Offices: The University Press of Kentucky
663 South Limestone Street, Lexington, Kentucky 40508-4008

03 02 01 00 99   5 4 3 2 1

Library of Congress Cataloging-in-Publication Data
Freedman, Jean R. (Jean Rose)
     Whistling in the dark : memory and culture in wartime London /
Jean R. Freedman.
          p.   cm.
     Includes bibliographical references and index.
     ISBN 0-8131-2076-4 (cloth : alk. paper)
     1. World War, 1939-1945—England—London.   2. World War,
1939-1945—Personal narratives, British.   3. London (England)—
History—1800-1950.   I. Title.
     D760.L7F74   1998
     940.53′421′0922—dc21   98-27439

This book is printed on acid-free recycled paper meeting
the requirements of the American National Standard
for Permanence of Paper for Printed Library Materials.

Manufactured in the United States of America

To my parents,
Myrle Neistadt Freedman and Leon David Freedman,
and to the memory of George Wagner

We are all going to have whistles as Mr. Bendall thinks if we are buried, it will be so useful to whistle to our rescuers. This I consider quite useful, and if buried shall whistle with all my might.
                    —*From the diary of Vere Hodgson, 28 February 1944*

Before he can open the door, we hear a high pitched whistling, rushing noise, and we know it's close. There's an explosion and one hell of a draught, as if someone has left all the doors open. We are both still standing, and Eddie has the door handle in his fist, but the door has gone away. "It blew out of me hand." He sounded offended.
                    —*From the diary of William Bernard Regan, Christmas 1940*

Contents

Illustrations follow page 106

Acknowledgments

A book is a collaborative endeavor, born in the mind and nurtured by readers, writers, scholars, editors, and communities of people, both living and dead. When the book is ready to face the world on its own, it is important for the author to thank those who have contributed to its growth. My first thanks go to the people of London—those who took the time to speak with me during the course of my research, those whom I met through books and archival documents, and the unknown many who kept London going during World War II. I owe a particular debt of gratitude to the people whom I interviewed during the course of my fieldwork. The men and women who shared their experiences of wartime London gave me friendship as well as information, and their presence gives an immediacy to my work. Their words and their memories show that the past still lives within the present.

This book began as a doctoral dissertation at Indiana University. Warm thanks go to my dissertation director, Ruth M. Stone, and to the members of my dissertation committee, Richard Bauman, John Bodnar, and Henry Glassie. Thanks are also due to Sandra Dolby and Roger Janelli, whose seminars allowed me to explore aspects of this research at an earlier date. Special thanks go to Harry Geduld, who allowed me access to his personal library with its fine documentation of wartime London and who shared his own memories of that era.

Scholars from around the world have also been generous with their time. Alice Prochaska and Elizabeth Russell provided a wealth of useful information during my preliminary field trip to London in 1991. David Edgerton and Keith Robbins sent me copies of their publications, which have great relevance and interest for my own work. Alessandro Portelli wrote me a detailed and encouraging letter in response to questions that I had while in the field. Venetia Newall had many helpful suggestions for my research and shared her own experience as a folklorist in London.

Many organizations helped me in the course of my research. The London Goodenough Trust provided the optimum place for a foreign scholar to live in

London. The archivists and curators of the Imperial War Museum, the London Museum of Jewish Life, the National Film Archive, the National Sound Archive, and the Public Record Office at Kew were infinitely patient and helpful in finding the massive amounts of information that I needed. In addition, Rickie Burman of the London Museum of Jewish Life and Joy Price of the Grange Museum introduced me to many people who remembered and told me about wartime London. The Institute of Historical Research provided me with a library, the opportunity to meet other scholars, and a very stimulating series of seminars. The Folklore Society gave me the opportunity to meet and share ideas with British folklorists. Thanks also to the British Broadcasting Corporation (BBC) for their splendid documentation of the war years and for their help with information of various kinds.

Funding for my fieldwork was provided by a dissertation year fellowship from the Indiana University Graduate School and a graduate student research fellowship from the Indiana Center on Global Change and World Peace. A Mellon doctoral dissertation write-up fellowship, administered through the Indiana University Department of West European Studies, financed the final year of writing. I would like to gratefully acknowledge all of these funding sources.

Copyright holders have been extremely generous in granting me permission to quote from published, broadcasted, and archival sources. For permission to quote from unpublished papers located in the Imperial War Museum, I would like to thank the copyright holders for the papers of George and Helena Britton, Oswald Edwards, Vere Hodgson, Josephine Oakman, William Bernard Regan and Violet Ivy Regan, and Len Waller. The Public Record Office at Kew allowed me access to a variety of documents, which are listed separately in the references section. Crown copyright material in the Public Record Office is reproduced by permission of the Controller of Her Majesty's Stationery Office. April Young Limited, agent for the late Ted Kavanagh, has kindly allowed me to quote from four wartime "ITMA" programs written by Mr. Kavanagh. These programs are listed separately in the references section. Two wartime broadcasts by the late J.B. Priestley ("Postscript to the News: The Epic of Dunkirk," broadcast on 5 June 1940, and "Journey into Daylight," broadcast on 11 May 1945) are reprinted by permission of the Peters Fraser and Dunlop Group, Ltd.

At the University Press of Kentucky, I have been privileged to work with a staff blessed with talent, patience, and a sense of humor. My thanks to them all. Thanks also to Leslee Anderson for her sterling job of copyediting the manuscript. The anonymous referees who recommended this work for publication made useful and insightful comments that have greatly benefitted the text.

Friends on both sides of the Atlantic helped in numerous ways. I have benefitted from conversations with, among others, Harris M. Berger, Donald Braid,

Giovanna Del Negro, Michael Golberg, Sally Hunt, Doreen Helen Klassen, Bertha Klempman, Jennifer Livesay, Lisa A. McNee, Judith S. Neulander, Kenneth D. Pimple, Jill Terry Rudy, and Clover Williams. Very special thanks to Jessica Bolker, who read and commented on a copy of the entire manuscript and whose interest in my project has been unflagging. Special thanks also to Shoshana Keller, who showed me wonderful articles that I might otherwise have overlooked, and to Gunde M. Iwersen, who helped translate a wartime broadcast that was at least six generations removed from the original.

Very special thanks go to my family, who have listened with patience and interest as this project grew and changed during the past decade. My brother, Carl Freedman, read and commented on parts of this manuscript, and contributed invaluable insights into British culture and literary theory. My parents, Myrle and Leon Freedman, have been a consistent source of encouragement, support, and love. Their stories of the war years are the original source of my interest in World War II. In addition, my mother read and commented on an entire draft of the manuscript. Finally, the warmest thanks go to my husband, Jonathan D. Pollock, whose love, encouragement, and staunch good humor have filled my life with a world of sunshine.

1

Introduction

"You are very much older than I am," said Winston. "You must have been a grown man before I was born. You can remember what it was like in the old days, before the Revolution. People of my age don't really know anything about those times. We can only read about them in books, and what it says in the books may not be true. I should like your opinion on that."
—George Orwell, *1984*

Winston Smith gave up too easily. In the same city where he found a man's memories to be only "a rubbish heap of details," I found a great deal more. My interviewees were conscious and intelligent witnesses to history. Over countless cups of tea in sitting rooms, senior citizens' centers, churches, and synagogues, they shared thoughts, ideas, and experiences; they allowed me to question and tape-record their lives. This is as close as we can get to the past; no museum reconstruction, no Cecil B. DeMille film, no fake verisimilitude can render history more truly than the words of those who were there. They may have forgotten, they may have misunderstood, and they may have confused their experience with the experiences of others, but they are, indelibly and unshakably, witnesses to the past. I have sifted and compared their memories with other forms of testimony in order to gain a more nuanced picture of life in wartime London and to pose the question, "How does the standard image of wartime London match with memory and experience?"

This book is a study of London during World War II. More precisely, it is a study of representations of wartime London. Few historical images remain more evocative: wartime London is consistently portrayed as a place of courage, humor, unity, and defiance, an island of warmth and civilization threatened by the cruelty and barbarism of Nazism. The building blocks of this picture include visual images (photographs of shelterers singing and pouring tea while bombs rained outside or the unscathed, ghostly outline of St. Paul's amid the wreckage of the East End), musical celebrations ("London pride is a flower that's free"),[1] personal stories, and political oratory. My research will focus on the ways that speech, narrative, and music helped to develop this image during wartime and to retain it in memory. This image is the standard by which postwar Britain is measured, for it is the image of the "finest hour."

Since the 1960s, scholars have begun to chip away at this image, to investigate incidents in which Londoners were neither brave nor unified, and to point out that the "finest hour" lasted nearly six years. Yet the image remains powerful, especially to the generation that actually experienced wartime London. Politicians of virtually all political stripes have invoked this era as an Eden from which the present has slipped; they pick and choose amid wartime attributes to find ones that support present-day political movements. As an era that combined modified socialism with unquestioning patriotism, wartime can provide political sustenance for an extremely broad range; the fact that it continues to do so, more than fifty years after the end of the war, is a remarkable phenomenon.

Debates about "what really happened" in wartime London are legion. In a way, these debates are unresolvable, because wartime London was not, in current fashionable parlance, a "moment." The finest hour lasted for years and involved millions of people. Many descriptions of wartime London are simultaneously true and false; during wartime, unity coexisted with selfishness, courage with cowardice, humor with fear. At the same time, the power of wartime images remains too pervasive for us to be able to treat them simply as propaganda ploys. The contradictions surrounding wartime London cannot be adequately explained away by attributing all inconsistencies to faulty memory or wartime censorship. Some memories are, of course, incorrect; some facts were concealed by government censors. But the consistent strength of wartime images demands a better explanation.

Books about wartime Britain are many, yet several curious gaps remain in the scholarly literature. Though memories of wartime are very much alive in Britain— and hence are a constant subtext to written material about this era—there has been little attempt by scholars to tap this rich source of information. Likewise, there have been few serious treatments of the phenomenon of wartime memory. The few that do exist treat memory with derision and condemnation and consider it of little value as a scholarly resource.[2] Despite a wealth of available materials, scholars of wartime Britain have been extremely chary of the use of oral and memory-based sources and have often treated the witnesses of this era as the chief obstructions to a clear view of it.[3] In *The Cheese and the Worms*, Carlo Ginzburg laments the fact that he cannot talk with sixteenth-century peasants, yet many historians who *can* talk with wartime Londoners try to avoid them. Whereas Ginzburg saw the written records of sixteenth-century Europe as biased, indirect, and partial representations of people's lives, historians of wartime Britain tend to exhibit a bewildering faith in equally fallible documents. The few existing oral histories of wartime Britain are essentially popular works, with scant contextual information and virtually no analysis. Even the best of them tend to be modified transcripts appended to headnotes or overly simplified narratives laced with quotations.[4] When one considers the splendid oral histories that focus on Italy and Germany during the same period, the lack of similar scholarly attention to Britain becomes especially puzzling.[5] Because World War II is so well-documented and because so many witnesses to that era are still alive, a golden opportunity exists to explore the dialectic between wartime documents and postwar memory, between oral and written artifacts, between the voices of the powerful and of the obscure. This book is one attempt to do so.

A second lacuna in the scholarship of wartime Britain relates to the use of wartime expressive culture. Cultural forms (such as music, theater, film, speeches, personal stories, radio drama, and so forth) are mentioned in virtually every account of civilians' experience of wartime Britain, and they figure quite prominently in popular literature and memoirs.[6] Scholarly work has been done on wartime literature, but more ephemeral arts, such as music and popular culture, have been given scant attention. To my knowledge, the only scholarly analysis of wartime music is in Brian Murdoch's *Fighting Songs and Warring Words*. Murdoch, a scholar of German literature, covers music and poetry of the two world wars and gives a brief look at the atomic future. His book is excellent but has only 226 pages of text, so it is necessarily superficial about any one topic. Since cultural forms were considered fabulously important by wartime propagandists and since they figure prominently in wartime documents and in postwar memories, I have chosen to focus on the use and importance of speech, narrative, and music in the creation and maintenance of wartime images. The ephemeral nature of many of these artifacts is an indication of the fact that they belong to the performing arts. As such, they were conduits of communication between performers and audiences, senders and receivers; their living nature gives them an immediacy that more contemplative arts may lack.

In this book, I will examine images of wartime London as they were created and used during the war and as they have been remembered in the 1990s. I have researched official propaganda and secret government documents, wartime diaries and postwar memoirs. I have also spoken to many people who do not appear in written sources but who remember wartime London and its attendant glorification. The contradictions among all these sources, between wartime documents and postwar memories as well as among the memories themselves, may help us to understand the contradictions and debates about "what really happened" in wartime London. This methodological combination of ethnography and archival research has been successfully conducted by oral historians and folklorists, such as Alessandro Portelli, Luisa Passerini, Lynwood Montell, and Gladys-Marie Fry. I believe it is useful to consider oral and written documents as existing in counterpoint, rather than harmony, to one another. In harmonic music, one melody line is dominant, and other notes that exist simultaneously are intended to enhance the dominant melody. In contrapuntal or polyphonic music, by contrast, two or more melody lines exist simultaneously, each with its own integrity and importance. If we view oral and written sources as contrapuntal, then we cannot prejudge one to be the more important or more valuable; we are forced to look more closely.

It is common in ethnographic work conducted by anthropologists and folklorists to invent pseudonyms for one's interviewees.[7] Oral historians are less comfortable with such an alteration of historical particulars. I concur with Henry Glassie (personal communication) that all ethnography is a form of history and that altering people's names lessens a work's historical accuracy. I also believe that such modifications indicate an unspoken belief that "ordinary people" are somewhat interchangeable and that their individual identities are less important than those of historical actors such as Winston Churchill or Julius Caesar. However, there are often good reasons to change or modify people's names. Using people's real names might, in some cases, damage their reputations, invade their privacy, or even risk their safety. Therefore, I left the choice of names up to my interviewees. Many were happy to be known by their full names; others preferred, in the interest of privacy, to be known by first names only or by initials. Only one chose a pseudonym: the regional appellation "Geordie." Though the main body of this text uses American spelling, I have chosen to use British spelling when rendering the spoken words of my British interviewees. These words are the springboard of my analysis; they present an eloquent, if sometimes discordant, counterpoint to the many written works that have ignored them.

4 April 1993. London, England. "And that reminds me of a story." Ettie Gontarsky put down her teacup and settled comfortably in her chair. We had finished supper—the fish, the salad, the homemade biscuits—and were relaxing with a second cup of tea in her sitting room, thirteen stories up in a central London high-rise. From her sitting room window, we could see a magnificent panorama of the city below, stretching in seemingly endless direction, dominated by the gleaming silver dome of St. Paul's Cathedral. Ettie was justifiably proud of her view, and the one from the kitchen was just as good; from there, you could see Big Ben and the Houses of Parliament.

Ettie and I had met only a few days earlier and had liked one another at first meeting. We had much in common: we were Jewish women of East European background, secular tastes, and progressive politics. We were both living in central London, had a taste for music, books, and theater, and also enjoyed quiet evenings of talk and Scrabble and strong English tea. But the differences between us were equally great. At the time, she was seventy-nine and I was thirty-three. She was English; I, American. I was a sojourner in the city where she had lived all her life. Ettie had left school at the age of fifteen to become a fashion designer; I was a Ph.D. candidate interviewing her for my dissertation.

Our similarities made the interview comfortable and enjoyable, but the differences were the reason I was there. In this situation, I was the student and she the teacher; I was the seeker, while her experiences were what I sought. I was her inferior in terms of age and knowledge; I wanted to learn things that she already knew. Yet in terms of outward status, our positions were partially reversed. We both recognized that her working-class background had taught her many things that I had yet to know, but my middle-class birth gave me the false status of caste. University education was the common path for middle-class Americans in the latter part of the twentieth century, but for working-class English girls of the 1930s, education was discouraged, expensive, and for most, just out of reach. That Ettie's formal education had ended at the age of fifteen was her own choice, but it was a choice not entirely without regret, a choice she remedied by taking individual classes throughout her life. Age, too, has uncertain status in present-day Western societies. Though age should command respect, all too often it receives only lip-service courtesy; in societies where euthanasia is touted as "kindness" and "dignity," a seventy-nine-year-old woman might be considered a less competent subject than a thirty-three-year-old one.

All these disjunctures between us were part of a familiar pattern, part of a good interview. As Alessandro Portelli tells us: "Only equality prepares us to accept difference in terms other than hierarchy and subordination; on the other hand, without difference there is no equality—only sameness, which is a much less worthwhile ideal. Only equality makes the interview credible, but only difference makes it relevant. Field work is meaningful as the encounter of two subjects who recognize each other as subjects, and therefore separate, and seek to build their equality upon their difference in order to work together" (1991, 43). Ettie and I worked together because we believed that wartime London, one of the best-documented subjects of the twentieth century, contains many hidden and little-known stories that have a value and importance of their own. Throughout my fieldwork, I deliberately sought the people whose stories I could not find in printed and archival sources, and much later I realized that these were people who were like myself.

I was born, by some reckonings at least, at the very end of the postwar baby boom. In my childhood, the war was safely tucked in the past, a part of history that no child could remember and every adult could. The war was still present in ways that seemed unremarkable and relatively unimportant: my parents' wedding photograph with my father in the uniform of the U.S. Navy, his leftover navy hammock, his sturdy navy blankets. Their tales of youth were exciting and disturbing yet never real enough to be frightening—until perhaps the day when some old friends came to dinner, and I saw for the first time the small blue tattoo that brands the former inmate of a concentration camp.

The postwar years were good to America. The prewar inequities and viciousness that my parents described—the Great Depression, the widespread hunger, the legal racism, the sly anti-Semitism—seemed incredible. By contrast, the war seemed a great improvement. Like all children of those who had lived through World War II, I heard many stories of the war years. My interest in World War II came originally from these stories. As Jews and antifascists, my parents saw World War II as a bitterly necessary event; the triumph of Nazism would have destroyed them and everything they held dear. They did not see World War II as a jingoistic attempt to assert the superiority of American weapons or American capital; rather, it was a fight for survival: the survival of decency, tolerance, and reason. That this view is unfashionable today does not, I think, make it invalid, and it was this perspective that I took to London in 1992.

For eleven months, I sought people who experienced wartime London as they—or I—might have done. I found, of course, all kinds. My interviewees were Protestants, Catholics, Jews, and atheists. Their political heroes ranged from Enoch Powell to La Pasionaria. Though all had lived in wartime London, not all were native Londoners; some had come from the industrial cities of the north of England, others from Scotland, Wales, and Ireland. One was born in Spain, where her father had been a journalist prior to the Spanish Civil War; two were refugees from Germany. But none were stereotypical wartime Londoners; all had individual and distinctive points of view.

Every fieldworker must wrestle with the problem of finding interviewees and then interpreting the commentary gleaned from interviews. The theoretical and methodological difficulties are many. How can we draw generalizations based on a small sample of people who are, in many cases, only giving us their opinions? How can we know if the people whom we interview are "representative" of the larger population? If we cannot draw larger conclusions, then what is the value of our work? I suggest that we can connect the words of our interviewees with larger social and political events by analyzing patterns that emerge in the interviews and by comparing oral testimony with written documentation. I also suggest that asking people to be representative of others may be a false or impossible goal. The only way to find a truly representative group is to take a statistically random sample, an impossible task in my case, for much of the population in question was dead and many others had left the city. Rather than suggesting that my interviewees speak for all wartime Londoners, I have instead emphasized their individuality and distinctiveness. If the biases are openly acknowledged, a nonrepresentative sample may be important in its own right.

Since bias was inevitable, I have tried to make mine purposive and meaningful. Because I could not interview everyone who had lived in wartime London or make my selection statistically representative, I chose to interview people whose views were underrepresented in the printed and archival literature. To address some of these lacks, I chose to concentrate on women, Jews, and the working class. My sample ended up being 40 percent Jewish and 80 percent female. Class membership can be measured with less precision, but approximately 70 percent of my interviewees were from working-class families.[8] Written sources (with the exception of local histories and popular oral histories) are heavily biased in favor of upper-class and middle-class experience, however much they may praise the "cheerful Cockneys." My interviews were heavily biased toward working-class subjects, though I did interview middle-class people as well.[9] Although much has been written about the working class in propagandistic formulations or in very general terms such as unemployment statistics, there is little published work by working-class Londoners themselves or by people who address working-class experience. Likewise, there is virtually nothing in print about the Jewish experience in wartime London, with the exception of two recent and excellent works by Tony Kushner: a pamphlet entitled *The Heymishe Front*, published by the London Museum of Jewish Life, and a book on wartime anti-Semitism entitled *The Persistence of Prejudice*.[10] Because of this lack of information and because Jewish life and identity were crucial issues during this period, I made an effort to learn about the experiences of Jews in wartime Britain. Women were also a central focus in this study, for they are another group that has been underrepresented in the written literature despite the fact that women were more likely than either men or children to remain in London for the entirety of the war.[11] There are scholarly and popular works on women in wartime, but not in proportion to their numbers or to their contributions. Finally, there is a bias in my sample that is impossible to overcome. Because I researched an era fifty years in the past, all of my interviewees were young at the time of the war.

Though several of my biases were deliberate, it is not my intention to articulate a specifically working-class, Jewish, or female experience of wartime. Rather, I wish to understand how these perspectives were part of the experience of wartime London as a whole. As E.H. Carr aptly put it, "History has been called an enormous jig-saw with a lot of missing parts" (1961, 12). I hope that my work will restore a few more people to their rightful places in the puzzle. It is important to remember that women, Jews, and working-class people did not exist in isolated communities but constantly interacted with men, Christians, and people of the middle and upper classes. By focusing on those whose experience has not been well documented, I hope to show that this experience is important in its own right and that it provides a richer and more nuanced picture of wartime London as a whole.

The most serious bias in my sample is, I believe, the dimension of age. Oral history of fifty years past is automatically skewed toward those whose luck, health, and longevity have brought them to a point in which they can remember what others cannot. Doing such a project is like visiting the country of the young, a place of relatively little responsibility, peopled by those who have a hearty interest in sexuality and a faint disdain for death. I have tried to remedy this bias with printed and archival material that discusses the experience of the middle-aged and the elderly. But it should be borne in mind that the wartime rhetoric of defiance, courage, and ultimate confidence was designed to resonate most strongly with the age group that I studied—the age group of soldiers and their friends and siblings.

In *What Is History?* E.H. Carr wrote, "By and large, the historian will get the kind of facts he wants. History means interpretation" (1961, 26). Some scholars may disagree with this dictum, believing that historians should only report the past and not judge it. Yet no one can report everything about the past, and the very act of choosing which data are essential and which are not is a judgment call. Steven Jay Gould's comments about science are instructive here, particularly if we use "science" in its nineteenth-century sense, to refer to any systematic body of knowledge obtained by empirical means: "Science, since people must do it, is a socially embedded activity. It progresses by hunch, vision, and intuition. Much of its change through time does not record a closer approach to absolute truth, but the alteration of cultural contexts that influence it so strongly. Facts are not pure and unsullied bits of information; culture also influences what we see and how we see it. Theories, moreover, are not inexorable inductions from facts. The most creative theories are often imaginative visions imposed upon facts; the source of imagination is also strongly cultural" (1981, 21–22). In rejecting the idea of absolute objectivity, Gould does not reject the notion of the fact: "I do not ally myself with an overextension now popular in some historical circles: the purely relativistic claim that scientific change only reflects the modification of social contexts, that truth is a meaningless notion outside cultural assumptions, and that science can therefore provide no enduring answers. As a practicing scientist, I share the credo of my colleagues: I believe that a factual reality exists and that science, though often in an obtuse and erratic manner, can learn about it" (1981, 22).

In historical research as well, our own assumptions and premises, both cultural and personal, will influence our conclusions and the ways in which we interpret data. Yet we can recognize that things did happen in the past, and that time, patience, and work can tell us something about them. Carr noted that interpretation is the creative task of the historian; he also recognized that such creativity is worthless if one does not use the proper tools: "The historian is engaged on a continuous process of moulding his facts to his interpretation and his interpretation to his facts. It is impossible to assign primacy to one over the other" (1961,

35). This recognition that absolute objectivity is never humanly possible is not to suggest that all interpretations are equally valid. I cannot do better here than to quote David Lowenthal: "No absolute historical truth lies waiting to be found; however assiduous and fair-minded the historian, he can no more relate the past 'as it really was' than can our memories. But history is not thereby invalidated; faith endures that historical knowledge casts *some* light on the past, that elements of truth persist in it. Even if future insights show up present errors and undermine present conclusions, evidence now available proves that some things almost certainly did happen and others did not" (1985, 235).

Though my research is historical in the sense that it focuses on past events, the theoretical base is broadly conceived and interdisciplinary. My work is heavily indebted to the fields of folklore, ethnomusicology, history, literature, social theory, and cultural studies. I have been unable to find a single discipline sufficient to describe and comprehend human behavior and creativity. The world that my interviewees described did not fit neatly into a single disciplinary bailiwick. The concepts with which I am centrally concerned—memory, expressive culture, and politics—are those that invite contributions from many different vantage points. In order to give attention to my interviewees' concerns while at the same time retaining scholarly coherency and rigor, I have borrowed from the work of several scholars whose writings embrace a wide range of human concerns. I shall briefly discuss some of the more central concepts of this book.

Hegemony

One of my initial problems was finding a way of studying politically motivated expressive culture. Many studies of political art treat these forms either as "propaganda" (if produced by the ruling classes) or as "protest" (if produced by the subaltern classes). These formulations are perfectly good in many situations, but they are insufficient to describe the case of wartime London. In wartime Britain, many cultural forms and events (films, slogans, song rallies, and so forth) were produced by the government with the intent to influence political behavior and thought, yet people were free to disagree with them or to ignore them. Though governmental directives obviously had considerable influence (and in many cases, legal consequences), wartime Londoners did not blindly or uncritically accept them. In many cases, private citizens found common ground with governmental ideas through such shared concerns as "patriotism" or "freedom." Wartime censorship prevented resistance from going beyond a certain point, yet private citizens continued to argue with their government by writing letters, staging rallies, producing parodies, and discussing policy with their friends. In fact, a certain amount of disagreement with governmental directives was not only tolerated but touted as an example of the

British tradition of free speech. Thus wartime cultural forms were often neither simple propaganda or simple protest but something in between.

Antonio Gramsci's writings on hegemony provide the theoretical framework that best describes this cultural give-and-take. Hegemony describes a relationship based on shared concerns among groups that hold unequal amounts of power. Yet Gramsci is careful to differentiate hegemony from domination, which is power held by brute force. According to Gramsci, "The supremacy of a social group manifests itself in two ways, as 'domination' and as 'intellectual and moral leadership.' A social group dominates antagonistic groups, which it tends to 'liquidate,' or to subjugate perhaps even by armed force; it leads kindred and allied groups" (1981, 197). The leading (hegemonic) and allied (subaltern) groups are bound together by shared values and concerns. These groups are unequal partners, but because hegemony exists as a process rather than a static entity, the opportunity for change is both possible and inevitable. As Raymond Williams notes, hegemony is not a static set of rules or dictates but always a process. According to Williams, hegemony is "a realized complex of experiences, relationships, and activities, with specific and changing pressures and limits. . . . It has continually to be renewed, recreated, defended, and modified. It is also continually resisted, limited, altered, challenged by pressures not at all its own" (1977, 112).

Hegemony is more than a set of political constructs or principles. It is the totality of acts, practices, utterances, and beliefs that maintains society in an agreed-upon yet unequal division of power. It goes beyond legal mandates and economic systems; it requires the help of art, religion, education, and the informal practices of everyday living. This breadth is what gives the concept such utility in the study of expressive culture. Williams writes: "Cultural traditions are seen as much more than superstructural expressions—reflections, mediations, or typifications—of a formed social and economic structure. On the contrary, they are among the basic processes of the formation itself and, further, related to a much wider area of reality than the abstractions of 'social' and 'economic' experience" (1977, 111). Artistic work, leisure-time activity, and everyday experiences are not epiphenomena of politics or economics but play an essential role in maintaining or resisting such political and economic arrangements. The importance of cultural forms also lies in their ability to articulate intellectual and moral leadership and thus to create ideology, the intellectual glue that binds together different sectors of society.

Ideology

The word "ideology" has an unhappy history. The original meaning of the term, as proposed by its founder Destutt de Tracy in the late eighteenth century, was the scientific study of ideas as natural rather than metaphysical phenomena. Yet ideology quickly lost its neutral, scientific connotation and came to mean that which is *opposed* to science or, more generally, to truth (Williams 1977, 56). Napoleon attacked it as unenlightened self-interest; Marx condemned it as false consciousness. The negative connotation of ideology continues in the work of thinkers such as Louis Althusser, Jürgen Habermas, and John B. Thompson, who stress the linkages between ideology and systems of domination. Other scholars, such as Clifford Geertz and Paul Ricoeur, have argued for a more neutral definition of ideology, one that calls attention to ideology's role in constituting symbolic systems that allow people to function normally in society. According to Ricoeur, ideology is essential to political life because "every system of leadership summons not only our physical submission but also our consent and cooperation. Every system of leadership wants its rule to rest not merely on domination, then; it also wants its power to be granted because its authority is legitimate. It is ideology's role to legitimate this authority" (1986, 13). Thus ideology asserts that the system's leaders are worthy of being followed and the course they promote worthy of being taken.

The Gramscian definition of ideology emphasizes its linkages with political power: ideology is not simply a set of ideas but the set of ideas that validates and extends the ruling class's hegemony. Power in the hegemonic sense is secured by the creation and dissemination of an ideology that all groups share. Chantal Mouffe explains the importance of ideology in the Gramscian schema:

> For Gramsci . . . hegemony is not to be found in a purely instrumental alliance between classes through which the *class demands* of the allied classes are articulated to those of the fundamental class, with each group maintaining its own individuality within the alliance as well as its own ideology. According to him hegemony involves the creation of a *higher synthesis*, so that all its elements fuse in a "collective will" which becomes the new protagonist of political action which will function as the protagonist of political action during that hegemony's entire duration. It is through ideology that this collective will is formed since its very existence depends on the creation of ideological unity which will serve as "cement." [1981, 224–225; emphasis in original]

Yet Gramsci, in distinguishing between domination and hegemony, leaves a window of hope that political power may someday be in the hands of decent and honorable people; the ideology in question might be a benevolent one.

Cultural forms are a vitally important part of everyday life, be they high art, folk art, or artful forms of ordinary communication. What makes them important for our purposes is the fact that they are cultural and ideological formalizations of something beyond themselves; in the language of semiotics, they are "cultural signs." However these signs are manifested—as words, pictures, or air-raid sirens—they are the tools of thought made material. They are among the items that must be manipulated and disseminated in the service of a political ideology. The process of producing, judging, sharing, and negotiating signs is a fundamental part of any political movement. It is a process by which people seek to understand, to influence, to resist, to join, to help, or to destroy others. V.N. Vološinov writes: "Every sign, as we know, is a construct between socially organized persons in the process of their interaction. Therefore, *the forms of signs are conditioned above all by the social organization of the participants involved and also by the immediate conditions of their interaction.* When these forms change, so does sign. And it should be one of the tasks of the study of ideologies to trace this social life of the verbal sign" (1973, 21; emphasis in original). As Vološinov explains, signs are essential to ideology; they are the conduits along which ideas are shared, exchanged, rejected, and changed. They are the means by which ideas are expressed, protest lodged, and consensus negotiated.

One of the most important contributions of the ideas of ideology and hegemony is their emphasis on the necessity of "ordinary people" in historical events. These ideas are especially germane to the study of the Second World War. World War II was a total war, a war in which entire populations—not just a small cadre of professional soldiers—had to be mobilized. To understand World War II, one must look beyond military hardware and tactics to the people who made and used these weapons and the meanings they assigned to the struggle they fought. To understand Britain during World War II, one must also examine the lives and opinions of those who stayed in Britain and fought on the "home front," those who put out the incendiary fires, harvested the crops for conscripted farmers, cared for the wounded, and buried the dead. This was a time when vast numbers of ordinary people were the great actors in a world drama. They were the ones who made history, but not, as Marx reminds us, "under circumstances chosen by themselves" (1959, 320).

The Past

In 1824, Leopold von Ranke published his famous dictum that the task of history was to represent the past "as it really was" (*wie es eigentlich gewesen*). Most twentieth-century historians have abandoned Ranke's directive, believing that such completeness is not possible, and have adopted more cautious and less optimistic stances. Scholars no longer expect to capture and view the past as a complete and static panorama; instead, we work somewhat like archaeologists, taking shards of evidence and fashioning them into a coherent and logical story. In a famous riposte to Ranke, Walter Benjamin asserted: "To articulate the past historically does not mean to recognize it 'the way it really was' (Ranke). It means to seize hold of a memory as it flashes up at a moment of danger" (1968, 255).

Wartime London was a complex of such moments of danger, and memories of this era are as varied as they are abundant. In addition to personal memories, the scholar is confronted with a forest of papers, films, radio programs, diaries, letters, posters, paintings, newspaper articles, and other forms of documentation. The past is gone, but cultural representations of the past remain, some newly minted, some as old as the event in question. It is my thesis that these cultural representations are not the secondary phenomena that surround history, not the chaff to be examined once the wheat has been consumed. Instead, they are the raw material out of which history—our understanding and interpretation of the past—is formed. Cultural forms are the means by which people know history (speech, radio, film, newspaper account), present history (narrative, epic, saga), and commemorate history (parade, pageant, festival, ritual). To study cultural forms as they have served political and historical events (stories of national heroes, songs of resistance fighters) is to take an important first step, but to take no others is to further the view that cultural forms are the eternal handmaidens of life, secondary to the great events of history that sweep by us like soldiers on parade. But who has ever seen a historical event? One may have seen parts of it from one's place on the battlefield or the Senate floor or the picket line, but the very act of characterizing such an experience as a "historical event" is to move from history as lived to history as narrated. And most people do not know history from the battlefield or the Senate floor but from the classroom, the textbook, the newspaper, the personal account—the cultural forms that give shape and meaning to experience and, in turn, are part of experience. Raymond Williams writes: "Many people seem to assume as a matter of course that there is, first, reality, and then, second, communication about it. We degrade art and learning by supposing that they are always second-hand activities: that there is life, and then afterwards there are these accounts of it. . . . What we call society is not only a network of political and economic arrangements, but also a process of learning and communication" (1966, 19). Cultural forms are active, rather than merely reflective, means of interpretation, analysis, education, indoctrination, and resistance.

The cultural forms with which I am chiefly concerned are those that involve words and sound: political speeches, popular slogans, personal narratives, songs, and so forth. Some of these forms were created during wartime; others are more recent commentaries on the war. Among the cultural forms that I analyze are the stories told to me by people who had lived in wartime London. As many oral historians note, the very orality of such source material can provide a radical challenge to previously held assumptions. Paul Thompson writes: "Since the nature of most existing records is to reflect the standpoint of authority, it is not surprising that the judgement of history has more often than not vindicated the wisdom of the powers that be. Oral history by contrast makes a much fairer trial possible:

witnesses can now also be called from the under-classes, the unprivileged, and the defeated. It provides a more realistic and fair reconstruction of the past, a challenge to the established account. In so doing, oral history has radical implication for the social message of history as a whole" (1988, 6).

Though oral testimony may challenge, even contradict, accepted historical narratives, we cannot ignore these narratives, nor do contradictions necessarily render them invalid. It is important to look at the ways that historical narratives affect the populations that they purport to represent, even if individual actors are ignored or subsumed into mass categories. All of my interviewees were well aware of the standard narratives of World War II, and their memories were sharpened, sometimes in disagreement, sometimes in accord, with well-known historical images. My interviewees held a wide variety of political opinions, and many had become politically active during wartime because of a sense of living through a period of epochal change. Even those who were too young or too uninterested to hold strong political views could not escape being drawn into world affairs. As evacuated children, young women whose husbands and boyfriends were fighting overseas, or workers who dodged shrapnel and avoided bomb craters on their way home through the blackout, they could hardly avoid having opinions about events of political and historical moment. Indeed, a large part of the governmental propaganda campaign was aimed at making ordinary people feel their own importance in the war effort; the British Ministry of Information named World War II a "people's war." My interviewees' names might not have appeared in history books, but as wartime Londoners, they knew that they had made history.

2

London Can Take It
Ideology and Wartime London

A chronicler who recites events without distinguishing between major and minor ones acts in accordance with the following truth: nothing that has ever happened should be regarded as lost for history.
　　　　　　—Walter Benjamin, "Theses on the Philosophy of History"

In 1939 London was the largest city in the world, the world's busiest port, and the home of more than eight million people. Greater London consisted of many urban boroughs and two administratively designated "cities": the ancient city of London, consisting of one square mile and home to its financial district, and the adjacent city of Westminster, where most government business was enacted. Around the core of these two cities the boroughs spread in concentric circles for miles, each with its own personality and self-contained neighborhoods. Financially and commercially, London was one of the most powerful cities on earth, though no longer the undisputed leader, for it had a serious rival in New York. Governmentally, London was the capital of the United Kingdom and the headquarters of an empire that numbered half a billion people. Artistically, London had a long history of literary and theatrical importance, the home of Keats and Dickens, the site of Shakespeare's opening nights. Few Londoners would dispute Samuel Johnson's dictum that "when a man is tired of London, he is tired of life."

London was the heart of a society that was simultaneously extremely stable and extremely fluid. Governmentally, it was quite stable: for centuries, England had been a constitutional monarchy, though its monarchs had increasingly limited power and its constitution has never been written down. Since the late seventeenth century, England has continuously been a parliamentary democracy, suffering none of the violent revolutions that had characterized French or German or Italian politics in the intervening centuries. The formation of Great Britain as a political entity had been accomplished without bloodshed or conquest; it was a union of governments rather than the eradication of any. Yet economically, Britain had changed almost beyond recognition in the preceding centuries, embracing industrial capitalism with a swiftness and ferocity that taxed its existing institutions nearly to the breaking point. Villages turned into towns and towns into suburbs; cities grew with alarming speed. The Industrial Revolution was a decidedly mixed blessing, destroying the health of many who sought its benefits, freeing others from the drudgery of life on the farm, allowing women the independence that could be bought with wage labor, furthering class mobility but also breaking traditional bonds of trust and reciprocity, creating the technology for clean water and sewage removal while simultaneously poisoning the air. But mixed blessing or not, the Industrial Revolution was the central fact of modern British society.

A nation so changeable and yet so resistant to change is likely to abound with contradictions. Britain had a long history of democratic self-government and respect for individual rights, from the Magna Carta to the Bill of Rights of 1689 to the writings of John Locke to the untrammeled debate in Parliament. Yet in 1939 Britain was the head of an empire that denied self-government to approximately 500 million people. It was a nation that had made remarkable contributions to science and the arts, a nation of famous schools and some of the best and oldest universities in Europe. Yet it was also a nation in which a large portion of the population left school at fourteen and only a tiny minority went on to the university level. It was a nation that had made the step from feudalism to capitalism early, so that class mobility had been possible for centuries. Yet by custom and practice it had one of the most entrenched class systems in Europe; and many scholars of class, including Karl Marx at his desk in the British Museum, had used it as a model. It was one of the most urbanized and industrialized nations in the world, yet it cherished a self-image of village greens and country lanes. It was a nation that sent travelers and adventurers to the other side of the globe, yet most of its citizens never ventured far from their hometowns.

It is always dangerous, especially for an outsider, to try to sum up an entire society with a single word, but I would venture to suggest the word *tolerance* to describe the British ethos that prevailed in 1939. Tolerance had built a nation with a highly cherished tradition of freedom of speech, so that virtually all opinions, even the most radical, could have their say. Tolerance made it possible for a nation with two established churches (one in England, one in Scotland) to have almost no restrictions on freedom of religion. Tolerance created a democracy that sought to incorporate, rather than to deny, opposing points of view; for centuries, the genius of British politics had been one of compromise, of coalition governments and merging political parties and long legislative debates. Tolerance viewed eccentricity as harmless, if not charming; tolerance encouraged artistic and intellectual creativity. Yet tolerance has its dark side too. Tolerance yields too easily to an apathy that cares for nothing outside the home district or the family circle. Instead of protesting injustice and oppression, tolerance often turns away from these evils, tacitly or actively accepting practices that should not be tolerated. Tolerance does not preclude prejudice; often it treats bigotry as simply another point of view that should be heard. All of these attributes of tolerance were apparent in Great Britain in 1939.

To many, the twentieth century had been a disappointment to Britain. The Edwardian era was glamorous and exciting to those who could afford it, but it was also a time when approximately 30 percent of the population lived in poverty (Havighurst 1985, 46). Even those at the top of the social ladder knew that Britain was no longer the supreme power it had been under Victoria. World War I was a great scar in the national consciousness and in the lives of many people. Six million British people served in uniform in World War I; of these, 750,000 died and 1.7 million were wounded. Civilians suffered and died as well: 1,413 had been killed in air raids over Britain (Havighurst 1985, 131). Yet when it was all over, few could adequately explain what the fighting had been about. The 1920s brought unemployment, industrial unrest (culminating in the General Strike of 1926), and the beginning of "the troubles" in Ireland. The worldwide depression of the 1930s only increased Britain's economic ills. By 1931 millions were out of work, production was declining, and the deficit was climbing; government policies were inadequate to ease human suffering or to improve Britain's sluggish economy.

On the other hand, the twentieth century had brought advantages as well. Britain was a far more democratic place in 1939 than it had been in 1900: universal adult suffrage, of both men and women, with or without property, was the law. Social programs, such as unemployment insurance and old age pensions, had been put into effect. The Labour Party was a new and increasingly powerful political force, representing the interests of labor unions and the working classes. Real wages increased. By 1939 the economy was improving, and it looked as though Britain might get back to normal. Many Britons wanted only peace and to be left alone.

But the world was not peaceful during the 1930s. In 1931 Japan invaded and occupied Manchuria. In 1933 Adolph Hitler became chancellor of Germany, instituted terrorism at home, and began rearmament, in direct violation of the Treaty of Versailles. Italy (Fascist since 1919) invaded Ethiopia in 1935, and in 1936 Hitler's troops occupied the Rhineland. In 1936, the Spanish fascist Francisco Franco (with the help of German Nazis and Italian Fascists) led a rebellion against the democratically elected government of Spain, which was eventually defeated in 1939.

These events garnered relatively little response from the international community. The League of Nations condemned the invasion of Manchuria, but virtually nothing was done, leaving Japan free to continue its invasion into China. In Britain, the rearmament of Germany was condemned because it violated the Treaty of Versailles, but soon the treaty was altered and negotiations with Hitler became the common political road. The League of Nations also condemned the invasion of Ethiopia; yet only months after its occurrence, the British foreign secretary, Sir Samuel Hoare, and the French foreign minister, Pierre Laval, agreed to give approximately one-half of Ethiopia to Italy. The Hoare-Laval proposal was never put into effect because of the weight of public opinion against it, and other solutions were offered, including economic sanctions and military action. In the end, nothing was done, and in 1936 Italy annexed the entirety of Ethiopia. Thousands of individuals from the United States, Latin America, and Europe went to Spain to fight in the International Brigades of the Spanish Civil War, yet no government sent similar support. The Western democracies were conspicuous in their lack of support; Britain, France, and the United States declared a policy of "nonintervention" and refused to sell arms to either side, while Germany and Italy armed the fascist rebels.

Throughout the 1930s, Britain attempted to solve problems by negotiation and compromise. For much of the decade, the government itself was a compromise, the so-called National Government, a coalition of the major political parties (Conservative, Liberal, and Labour), headed first by Ramsay MacDonald, the first Labour prime minister, and later by the Conservative Stanley Baldwin. The danger of Hitler was dealt with by trying to negotiate and contain the problem—and keep it far away from Britain. Anthony Eden, then a rising young Conservative politician, was uneasy about Germany's annexation of the Rhineland but was not in favor of making too much of it; on 26 March 1936 he said, "It is the appeasement of Europe as a whole that we have constantly before us" (quoted in Havighurst 1985, 252). Many British politicians agreed, and the tenor of public opinion encouraged appeasement. Memories of World War I were still bitterly sharp; to many, anything was better than war. Alfred F. Havighurst describes the political atmosphere of the early 1930s, which led to the policy of appeasement: "If the Cabinet wavered between complacency and confusion on foreign policy, so did public opinion. Noel Coward's *Cavalcade* was shot through with vague pacifism. No matter how serious the international situation, war was not the solution. This position came more from timidity, even outright fear, and from lack of self-confidence than from pacifist views held by conviction. Aggression and force were abhorred, but why should they involve Britain?" (1985, 241).

When the Conservative Neville Chamberlain replaced Stanley Baldwin as prime minister in 1937, he and his ministers continued Baldwin's policy of appeasement. When Kurt von Schuschnigg, the Austrian chancellor, appealed to Britain for help against the Nazis in March 1938, he was coolly rebuffed. When German troops occupied Austria several days later, the British government made a mild protest but took no action, suggesting only that Hitler behave better when dealing with Czechoslovakia. In an attempt to provoke such behavior, Chamberlain flew to Berchtesgaden and discussed a Nazi takeover of the Sudetenland. From 28–30 September 1938, Chamberlain met with Hitler, Mussolini, and French premier Edouard Daladier in Munich. The four leaders agreed to give the Sudetenland to Germany in exchange for a promise that the Nazis would leave the rest of Czechoslavakia alone. Chamberlian returned to London, triumphantly bearing the paper on which Hitler had sealed his pledge, and declared, "I believe it is peace in our time." When Nazi troops arrived in Prague in March 1939, the Chamberlain government seemed genuinely shocked, apparently unaware of the maxim that there is no honor among thieves. Chamberlain continued to argue for peace while simultaneously preparing for war; he had finally decided that "I cannot trust the Nazi leaders again" (quoted in Havighurst 1985, 278). He turned to France for help, rejected the idea of a security conference with the Soviet Union, and guaranteed to protect Poland, should it require help. Appeasement had failed.

The policy of appeasement had had its critics, and they became more numerous as time passed. Various left-wing groups had warned of the dangers of fascism for years, as had the then out-of-fashion Conservative Winston Churchill. The viciousness of fascist practice during the Spanish Civil War increased and strengthened the opposition to appeasement. On 20 February 1938, Anthony Eden resigned from the government, unable any longer to condone Chamberlain's policies. Duff Cooper, then First Lord of the Admiralty, resigned in protest after the Munich agreement. Public opinion began to abandon the stance of appeasement, or at least to question it. Anne Lubin, who grew up in the East End of London, was only fifteen years old at the time of Munich, but she remembers it very well indeed: "I can remember feeling absolutely both shamed and relieved . . . when Chamberlain came back with his bit of paper. . . . I felt, although one was relieved that there wasn't going to be a war, you knew in your heart there was going to be one sooner or later. I can still remember with what bated breath we waited in 1938" (personal interview, 21 January 1993). Angus Calder concurs: "Once their gasp of relief had subsided, the British people felt uneasy once more. Shame on the one hand, fear on the other, had not been appeased" (1969, 26).

The spring of 1939 was a time of uncertainty. Britain was at peace but was preparing for war: the production of aircraft increased, a peacetime draft was instituted, and pledges of military help were issued to Romania, Greece, and Poland. And it was to Poland that Hitler turned his sights. Chamberlain had rejected offers of mutual assistance from the Soviet Union, and by the summer it was too late; on 23 August 1939 the Molotov-Rippentrop nonaggression pact was signed between Germany and the Soviet Union. Hitler now felt free to invade Poland and did so on 1 September 1939. Mindful of the pledge to defend Poland, the Chamberlain government demanded that German troops withdraw from Polish soil. They did not.

At 11:15 A.M. on 3 September 1939, Prime Minister Neville Chamberlain announced that the United Kingdom was at war with Germany—ostensibly because Germany had not removed its troops from Poland, which the United Kingdom had pledged to protect. In reality, Great Britain was becoming aware that it was one of the few European nations neither in accord with Hitler (by alliance or agreement of nonaggression) nor occupied by Hitler.[1] As Harold Nicolson put it, "It was now clear that Herr Hitler was out for loot and conquest. The dreadful day might come when he would cease murdering small and distant countries of which we knew little, and start attacking us" (1939, 104). In other words, British interests were at risk. Britain began the war by fortifying the home front and preparing for battles abroad; the blackout, the evacuation of children, and the conscription of men were firmly in place in the early weeks of the war. (Women were not conscripted until 1941.) It seemed to many British people that the war did not really begin until the spring of 1940, but even those early months (often called "the Bore War" or the "Phony War") were not without dangers. On the first day of the war, a U-boat sank the passenger ship *Athenia* off the British coast, killing many on board. On 14 October a U-boat sank the British battleship *Royal Oak* in its harbor in Scapa Flow, Scotland. Scotland was also the site of one of the first air raids of the war; on 16 October, German planes bombed ships in the Firth of Forth, killing twenty-five sailors and spraying Edinburgh and its environs with shrapnel (A. Calder 1969, 60).

By the spring of 1940, no one thought that the war was phony. By May Germany had invaded and defeated Denmark, Norway, Belgium, the Netherlands, Luxembourg, and France, leaving Britain to "stand alone" against the Nazis. Confidence in the Chamberlain government was at an all-time low. The prime minister seemed weak, inept, and out of touch with the people he was supposed to lead. Chamberlain offered to form a coalition government with the other major parties, but leaders of the Liberal and Labour Parties refused to serve under Chamberlain. They did, however, agree to serve under Winston Churchill, who became prime minister after Chamberlain's resignation on 10 May 1940. Speaking in the House of Commons on 13 May, Churchill declared that he had nothing to offer but "blood, sweat, toil, and tears," but he intended to achieve "victory at all costs." On 19 May, after the fall of Belgium and the Netherlands, during the final days of the Battle of France, Churchill spoke in a world broadcast. He talked about the unity of the British people and the assurance of final victory, themes that were to be important throughout the war. His gift for language and his belief in the nobility of his nation's cause are apparent: "Having received His Majesty's commission, I have formed an administration of men and women of every party and of almost every point of view. We have differed and quarrelled in the past; but now one bond unites us all—to wage war until victory is won, and never to surrender ourselves to servitude and shame, whatever the cost and the agony may be. This is one of the most awe-striking periods in the long history of France and Britain. It is also beyond doubt the most sublime" (quoted in Eade 1951, 184).

Morale began to improve almost immediately. The Ministry of Information's morale log of 21 May 1940 noted that "the belief that Britain will triumph eventually is universal" (INF 1/264, 97/15 H.I.). Yet fear and uncertainty remained; on 25 May 1940 the Ministry of Information reported that in London "feeling in the main seems to combine fatalism, determination and depression, all of which will seem to be attributable to the extreme state of uncertainty about the present situation" (INF 1/264, 97/15 H.I.). For many, the tension and anxiety of the "phony war" were worse than the days that followed. In the summer of 1940 the Battle of Britain was fought in the British skies. By September the blitz had begun: German bombs fell on British airfields and cities, with particular violence on London, and Great Britain was at war indeed, a war that was to last nearly six years and affect every sector of British society. During this period, morale actually increased in many areas, and Churchill's leadership is often cited as a reason.

Churchill was, in many ways, a curious choice for a war leader. In May 1940 he was sixty-five years old, an age at which most men would think of retiring. He had distinguished himself as a soldier before going into politics; as a politician, he had made enemies on all sides. He began as a Conservative in 1900, became a Liberal in 1904, and returned to the Conservative fold in the 1920s. Both Tories and Liberals felt betrayed by his vacillation; Labour hated him for other reasons. As a Liberal member of parliament, he had been a close associate of David Lloyd George; in 1908 Churchill suggested the implementation of unemployment insurance, a national health insurance, state-run enterprises, and other solutions later to become cornerstones of the welfare state (Charmley 1993, 54). Yet as home secretary, in 1910 he sent policemen to quell industrial strikes, though the story of his sending troops against striking miners in Tonypandy is apparently false. His bellicose part in breaking the General Strike of 1926 seemed to seal his fate as an enemy of Labour. Perhaps his most unforgivable mistake had occurred in 1915 when, as First Lord of the Admiralty, he was responsible for the failed attempt to take the Dardanelles, an operation that resulted in great loss of life.

Thus it might seem surprising that the preferred choice for the leader of a coalition government should be someone who had offended virtually every political party in the country, that a war leader should be an old man famous for a military disaster. Nonetheless, there was something uncannily correct in this choice. His opposition to Hitler was genuine; Churchill had long opposed the policy of appeasement, to the detriment of his own career. Though he judged himself a man of action, Churchill's primary talents were not for strategy, either military or political. His primary talent was for words, as he himself had discovered as a Victorian schoolboy, struggling with Latin and mathematics, inept at games. He could write and he could also speak, as millions of wartime listeners would attest. As a soldier and a politician, he loved a fight, but his most accurate weapon was the word.

Successful warfare demands unity, yet Great Britain in 1939 was divided by class, region, age, religion, ethnicity, and politics. In order to unite this disparate populace, British propagandists depended heavily upon the weapons of intellect and persuasion. Unity was secured by the careful creation of an ideology that stressed support for the war effort. Every form of communication contributed to the formation of this ideology, from Churchill's famous radio broadcasts to the most casual of personal conversation. Books, films, radio, and overseas letters were censored. Government organizations, such as the Wartime Social Survey, and private ones, such as Mass-Observation, sent workers into London neighborhoods in order to gauge the tenor of public opinion and to assess the needs of the population.[2] The government could then plan policy accordingly, not always in accordance with the wishes of the people but with knowledge of those wishes in mind. (See also Mack and Humphries 1985.) The most famous wartime slogan—"Careless talk costs lives"—emphasized the danger that could arise from casual conversation and simultaneously recognized the importance of cooperation with ordinary citizens. Thus ideology—the creation of the "collective will"—involved an extensive give-and-take between the government and ordinary citizens.

Wartime ideology was not only an expression of support for the war; it was also a means of creating unity among a diverse people whose help was essential to successful prosecution of the war. Politicians and generals may have been the leaders, but it was the efforts of those they led that accomplished most of the work. Alex Callinicos's idea of "collective agents" is instructive here, particularly the kind of collective agents he calls "collectivities." He writes, "A collectivity exists where persons coordinate their actions because they believe themselves to have a *common identity*" (1988, 135; emphasis added). Callinicos identifies classes and nations as the most important examples of collectivities and distinguishes them from organizations as follows: "The difference between organizations and collectivities is that the former have a structure while the latter need not. In particular, any organization has some procedure through which decisions binding on all its members are arrived at. . . . A sense of collective identity by contrast does not entail the existence of any such procedure" (1988, 136).

While members of organizations act according to rules and regulations, members of collectivities act according to fellow feeling. A nation-state, of course, has properties of both a collectivity and an organization; in wartime Britain, hegemony was secured by institutional regulations as well as freely given public support. The government instituted rationing, conscripted soldiers, and censored books, but it could not legislate "morale," nor could it dictate the cheerfulness and humor that wartime Londoners displayed with such pride. Whereas organizations are based on acknowledged and regulated codes, collectivities draw their strength from ideology.

The common identity of which Callinicos speaks was an important component of British wartime ideology. Shared identity must be carefully constructed; it neither exists naturally nor can it be imposed by force. Rather, it appeals to our free will—to a freely chosen and personally affirmed sense of self. As Callinicos writes, "A particular ideology invites us to accept a particular kind of social identity" (1988, 156). Each person has many identities based on different factors: family, ethnicity, gender, religion, and so forth. In political movements such as war, it is necessary to create a sense of shared political identity that I term the "political self."

It is assumed that few people, outside of a few professional soldiers, will want to go to war simply for the love of fighting. Thus an ideology of warfare must address the question "Why are we fighting?" Before this question can be answered, it is necessary to determine who "we" are and to differentiate "us" from "them" (the enemy). Political selves are created as actors for specific political purposes. Since each person has several elements of identity, the political "we" must assert the primacy of one of these factors, either for all time or for a particular political crisis. Since this factor is shared by individuals who differ in other particulars, political identification must declare unity in spite of, or superseding, the fact of difference.

Twentieth-century rhetoric allows two primary justifications for warfare: freedom and self-defense. Of these two principles, self-defense is generally considered the less problematic, though the definition of the self is not as straightforward as it seems. Defending one's family, one's companions, and one's country from attack is usually deemed justifiable violence or self-defense; thus the purview of the self extends beyond the boundaries of one's body. During World War II, an American soldier whose home was thousands of miles from Pearl Harbor was considered to be fighting in self-defense, because his country—his political self—had been attacked.

Freedom, that other justification for virtually everything, is a trickier concept, since it is not a quality that exists by itself. One cannot simply be free; one must be free of something or free to do something. Although all sides invoked freedom as a reason for fighting World War II, this freedom was predicated on being "free" of very different things: of fascism, of communism, of capitalism, of oppression, of Germans, of Jews, of imperialism, of internationalism, of murder, of parliamentary democracy, of German/Japanese/American/British bombs. Hitler defended the murder of Jews by declaring them a foreign people (a political "they") who had invaded German life; according to this argument, Aryans (the political "we") were urged to *defend* their country, their purity, and their way of life (their political selves) by *freeing* themselves of a foreign element.[3]

In Britain, wartime unity was built in many different ways, but the notions of freedom and self-defense were never far from the surface. As the political self expanded to include more than the individual, so did the doctrine of political self-defense. In a speech given soon after the fall of France, Churchill suggested that all decent people, including those who could no longer fight for themselves, depended upon Great Britain to fight for them:

What General Weygand called the Battle of France is over. I expect that the Battle of Britain is about to begin. Upon this battle depends the survival of Christian civilization. Upon it depends our own British life, and the long continuity of our institutions and our Empire. The whole fury and might of the enemy must very soon be turned on us. Hitler knows that he will have to break us in this island or lose the war. If we can stand up to him, all Europe may be free and the life of the world may move forward into broad, sunlit uplands. But if we fail, then the whole world, including the United States, including all that we have known and cared for, will sink into the abyss of a new dark age made more sinister, and perhaps more protracted, by the lights of perverted science. [Eade 1951, 206–7]

In this speech, the political "we" embraces all citizens of Britain ("our own British life"), all denizens of the empire, all Christians, and finally the whole world. Though there is some sense of being tied by commonality ("all that we have known and cared for"), there is a greater sense of being united in opposition to a common enemy. Here, the political "we" is most strongly constructed in opposition to a political "they."

Not all commentators tried to reach as broad-based a constituency as did Churchill. More particularist writings shed light on ways in which narrower political "we's" were constructed. For Harold Nicolson, writing several months before the speech quoted above, the political "we" was coterminous with the nation-state. In his book *Why Britain Is at War*, Nicolson invoked the concepts of self-defense and freedom—but freedom only for the British people. Unlike Churchill, he did not invoke the qualities of goodness, honor, or Christianity; it was the defense of Britain that mattered. Nicolson stated quite plainly that what Hitler did in his own country was his own affair:

We are not . . . at war with Hitler because of his contempt for the virtues of the German people, or the masses in general. We may regret that he should have seen fit to crush all independent thought in his own country and have employed the magnificent machine of German state education for the production of a generation believing only in the harsh majesty of force. We may regret that in the twentieth century any Government can have imposed upon its fellow citizens such cruelties as Hitler has imposed upon the Jews and socialists. . . . Yet we are not concerned in this particular quarrel; it is a quarrel between his countrymen and himself; it is to them that he will one day have to render account. [1939, 37]

German Jews and socialists were not part of Nicolson's political "we," nor were the "masses in general." It is nearly one hundred pages later that he explains why Britain is at war, and the reason is self-preservation. Nicolson writes: "Before he agrees to make war the Briton must have (a) a sense of personal danger and (b) a sense of personal outrage. His deep instinct of self-preservation, and his long moral tradition must simultaneously be aroused" (1939, 129).

He cited 15 March 1939—the day Hitler took Prague—as the day when these two emotions simultaneously became aroused in the majority of the British people. Nicolson explained the process as follows: "Until March 15th last it was believed by the Prime Minister and his intimate advisers that if we could only avoid a head-on collision our own life might be preserved. After March 15th they cherished no such illusions. The tiger was not merely attacking the native huts down in the village; he was fixing lustful eyes upon our own large bungalow. Hitler was out for loot. And since the British and French Empires offered the richest loot in the world, it was probable, it was even certain, that in the end we also should be attacked" (131–32). Using similarly imperialist language, Nicolson spoke to the conservative interests of the nation. He explained British self-defense as the defense of certain freedoms for the British people, including the freedom to own property and a good portion of the world.

A very different view was offered by W.J. Brown, general secretary of the Civil Service Clerical Association. The purpose of his book *What Have I to Lose?* was to provide a left-wing antidote to Communist propaganda that, prior to the invasion of the Soviet Union, asserted that the British working classes would do as well under Hitler as under the British ruling classes. Brown's notion of "collective thought" is strikingly similar to Gramsci's idea of "collective will": "In such a [total] War, psychology is as much a military factor as are Guns, 'Planes, Ships, and Tanks. The morale of a nation is as important as the movements of its Armies and Navies, and the flights of its Aerial Squadrons. On the *collective thought of a nation* depends the willingness of the soldier, the sailor, and the airman to risk his life; the willingness of the workers to endure day after day, week after week, month after month, the hard labour of field, factory, and workshop" (1941, 9; emphasis added).

Brown's political "we," like Nicolson's, embraced the entire British people but used very different arguments and spoke to very different interests. Nicolson directed his arguments to the conservative wing and explained how the war would help the propertied classes; Brown addressed his arguments to the progressive wing and explained how the war would help the working classes. One might say that, for Brown and Nicolson, the primary political "we" was composed of class identification; and for purposes of winning the war, each decided to bind the interests of his own class with that of others, temporarily expanding the political "we." Brown's personal identification is spelled out quite clearly:

I write as a Trade Union Secretary. I aspire to see an order of society in Britain radically different from the order of society which now exists. . . .

But I know that Britain is older than the industrial system. It existed before that system came; it will exist long after it has gone, or at least has been transformed out of recognition.

But I feel with every fibre of my being that, if Britain and the British are to survive as a free country and a free people; if the Trade Union Movement is ever to reform the Industrial System and to win full recognition of the rights of Labour; if to Political Democracy there is to be added what we now lack, namely, Economic Democracy; if the dream of a just order of society is ever to be achieved; then Hitler and Hitlerism must be beaten, and not merely beaten, but beaten decisively and overwhelmingly. [1941, 11–12]

Brown's book, in response to left-wing antiwar propaganda, addressed his two intertwining political "we's"—the working class and the British people. In addressing the former, he pointed out that a Nazi defeat of Britain would neither help workers nor further revolutionary communism. He combined the two political "we's" by pointing out that the working class in Britain had a higher standard of living than the working class in Germany. And Brown decried the things that would happen to Britain—the whole of Britain—should it be defeated in the war:

If Hitler won, there would be a Britain with its industries shut down, as the general industries of Poland have been shut down. There would be a Britain reduced to the level of an agricultural community producing food supplies for the German "master-folk." In this Britain there would be only so much education as was necessary to make the population efficient serfs. In our papers we should read only what the Government (German or German-controlled) wanted us to read. Access to the great books of the world would be forbidden us. . . . A darkness more black than any *we have ever as a people* undergone would settle about the land; a tyranny worse than any *we have as a people* ever endured would regulate every detail of our slave lives. [1941, 43–44; emphasis added]

In describing the horrors that would befall British life, Brown made it clear that British institutions and British autonomy would effectively be eradicated. Likewise, Brown listed the freedoms that would be destroyed by Nazi conquest, freedoms that he considered necessary to ameliorate the class system and bring about economic justice: "freedom of thought, freedom of speech, freedom of industrial and political organizations" (44). Again, freedom and self-defense were the goals invoked; they were the rights to be defended by the British working class.

Having heard from the right and the left, I should now like to turn to the center. In an extraordinary little book entitled *What Is at Stake, and Why Not Say So?* published in 1941, C.E.M. Joad declared that he was fighting for "the liberal tradition." He explained that he did not mean "liberal" to refer to "the tenets of a political party now largely defunct, but a particular attitude to the individual, to the State, and to the individual's relations to the State" (1941, 11). As in the phrase "liberal arts" or "liberal education," Joad used the term in a way that stressed its Latin root, *liberalis*, meaning "of a free man." Though he recognized that many were fighting to retain Britain's position as an imperial power, his own battle was in defense of freedom. Joad insisted that his was "a war of ideas," yet it is clear that these ideas had extremely practical consequences. He was not concerned with some Platonic ideal of "liberalism," but with retaining his own freedom and that of his compatriots.

This viewpoint is especially apparent in the section on patriotism, in which Joad combines love of country (self-defense) with the liberal tradition (freedom):

> It is sometimes charged against the upholders of the liberal tradition that they are lacking in patriotism. As a humble follower in the same tradition, I repudiate the charge; for we, too, are lovers of our country. Ours is not the patriotism which measures national greatness in terms of wealth or territory, which reverences aristocrat or plutocrat, which prides itself on its ability to hold down a reluctant India or to add a new colony. . . . Ours is a patriotism which expresses itself in the love of a country and a way of life. The country is England, an England which is a small island and not a great empire. . . . The England that I love is a land of green fields, of winding lanes, of streams and copses and little hills, of market towns and cathedrals and old universities and of people who are engaged in the immemorial pursuits of the land. . . . Now this England, this *little* England that I love so much that time and again, having gone abroad for a holiday, I have come scuttling home before half of it was done in a frenzy of nostalgia for the grey skies and the soft air I know so well, this England is in danger; to think of it being violated by the Nazis fills the heart with a sick dismay. [1941, 19–20; emphasis in original]

Here, the political "we" is conterminous with England—not England the powerful but England the free. But the political "we" is not England alone; it is all free people and all free ideas. In discussing how England (which he uses as a synecdoche for Britain) can get help from the people of occupied countries, Joad writes: "We must somehow contrive to convince them that this is not a struggle on the part of England to retain her empire against Germany's attempt to wrest it from her, but a struggle to save civilization against a barbarism that would destroy it. If we can do this, then all those who on the Continent of Europe hate oppression, love liberty, and care for civilized ways of living will rally to our aid" (46). As the political "we" embraced all of "liberal England," it also embraced all civilized peoples and all who loved liberty.

Joad's book is an extraordinarily frank and thoughtful piece of wartime writing. With wit, irony, and careful reasoning, he demonstrated that support for World

War II did not have to be based on mindless jingoism or imperialist arrogance. Joad's explanation of the intellectual road that led him to his wartime convictions is particularly poignant: "It is because I know that this is not a struggle which requires me to hate every man born in Germany because he was born in Germany, but only to hate certain ideas which aim at the imprisonment of the minds of civilized men and the destruction of the way of life which has made them civilized, that I have abandoned a pacifism which has served me as a political standby for the last twenty-five years and thrown in my lot with those who insist that the Nazis must be defeated" (1941, 63).

Another interesting permutation of the political "we" was demonstrated by the American writer Margaret Culkin Banning, who went to London in the summer of 1942. The United States had been in the war for less than a year, and Banning discovered that the process of "identification" had not been solidified in the States as it had in Britain. She shows that the political "we" can be based on gender. In a letter to her daughter, Banning wrote:

> Too many women in the United States still don't realize that the outcome of the war involves keeping or losing everything of value they have—decent jobs, the right to study, self-respecting husbands, children who aren't war matériel. I needn't write my favorite speech on women to you tonight, but have you ever forgotten that day at the Olympic games in Berlin when we realized that the only thing German women were allowed to do in the events was to clean up after the horses?
>
> I wonder if all British women know it's a fight for survival of all the privileges women have gained—so slowly—since it was discovered that they were teachable? [1943, 6–7]

Banning's fight was, in part, against the Nazis' denigration and exploitation of women. For her, the political "we" comprised all women.

Thus far I have dealt largely with works of propaganda, works that were consciously intended to build and create a strong political "we." It is interesting to see echoes of these sentiments in the casual words of ordinary people, as recorded in popular literature of the day and in memory. One of my interviewees, Shirley Ann, was a child in a working-class London home during the war. Nearly fifty years after the war's end, memories of wartime unity remained strongly with her: "I mean I was only a tot at the time but I can yet remember that sort of feeling because Mum used to tell us, you know, 'Go, you know, don't ever worry because we're all in it together.' You know. And you just felt that, you know, like one big family in a way. You could trust people" (personal interview, 18 February 1993). Fred Mitchell concurs with this opinion and gives a practical explanation for this sudden show of fellow feeling: "When there's a common enemy everyone unites. . . . I mean, neighbours which were at each other's throats before the war, were very, you know, were great friends and helped each other out. . . . And after the war ended they were at each other's throats again" (personal interview, 18 May 1993).

Books published during the war show no such pragmatic cynicism, nor do they look toward a peacetime wherein this unity would dissolve. They do, however, stress the important military value of a unified populace; indeed the very fact of their publication made them wartime weapons. In a book of letters entitled *Home Front*, edited by Richard S. Lambert, a letter writer from Musselburgh (in southern Scotland, near Edinburgh) commented on the unity he felt among the British populace:

> The temper of the nation is very different from last time. There is no light-heartedness; no singing on the march; no cheering or flag-waving. But in place of it, there is the grimmest determination. Nobody has wanted this. But, as one man, the whole nation, united in a way never before experienced in our lifetime, is determined that the World's Bully has got to be stopped. And the determination is not weakened in the slightest by the fact that people know, as they never knew in the last War, what it is going to cost. And there is also an assurance of ultimate success: in fact, we take success for granted. [1940, 4]

More simply, perhaps less ideologically driven, the same sentiment is expressed in a letter from Surrey (in southern England, near London): "I think this war has made us all feel more chummy towards one another, and we can't help feeling proud of our country and our Dominions at a time like this" (Lambert 1940, 5). The political "we" in these letters comprised the entire British nation and, in the latter example, the Dominions as well.

As the political "we" changed and shifted to incorporate new allies, Londoners built a collective identity based upon geography. As the political, financial, commercial, and symbolic center of the nation, London was the prime target of enemy attack. Even today, the most famous images of wartime Britain are London ones: people asleep on underground platforms or laughing in air-raid shelters, St. Paul's unscathed amid the smoking ruins of the blitz. In a retrospective account, Susan Briggs reports the comments of a City printer: "You know, mate, I ain't a religious bloke—I never go to church, and I don't pray or anything. But I should hate to see dear old St. Paul's hurt or damaged. Somehow—you know what I mean, mate—somehow—well, blast it all, it's *London,* ain't it?" (1975, 68). Using the symbols of their city, Londoners were able to create solidarity—a small-scale political "we"—among themselves. In so doing, they created an ideal Londoner who endured the war with stoicism, patriotism, hard work, and staunch good humor. The ideal Londoner never panicked (and looked with disdain on those who did), helped those who were in trouble, and never failed in his or her duties. Like

Julia, Winston Smith's lover in *1984*, the ideal Londoner always looked cheerful and never shirked anything (Orwell 1949, 101).

Since the blitz was a deliberate attempt to cause civilian terror, an important component of the ideal Londoner was the refusal to panic. Basil Woon, in a contemporary account of the blitz, described a sign flashed on cinema screens during air raids: "Walk, not run, to the exits. Do not panic. Remember, you are British!" (1941, 91). Woon's own comment on his fellow Londoners was: "Panic London? It's a laugh!" (1941, 17). J.B. Priestley, in a retrospective broadcast made soon after VE Day, described an attack on a fashionable nightclub during the blitz: "When the bomb fell, there was no screaming panic. But the young men fought the flames, and the girls tore strips from their evening dresses to bandage the wounded. We were, you see, better people than we'd thought" (NSA ref. nos. 8018-9 and MT8018).

Many personal memories report a similar refusal to panic. Anne Lubin, from a working-class home in central London, was a factory worker during the war. After telling me a story in which she had narrowly missed being hit by a bomb, she commented, "There wasn't a great deal of fear that I remember. I can never remember being panic-stricken or anything like that" (personal interview, 13 March 1993). Marian, a small child during the war, remembers with amusement that lacking adult understanding also meant lacking adult fear; she found air raids unpleasant only because she had to get out of her comfortable bed and go to a shelter (personal interview, 2 February 1993). Many people remarked on the human capacity for normalizing the abnormal, for getting used to whatever comes one's way. Eileen Scales, an office worker from a working-class home in south London, recalls: "Surprising how the air raids and things like that, how people did eventually carry on in quite a normal way. And you tended to get so used to the siren going and planes overhead that you, at first you would go into a shelter and sort of not venture out. But it became sort of so commonplace that you carried on as normal" (personal interview, 3 May 1993).

People did not, of course, always live up to this ideal. A Ministry of Information morale report from 7 June 1940 describes an example of less-than-exemplary behavior; at the same time, it posits this incident as an exception: "A false alarm on a housing estate of parachutists occasioned by a flock of pigeons resulted in about half the tenants rushing to the roof and the rest rushing to the shelters in the basement. In the melee several women fainted. These people are normally calm and collected" (INF 1/264, 97/15 H.I.). The records of the Tilbury Shelter, a huge shelter in London's East End, also recall incidents that contradict the image of the fearless wartime Londoner. A warden's report describes the following melee occurring during an air raid: "Police were unable to keep crowd in order or marshall them in properly. People were banging at doors, were trying to force entry all the time. Police ordered that only the wicket door should be opened; as the situation became impossible the big doors were opened within three to four minutes. Owing to the pressure of the crowd outside difficulty was found in swinging back the bar. Mrs. M. was called to the first aid post where she found a woman whose head was bleeding, had six stitches in her head. Unable to make a statement as she was hysterical" (private papers).

Postwar memory, unbound by the restrictions of wartime, is also filled with incidents of less-than-ideal behavior. Some of my interviewees referred to others who panicked in times of crisis (relatives, the elderly, Americans), while some admitted to panicking themselves. One woman remembered an incident in which her mother, a nervous person by nature, was awakened by an air-raid siren and, in her haste to get to the shelter, was preparing to leave the house in her underclothes. Yet my interviewee reports that even her mother got used to the raids and the uncertainty as time went on. It is interesting that many people remembered moments of panic—by themselves and by others—on the first day of the war, after the first air-raid siren (which, as it turned out, was a false alarm). As time went by, the image of the ideal Londoner solidified, and most Londoners adjusted to the exigencies of war—or, if possible, left town.

Once the blitz started, morale in many cases actually increased, as people tried to adapt their behavior to that of the ideal Londoner. A report from 26 August 1940 stated: "London has come through a weekend of extensive raids with courage and calmness. . . . East-Enders experiencing screaming bomb for first time expressed great fear but did not panic. Those in shelters remained, although they said it sounded as if the bomb was falling right on top of them" (INF 1/264, 97/15 H.I.). With the advent of the antiaircraft (ack-ack) guns, morale increased still more, as people began to feel that they were fighting back. A morale report from 12 September 1940 said: "Morale has jumped to new level of confidence and cheerfulness since tremendous A.A. barrage. This is true of every district contacted, including East End and areas badly hit yesterday, such as Woolwich and Lewisham. 'We'll give them hell now' is a typical working class comment to-day. . . . Kensington people rendered homeless in night joking when taken in by neighbours. In spite of little sleep, factory workers are turning up as usual and working well; employers reported to be very accommodating about time" (INF 1/264, 97/15 H.I.). Though incidents of panic and depression continued to be mentioned in the ministry's daily reports on morale, general morale was reported as excellent. The vision of the idealized wartime Londoner was not the fantasy of propagandists; praise of such behavior was a deliberate attempt to make it the norm.

Government sources were loath to mention the costs of the war, but such sentiments were not censored; in a way, they only made the Londoners' courage that much more noble. Kensington diarist Vere Hodgson wrote on 6 December

1942 of a book she liked entitled *The Front Line*. A quotation from the book summed up her feelings about the blitz: "There was never a trace of public panic; but the Blitz was not a picnic, and no fine slogan about taking it should obscure the realities of human fear and heartache." In a diary entry of 25 November 1940, Chelsea resident Josephine Oakman described a similar sentiment, with heartfelt mention of the human costs of war: "London has now had 10 weeks of blitz and I have heard no word of complaint and saw not a single case of panic during this terrible time. London can take it! But at a cost—of lost lives, broken hearts and limbs and destroyed homes. The Lord help them—these the victims of the air raids! On them the price does fall."

"London can take it" said the famous wartime slogan, and a film of that name was made by the Ministry of Information. London was strong and would not break. At a London County Council luncheon in the summer of 1941, Winston Churchill said, "London is so vast and so strong that she is like a prehistoric monster into whose armoured hide showers of arrows can be shot in vain" (NSA ref. nos. 3843-5 and T3843b1). The *News Chronicle*, at the height of the blitz, wrote:

> London's nightly ordeal by steel and fire continues. Bodies are weary and nerves are strained. Who can deny it? But London's spirit is unbroken.
>
> Morale, that war-winning quality, is maintained. With each new dawn, the citizens of the world's greatest capital take a new grip on themselves and on their circumstances. They feel themselves to be front-line soldiers and in this battle of will-power and endurance they do not weaken. [quoted in Woon 1941, 82]

The ability of Londoners to "take it" and "carry on" became a source of civic pride. A film entitled *Ordinary People: London Carries On* was made by the Ministry of Information in 1940 and 1941. Its purpose was to demonstrate the virtues of the ideal Londoner to the American public and, no doubt, to hasten America's entry into the war. The facilities of a firm called Bourne and Hollingsworth were used in making the film, and in return, Stafford Bourne was given a copy. He thanked the ministry in a way that equated the London of the film with the London he knew: "I shall value it [the film] highly, and perhaps in years to come shall show it from time to time to my friends and staff here, and feel some pride at the way all the millions of us Londoners stood up to the air raids" (INF 5/76). George and Helena Britton, residents of London's East End, described the hardships of wartime London in letters to their daughter in California. Despite their many criticisms of specific government actions, there is little sense of personal complaint. Their left-wing views show nothing but contempt for mindless jingoism; nonetheless, like other Londoners, they "carry on": "I can assure you that in whatever direction you go from the centre of London results of the bombing are manifest for five or six miles. Yet most of us are still alive and on the whole quite recovered and very cheerful" (17 February 1943).

Thus the ideology of wartime Britain was created in many different ways and by many different people. Government officials, trade union leaders, conservative property owners, and left-wing workers all expressed the sentiment that prosecuting the war was in their own best interest. This sentiment was based on different facts for different people: trade union leaders recognized that a Nazi victory would mean the end of free trade unions, while property owners realized that their property might well be confiscated and their privilege destroyed. Many different paths led to the same conclusion: Nazism was a threat and a danger that had to be stopped. In order to fight against a threatening political "they," it was necessary to form a strong political "we," a collectivity mighty enough to defeat an extremely powerful military force. The different paths that led to this conclusion were then superseded by a feeling of shared concerns. In emphasizing these shared concerns, wartime expressive culture promoted, even while it formed, a sense of unity. This unity of shared suffering, purpose, and hope became a source of strength, a resource upon which to draw, a personal identity. It was a source of national pride, something to be commented on and wondered at even long after the war was over. My next topic is the process by which this ideology was created and the many ways in which it is remembered.

3

Careless Talk Costs Lives
Speech in Wartime London

> Be careful. Should you omit or add one single word, you may destroy the world.
>
> —Talmud

In *The Dark Lady of the Sonnets*, George Bernard Shaw paints a delightful picture of the speech habits of Londoners: he shows the young Shakespeare walking around the city and writing down what people say. These notes become the dialogue of his plays; Shakespeare is depicted here as a great folk-poet, taking the living language of his people and crafting it into a work of his own, what Henry Glassie (personal communication) calls "the individual expression of the collective will" (or, in this case, "the collecting Will"). While Shaw's portrayal of London speech is (unfortunately) exaggerated, his emphasis on the vast interplay between written and spoken language is compelling. Shaw came from a country that had great commerce between the written and the spoken word, and he was exquisitely sensitive to verbal nuance in his adopted country, England. In *Pygmalion*, for example, Shaw described the relationships between speech style and social class forty years before the linguist A.S.C. Ross (1954) coined the terms "U" and "non-U." And while sixteenth-century Londoners may not have spontaneously recited Shakespearean poetry, twentieth-century Londoners certainly did: political speeches, films, memoranda, and even diaries from World War II are filled with Shakespeare.

"You taught me language," said Caliban to Miranda and Prospero, "and my profit on't / Is, I know how to curse" (*The Tempest*, act 1, scene 2). Language made Caliban a slave, for only through words could he understand orders. To Caliban and Prospero, language was a social and political tool, a means for accomplishing tasks or resisting demands. This perspective on language is shared by many contemporary scholars and was mightily utilized by World War II propagandists. In this view, language is the fundamental activity of human experience: clowns and poets may sport with language, demagogues may enslave thereby, and perhaps the truth will make us free. Within the disciplines of folklore and anthropology, the study known as the "ethnography of speaking" has laid special emphasis on the importance of speech in human interaction and on the potential artfulness of speaking in all aspects of human activity, whether or not such speech is specifically marked as linguistically interesting or special. Summing up the credo of the ethnography of speaking, Richard Bauman and Joel Sherzer write, "The unifying principle is that society and culture are communicatively constituted, and that *no* sphere of social or cultural life is fully comprehensible apart from speaking as an instrument of its constitution" (1989, xi; emphasis in original).

Historians of speech have stressed the importance of critically examining the language of historical documents rather than treating such language as a transparent means for expressing facts. Peter Burke cautions, "Without . . . knowledge of linguistic rules, explicit or implicit, historians run a serious risk of misinterpreting many of their documents" (1987, 9). Historians are also paying more attention to the language activities of the people that they study. Drawing upon the work of sociolinguistics, Burke writes, "Language is an active force in society, used by individuals and groups to control others or to defend themselves against being controlled, to change society or to prevent others from changing it" (13). Language is not just a means of describing or proposing an event; it is a means of enacting it.

"Rhetoric," said Aristotle, "is a counterpart of dialectic" (1975, 3). Throughout history, rhetoric has been an important component of political life. In classical Greece, it was an essential part of the education of a free man.[1] Rhetoric's unsavory reputation began during the Enlightenment, when rhetoric was attacked for its elevation of form above content. Enlightenment philosophers feared that rhetoric enabled one to persuade not on the basis of reason or the worthiness of the ideas presented but merely by the beauty of the language within which these ideas were couched. This criticism is, of course, a valid one, but it contains within it a naïve belief that form and content can somehow be separated, and that one can express ideas without the skilled use of language. The Enlightenment belief in the transparence of referential (as opposed to artistic or poetic) language has informed much modern scholarship. If one wishes to present ideas as facts rather than opinions, one is careful to avoid the linguistic elements that call attention to language itself. As Aristotle knew, this is an extremely efficacious rhetorical trope: to make language *seem* transparent, to not "betray the artifice," but to make the ideas appear to "speak for themselves." Yet such seeming transparence is the result of much skillful manipulation of language.

Rhetoric is in some sense a benign tool; it seeks to persuade with words rather than guns. At the same time, it is an instrument of control that costs little. Democrats use rhetoric in order to gain the goodwill of their people. Dictators use it to organize behavior without exhausting their treasuries. Rhetoric is essential to democracy, where many points of view must have their say; it is also essential to dictatorship, because it tells the masses how to behave. Kenneth Burke writes:

"Persuasion involves choice, will; it is directed to a man only insofar as he is *free*. . . . Only insofar as men are potentially free, must the spellbinder seek to persuade them. Insofar as they *must* do something, rhetoric is unnecessary. (1962, 574; emphasis in original). Of course, rhetoric may be used to create an illusion of freedom or choice where none exists. Yet even in the most unfree societies, such as absolute dictatorships, dictators must persuade others to carry out their orders; and in some sense, people are always free to disobey.

Whether rhetoric is used for vicious or beneficial purposes, its effectiveness depends on the successful manipulation of words in the service of a particular belief or ideology. V.N. Vološinov writes, "*The word is the ideological phenomenon par excellence*" (1973, 13; emphasis in original). During World War II, three masters of oratory (Churchill, Hitler, and Roosevelt) pitted themselves against one another. Using very different techniques, exquisitely sensitive to their audiences (even if these audiences were unseen), these rhetorical geniuses sought to change the lives of millions by the use of words. Political oratory represents an extreme and highly obvious use of words for ideological purposes. Yet all words—poems, plays, slogans, restaurant menus, even casual conversation—can be used in the service of a political cause. During times of crisis, such careful talk may be officially mandated or at least strongly encouraged. In this chapter, I shall look at some of the ways that words were used as political tools in wartime London.

In 1940 John Hargrave Wells Gardner, the author of an impassioned polemic entitled *Words Win Wars*, wrote the following: "In peace, as in war, our lives are conditioned, influenced and directed by words: words spoken one to another, words read in books and papers, words heard 'over the air,' in films, on the gramophone, in the schoolroom, in the lecture hall, from the platform, the stage, the soapbox at the street corner . . . even the word overheard in passing—the chance word—can change the whole course of our lives" (1940, 2). Gardner was, at this juncture, lamenting the ineffectual use of words by official propagandists, especially the Ministry of Information, the government propaganda ministry. He was writing during a crucial year in national and international affairs: it was the year that Churchill replaced Chamberlain as prime minister, the year of Dunkirk and the Battle of Britain, the year the blitz began, the year in which the Nazis conquered Belgium, the Netherlands, Luxembourg, Denmark, Norway, and France. It was also a pivotal year for the Ministry of Information: during 1940, the ministry changed ministers several times (McLaine 1979, 4), discovered that upper-class rhetoric would not work in every situation, and settled down to creating an ideology that would be acceptable to a diverse population under siege. Some of the subtlest and some of the most obvious changes in British society are apparent in the language of wartime—both the language that propagandists used and the language that they deemed acceptable.

Speech was manipulated in primarily two ways in wartime Britain: in one sense, speech was designed to curtail speech; in another, speech was designed to boost morale. The former strategy attempted to stop people from spreading rumors, giving away military secrets, or saying anything that might cause "alarm and despondency," to use the lovely official phrase. The latter strategy was intended to encourage, inspire, and cheer people who were living in a state of privation, danger, and uncertainty. Both verbal strategies promoted unity, courage, and the assurance of victory, and both made appeals to a wide variety of interests. What follows is a discussion of four wartime needs that predominated in verbal maneuvers: the need for silence, the need for unity, the need for humor, and the need to talk about the future.

The Need for Silence

> Speech is silver, silence is golden.
> —Swiss proverb, quoted by Thomas Carlyle

> That's a first-rate training they give them in the Spies nowadays—better than in my day, even. What d'you think's the latest thing they've served them out with? Ear trumpets for listening through keyholes! My little girl brought one home the other night—tried it out on our sitting room door, and reckoned she could hear twice as much as with her ear to the hole. Of course it's only a toy, mind you. Still, gives 'em the right idea, eh?
> —George Orwell, *1984*

Freedom of speech is an early casualty of war. Military victories depend on secrecy, and "careless talk" is the most obvious way that secrecy is broken. In Britain, freedom of speech was so ingrained and taken for granted that the government was forced to tread lightly, realizing that any abridgement of so entrenched a right might alienate people and actually lessen their support of the war effort. Thus, hegemony had to be achieved by convincing people that restrictions of speech were a temporary wartime necessity and would depend upon cooperation rather than coercion. The Committee of Imperial Defence stated this policy in a secret document on 15 July 1938, more than one year before the start of the war: "British subjects are unaccustomed to any form of official 'censorship' of their communications and publications. Every opportunity should therefore be taken to enlighten the public in regard to the importance of the war censorship to their own personal safety and interests, with a view to obtaining their co-operation and retaining their goodwill" (INF 1/159).

Censorship, when it did come, was not received quietly. Press censorship, for example, provoked a huge outcry among both British and foreign journalists. Press restrictions were supposed to be limited to material that would have military value to the enemy; only facts were to be suppressed, not opinions. Yet the definition of military value was up for grabs; similarly, the difference between fact and opinion was not always clear, and censors could act with annoying arbitrariness. It must be admitted, however, that criticism of the government continued throughout the war. Press censorship did not keep the *New Statesman* from describing the Ministry of Information as a "scramble of socially favoured amateurs and privileged ignoramuses," nor did it keep the *Observer* from describing the ministry's method of choosing staff as one of "stupefying absurdity" (McLaine 1979, 39).

Prohibitions on speaking focused on both factual information and opinions. Whereas giving away military secrets (genuine facts) could help the enemy, so could defeatist opinions or false information lower British morale. Edward Glover, a London psychologist, advised the Ministry of Information of the dangers of rumor: "What is the realistic objection to rumour? Simply that the morale of the country is damaged by it! Here is the crucial argument. At any time up to gaining of a decisive military victory, the war can be lost by a sudden and violent drop in civilian morale. Incidentally the peace can be lost immediately after a victory for the same reason. *If therefore a M.O.I. has any justification in wartime its function must be the maintenance, stimulation and useful canalising of morale*" (INF 1/318, H.P. 345, emphasis in original). Rumors abounded in wartime Britain: one of the most widespread claimed that German agents had parachuted into Britain disguised as nuns; they could be identified by their hairy wrists.[2] Yet stopping the spread of such rumors was not easy; the ministry's antirumor campaign was both unpopular and unsuccessful.

For one thing, the definition of rumor is problematic, as a Home Intelligence report of 24 May 1940 makes clear: "It is useless to warn people against *repeating rumours;* most people only repeat what they believe to be true and they repeat it because they have nothing more positive to talk about and their time is not being actively filled. Enemy agents may be at work and there is malicious gossiping but evidence before us at the moment suggests that most rumours are passed on by idle, frightened, suspicious people" (INF 1/264, 97/15 H.I.; emphasis in original). The problematic nature of rumor did not prevent the ministry from searching it out and prosecuting it. On 6 June 1940 an extract from the Log Book of the Anti-Lie Bureau lists the following under *Today's Rumours:* "B.E.F. Officers fought to be evacuated before their men. Story spread by a Mrs. Watson, 145 Empire Court, Wembley." The informant was listed as H.J. Keefe of Wembley, and the action taken as "Informed Scotland Yard, and asked them to send an Officer to reprimand and warn Mrs. Watson" (INF 1/264, 97/15 H.I.). With such activities going on, one is not surprised to learn that George Orwell had extensive experience with the Ministry of Information during the war.[3] A morale report, also of 6 June 1940, is filled with references to public depression and grumbling; it lists a harsher punishment for rumor-mongering: "Yesterday at Mansfield a civilian was fined 10 gns. [guineas] and 5 gns. cost for falsely attributing a rumour to Haw Haw. The case received wide publicity" (INF 1/264, 97/15 H.I.). Such policy showed that if careless talk did not cost lives, it could at least cost fifteen guineas—no mean sum in 1940.[4]

In addition to rumors, other forms of verbal misbehavior were punished, and people were prosecuted for spreading "alarm and despondency." Such limitations on speech were met with great hostility. Ian McLaine writes, "The public resented the well publicised spate of prosecutions for what was regarded as grumbling 'in the British tradition'" (1979, 83). The "Silent Column" campaign—a wordless response to the Fifth Column—was launched by the Ministry of Information in the summer of 1940. Its aim was to quiet those who spread depressing rumors as well as those who spread actual information. Silent Column posters depicted characters such as "Mr. Knowall," "Miss Leaky Mouth," and "Mr. Glumpot," who displayed inappropriate verbal behavior and could be countered by demonstrations of correct verbal behavior. For example, the description of Mr. Knowall reads: "He knows what the Germans are going to do and when they are going to do it. He knows where our ships are. He knows what the Bomber Command is up to. With his large talk he is playing the enemy's game. Tell him so" (McLaine 1979, figure 3). In a lighter and wittier vein were the many posters bearing the legend "Careless Talk Costs Lives." Fougasse's charming cartoon sketches show people talking, secure in their privacy, while Hitler lurks behind portraits and in wallpaper (McLaine 1979, figure 2b/c). Another poster shows a glamorous woman in evening dress (the dangerous spy and the silly gossip combined), who listens with interest while a soldier, a sailor, and an airman talk; the poster drives home its point with the legend "Keep Mum—She's Not So Dumb" (Cantwell 1989, plate 19). And perhaps the most clever of the slogans, certainly the one most remembered by my interviewees, exhorted British citizens to "Be like Dad—keep Mum!"

The Silent Column and antirumor campaigns were, in the words of Harold Nicolson, "a ghastly failure" (quoted in McLaine 1979, 83). People who spied on their neighbors and turned them in for verbal misconduct (dubbed "Cooper's Snoopers" during Duff Cooper's tenure as minister of information) were especially unpopular. The ministry's Daily Reports on Morale noted the growing resentment created by this unwonted truncation of normal speech. On 17 July 1940 and 20 July 1940, several verbatim comments from "ordinary people" were listed; these included: "The Silent Column campaign is a backhand. Although I agree that people shouldn't say dangerous things, this makes you feel you daren't say anything" and "We are fighting for freedom but losing what freedom we've got" (INF 1/264, 97/15 H.I.). On 22 July 1940, the following secret report was issued: "Strong resentment still felt among all classes at Silent Column Campaign and at police prosecutions for spreading rumours, which are considered 'ridiculous.' M.O.I. becoming unpopular again; much of this feeling directed against the Minister. Indignation expressed at what people say to be 'a policy which is turning us into a nation of spies.' Labour Party Candidates meeting agreed that prosecutions for idle talking were upsetting public morale seriously. People in new positions of minor authority accused of officiousness and bullying manner, reminiscent some say 'of the early days of the Nazis'" (INF 1/264, 97/15 H.I.).

It was clear that such purely negative propaganda was having, if anything, the opposite of the desired effect. On 19 July 1940 the ministry proclaimed that it had "no wish to stop people talking, nor expressing their opinions upon any subject" (quoted in McLaine 1979, 84). In August, it was decided that only the most serious cases would be prosecuted in the future (McLaine 1979, 84). A morale report from 2 August 1940 showed a compromise slowly growing between governmental dictates and citizens' desires. Though the ministry had been forced to bow to popular wishes, the populace was still considered mute and insensible; despite the many manifestations listed in ministry reports of outspoken criticism among young people, the intelligentsia, and the unnamed "ordinary people," the ministry still was having difficulty grasping the idea that the masses could think and articulate their thoughts: "There has been a great deal of popular satisfaction at the revision of the defeatist talk sentences, although there is little evidence that people at large are greatly concerned about the curtailment of civil liberties" (INF 1/264, 97/15 H.I.).

Despite the government's slowness in coming to terms with the articulate masses, compromise was being accepted by the government as inevitable. Compromise and negotiation are essential components of hegemony; whereas domination demands and goes in with guns, hegemony cajoles and wins the other side to its point of view. Fines and punishment were actually lowering morale and increasing the cleft between government and people; thus, some way had to be found to make people *agree* to the importance of speech restriction, and to police their own ways of speaking. Already in June 1940 the ministry was wrestling with this problem. Gavin Brown, a member of the editorial staff of the *Times*, wrote in a letter to the ministry:

> From many sources I have heard that the following remarks are being
>   made in public:—
> "We should be no worse off under Hitler."
> "If Hitler were here it would not affect you and me."
> "If Hitler ruled England, it would only mean that I should pay my taxes
>   to him instead of to the King."
>
> I am a serving Special Constable and if I could only catch one of
> these men or women first hand I should naturally know how to deal

with him or her, but unless I can get hold of definite names of persons it is not much use my reporting to my Police Inspector the mere fact that these statements are being made, and it struck me that it might, perhaps, be more a matter for the Ministry of Information than for the Police.

I thought that the Ministry might care to draw attention to the fact that these statements were being made and that the severest penalties would be imposed, or, conversely, it might like to issue some counter propaganda showing what would happen if Hitler did come here. [INF 1/257, H.7]

C.H. Wilson, in a letter to Sir Kenneth Clark, suggested that the latter course would be most effective in the majority of cases:

While only the strongest measures would be effective against deliberate rumour-mongers, our experience with rumour suggests that a larger and equally important body of people tends to defeatism simply through lack of any inspiring direction. I do not think that defeatism of this class can be countered by terrifying people. . . . All classes in this country should be reminded of the values of civilisation which they have so far achieved and . . . should be reminded of the achievements of labour, of their social services, their high standard of living, their tradition in public education, the emancipation of women, their industrial preeminence, and that they are a race of pioneers and leaders. They must be told that they are fighting for the preservation of these achievements and for their future development.

Side by side with these appeals could be given a picture of life under the Nazis. . . . The keynote of all this is that it is a People's War. [INF 1/ 257, H.7]

Wilson paints here with a remarkably broad brush, appealing to "all classes in this country," to women and men, to workers and industrialists, to nationalists, imperialists, and antifascists. He speaks of defending institutions that Conservatives had previously fought and of achievements that had pitted themselves against one another. But there is no trace of past conflict in Wilson's appeal; his all-inclusive "they" refers simply to the British people, who are to be both savior and saved. Wilson is moving past the purely negative verbal strategy of restriction and toward the more positive goal of unity.

Yet the goal of restriction was still present; it simply had to be accomplished by convincing people that such restrictions were in the best interest of British citizens and, indeed, of the world. Loyal British subjects should not listen to or repeat lies, rumors, dangerous information, or broadcasts from Haw-Haw; thus, they need a thoroughly truthful public source from which to glean and impart information.

Fortunately, such a resource was readily available: the British Broadcasting Corporation (BBC). A document entitled "The Fifth Column: How It Works," apparently written in response to Gavin Brown's letter, describes the BBC in its new, godlike role:

> It is the duty of every one of us to trust no-one, not even our next door neighbours, and to ignore completely every sort of talk or news that is not official. In other words believe the B.B.C.—the announcers now are all named and recognisable by their voices—and believe all other official statements. But always ignore everything else. Further, on no account embroider or add to any news you may be discussing by tying it up with your own theories of what may or may not happen. Finally, stick firmly to your duties and your jobs. People who are fully occupied have little time to talk. [INF 1/257, H.7]

A.P. Herbert translated this dour, Big-Brotherish dictum into a catchy bit of doggerel:

> Do not believe the tale the milkman tells;
> No troops have mutinied at Potters Bar.
> Nor are there submarines at Tunbridge Wells.
> The B.B.C. will warn us when there are. [quoted in A. Calder 1969, 134]

Such statements were still a bit heavy-handed. To enlist the British people as partners, rather than merely followers, it was necessary to show the actual dangers of careless talk and, at the same time, to show that restrictions on speaking should come from the people themselves. A series of films made by the Crown Film Unit presented the problems and showed the possible consequences of careless talk. Some of these films were cast essentially as spy thrillers, such as one entitled *Dangerous Comment,* which was made in 1939 and featured Ian Fleming (INF 6/525). At the beginning of the film, two British officials are discussing the problem of careless talk. One says, "In Germany, they cure wagging tongues in a concentration camp." "That's not our way," the other replies. "No, it's not," the first one agrees. The film goes on to show a disastrous string of events caused by careless words: a soldier tells his girlfriend of a surprise attack on Germany, the girlfriend tells a friend, who gossips at a bar where the barman is a German spy and manages to get information back to Germany, where it is the British fighters who are surprised. The film shows that careless talk is dangerous to the British people and that the British people alone can stop it—no concentration camps, no roundups in the night will be employed. The film is designed to show how one protects freedom of speech by voluntarily and temporarily curtailing it. Ideologically, the film declares that British ways are worth fighting for, and that careful words are a way in which everyone can join the fight.

If one should not speak improperly, then by the same token, one should not listen to improper speech. Whereas Miss Leaky Mouth and Mr. Glumpot were shadowy fictional characters, the chief verbal villain was not. Arguably the strangest radio personality of the war, William Joyce (better known as Lord Haw-Haw) was born in 1906 in New York, the son of an Irish father and an English mother. Though William's father had become an American citizen, he moved the family back to Ireland when William was three years old. The family opposed Irish home rule and moved to England in 1921. Joyce had a mystical, romantic attachment to "Britishness," though he never actually held British citizenship. He was first attracted to fascism in 1923 when he joined an obscure group called British Fascisti Limited; later, he was an ardent member of Sir Oswald Mosley's British Union of Fascists. Eventually, he found British fascism too liberal for his liking, became a dedicated National Socialist, and moved to Germany shortly before the war. Employed as a radio announcer of Nazi propaganda, he made regular broadcasts to Britain (usually beginning with "Germany Calling") and tried to convince the British that they were fighting on the wrong side. He was also a producer of programs for the New British Broadcasting Station, a Nazi project stationed in East Prussia that pretended to be the work of British Fifth Columnists (Cole 1964).

The nickname "Haw-Haw" was coined by Jonah Barrington, writing for the *Daily Express*, and it originally referred not to Joyce but to Norman Baillie-Stewart, another British subject who was broadcasting for the Nazis in Germany. The epithet referred to Baillie-Stewart's stage-aristocrat manner of speaking: "He speaks English of the haw-haw, damit-get-out-of-my-way variety" (quoted in Cole 1964, 115). When Joyce became the most prominent broadcaster of Nazi propaganda to Britain, Barrington appended the title and dubbed Joyce "Lord Haw-Haw," for the true identity of this Nazi broadcaster was a mystery at the time.[5] The link between accent and class is notoriously strong in Britain; Eliza Doolittle had only to change her clothes and her accent to be thought an upper-class lady. It is also interesting that "the most-hated man of the Second World War" (Cole 1964, 14) should be cast in the guise of a British aristocrat (which, of course, he was not). Some took umbrage at such a suggestion, forgetting perhaps that Oswald Mosley was a baronet. Yet, one wonders how much pent-up hatred of the complacent upper classes could be released by dubbing this famous traitor a lord.

Millions of people listened to the Haw-Haw broadcasts. The British government cannily did not jam the airwaves or forbid listening to German broadcasts, which was in sharp contrast to the German policy of (only partially successful) jamming the airwaves and severe penalties for those who listened anyway. Kenneth Burke writes: "The greatest menace *to* dictatorships lies in the fact that, through their 'efficiency' in silencing the enemy, they deprive themselves of competitive collaboration.... By putting the quietus upon their opponent, they bring themselves all the more rudely against the *unanswerable opponent*, the opponent who cannot be refuted, the nature of brute reality itself" (1967, 107; emphasis in original). The British government did not attempt to silence the enemy, but they did wish to make him unpopular while at the same time showing their tolerance for freedom of expression. In 1940 the British *Public Opinion Quarterly* wrote: "Haw-Haw's propaganda is listened to with enjoyment. It is common to hear people say that 'there is a great deal of truth in it'" (quoted in Rolo 1942, 73). With such opinions common in Britain, it was necessary to discredit Haw-Haw rather than to forbid listening to him.

But what exactly did Haw-Haw say? His reputation for both omniscience and threat was astonishing. He was supposed to have known that the Darlington Town Hall clock was two minutes slow (INF 1/264, 97/15 H.I., 5 June 1940) and that a gasometer in Ipswich was near a factory where girls slid down bannisters (Cole 1964, 155). The Ministry of Information was deluged with letters from people asking if their town, factory, cathedral, and so forth were going to be blown up; they had heard rumors that Haw-Haw had threatened these targets (INF 1/265, H.I. 1005/1, p. A). Few people had actually heard the alleged broadcasts personally; someone else had usually been the source of the information. Obviously, these "Haw-Haw legends" (as the ministry called them) were doing as much harm as the actual broadcasts. On 4 June 1940 the ministry released the following secret report: "The anti-rumour campaign should be intensified and occasion should again be taken to discredit the Hamburg broadcasts and the New British Broadcasting Corporation. In particular an early and renewed effort should be made to dispel the legend of Lord Haw-Haw's omniscience, as of his secret sources of information" (INF 1, 250, H. 1/1). The *Daily Mirror* mounted its own anti–Haw-Haw campaign by forming the Anti Haw-Haw League of Loyal Britons "who promised not to listen to German broadcasts or even any mention of the name Haw-Haw and to try to stop the spread of any harmful rumour." The newspaper supplied a notice, to be cut from the paper and placed on the radio, that said: "This set is Anti Haw-Haw. It hears no evil, speaks no evil." The Anti Haw-Haw League was no more popular than the antirumor campaign and ended on 26 July 1940, feeling perhaps that its work was done (Cole 1964, 157).

The wartime British press treated Haw-Haw as a great evildoer or a great joke. Interestingly, memories of Haw-Haw combine just this mixture of hatred and derision. According to Eileen Scales:

> *ES*: We hated him. We would hear all these lies which we said they
> were lies, you know, how many English planes had been shot down
> over Germany. I mean it was just all done to demoralise you really.
> And my father used to get very angry when he listened to him, and
> he said he was a man that used to stand at the corner of a street

where we lived just prior to the war. . . . William Joyce used to stand at the corner of this street surrounded by his Blackshirts . . . hated him. To think that—we were always under the impression that he was an Englishman—and to think that an Englishman should be such a traitor as to, you know, to broadcast against his country as he did. . . . It was just sort of propaganda to make you feel bad and to demoralise you and to make you feel that we were losing the war.

JF: Did it work at all?

ES: I don't think so. It certainly didn't with my family. I mean, they tended to laugh at him a bit although he made them angry to be a traitor. [personal interview, 5 March 1993]

Traitors are rarely funny, yet Haw-Haw was and is treated as a monstrous joke. Eileen Scales does not recall his propaganda efforts as successful—despite the fact that at the beginning of his broadcasts Britain *was* losing the war. Fred Mitchell's memories are similar: "Everyone used to listen to Lord Haw-Haw, didn't they? . . . I thought it was funny actually. I mean everyone used to go out and say, if we got a hold of him we'd skin him alive, you know. I mean, the general concept, we'd like to get hold of him and put him in a room with half a dozen of the women who'd lost husbands and sons" (personal interview, 18 May 1993).

In the case of Lord Haw-Haw, memory follows public presentation very closely: he was viewed as a nasty buffoon, vicious but fundamentally harmless. Mass-Observation noted that this public presentation was mirrored by wartime Londoners as well. On 9 September 1940 a group of waitresses at a Lyons Corner House greeted an alleged threat from Lord Haw-Haw with "much laughter": "Lord Haw-Haw says he's going to bomb all the Corner Houses next Sunday because they're Jewish!" (Harrisson 1990, 69). One has to look at formerly secret documents to realize that, at one time, Haw-Haw was taken very seriously indeed. Why was so much importance attributed to the fact that, of all of Goebbels's propaganda machine, people were listening to Lord Haw-Haw? Why was he credited with such omniscience, such intimate knowledge of the everyday workings of British towns? Why were his supposed bombing threats taken so seriously, despite the fact that they did not actually come to pass and that military maneuvers are rarely communicated to the enemy? (If Haw-Haw had announced genuine military targets, he would have been helping the British, not the Germans.) And finally, why did so many people listen to him?

Charles J. Rolo, writing in 1942, gives a partial answer:

Haw-Haw's initial popularity is easily explained. Throughout the fall and winter of 1939 and the spring of 1940, dissatisfaction with the Chamberlain regime had crystallized into a total loss of faith. When

Haw-Haw denounced the hidebound conservatism, the muddle-headedness and inefficiency of the "old gang," he was only giving pointed expression to the sentiments of the bulk of his listeners. His appeal vanished overnight when Churchill took over. With a leader they respected, and one who restored their confidence in themselves and in their cause, the British were in no mood to pay much attention to the strictures of a Nazi hireling. [1942, 73–74]

Yet, as we have seen, the Ministry of Information was paying close and concerted attention to Haw-Haw in the summer of 1940, after Churchill had become prime minister. (One also might add that Churchill was a Conservative, the grandson of a Duke, and a one-time member of the "old gang.") Though Haw-Haw's attacks on the British establishment were certainly one factor in his popularity (despite the fact that by his accent and titled nickname he was identified with them), other forces were at work as well—forces that could not be adequately discussed in 1942. I believe that Lord Haw-Haw became the focal point of fears held by both the British government and the British people, fears that could not be directly discussed because of prohibitions on speech.

"Joyce was a man who is remembered for what he did not say," writes J.A. Cole (1964, 158). The many Haw-Haw legends, regarding Joyce's knowledge of town clocks and alleged threats of bombing, were largely fabrications; Joyce said nothing of the kind. Yet the British people were constantly being told that Fifth Columnists were at work in Britain. The British people knew the strength of the German military; as Britain "stood alone" in the summer of 1940, it had seen German legions roll into France, Austria, Denmark, Norway, the Netherlands, Luxembourg, and Czechoslovakia with virtually no trouble. Such a military machine was capable of putting scores of Fifth Columnists in strategic places and of bombing innocent civilians. Though the sustained bombing of civilian targets ("the blitz") had not yet begun, precision bombing was in its infancy; by the summer of 1940, civilians had been killed by bombs during the Battle of Britain and in other raids on military and industrial targets. (There were also memories of the German bombing of London during World War I.) As reported in the Ministry of Information's morale logs, the anxiety and uncertainty of the pre-blitz period were in some ways worse than the blitz itself: people had no idea what to expect or what to do. By attributing such fearsome power and such nonchalant threats to Lord Haw-Haw, people could express their fear of the German military without actually referring to it. Haw-Haw became a symbol of German power and conquest and was hated and derided as such.

Why was Haw-Haw singled out? William Joyce represented the worst nightmare of the British government and the British people: the Briton turned traitor.

As it turned out, fascism never made much headway in Britain; the explanations range from British respect for law and order (the conservative explanation), British tolerance for difference (the liberal explanation), the presence of an active British trade union and left-wing movement (the socialist explanation), and the idea that fascism was undesirable because it was a foreign philosophy (the "fascist" explanation). But in 1940 there was no way of knowing how many people would go along with fascism in the case of a German invasion that, at the time, looked inevitable. Genuine traitors like William Joyce are relatively rare, but cowards and collaborationists are depressingly common; Britain had watched fascism spring like an evil weed in most of Europe. Even normally tolerant countries such as the Netherlands and Denmark had been defenseless against a combination of German troops and homegrown Nazis; and Britain's old friend, Norway, had coughed up Vidkun Quisling. Despite Churchill's promise to "fight on the beaches and the landing grounds," the British military had not bothered to defend the German invasion of the Channel Islands; no one had fought on the beaches and landing grounds of Jersey and Guernsey. No one knew how many other William Joyces would come out of the woodwork in the event of a German invasion. If Haw-Haw could be treated as a joke and a buffoon, a figure of ridicule and even of fun, then fear of what he represented could be muted and rendered manageable. But the hatred accorded him showed how real the fear still was.

Why did people listen to Haw-Haw? One reason was because they were desperate for information. The Ministry of Information wrote on 11 July 1940, "Some women who listen remark: 'We get our news first from German stations as long as Germany is winning the war'" (INF 1/264, 97/15 H.I.). Second, in the war of words, Haw-Haw provided a verbal target. I.E.W., a young teenager in 1940, remembers yelling at the radio such comments as "That's a load of lies" and "We're going to beat the living daylights out of you" (personal interview, 7 May 1993). There also were people who listened to Haw-Haw because they agreed with some of Haw-Haw's views, though it would be difficult in 1993 to admit to liking a famous British traitor. Yet in 1940 these views were real enough; Tom Harrisson of Mass-Observation reports wartime comments such as "He sounds such a nice man. It makes you think there must be something in what he says" and "I love him and his clever, tricky sayings. I love his voice and manner and would love to meet him" (1990, 316–17).

The popularity of Haw-Haw and the prevalence of rumors alerted the British government to the necessity of providing a more accurate or at least more easily controlled venue for information. In his "Memorandum on the Functions of the Ministry of Information," Edward Glover wrote: "Why give news at all? Primarily to satisfy the need for accurate information about the war. If no news were given, the people . . . *would manufacture their own news*, which would naturally take the form of unfounded rumours and suspicions" (INF 1/318, H.P. 345; emphasis in original). People, like nature, abhor a vacuum; if told nothing, they manufacture something to tell. If the government wished to quiet rumor, it also wished to gain the trust of the people, to make them feel partners rather than followers in a dangerous and important enterprise. Such trust could be gained only if people believed that they were being told the truth, as the following memorandum makes clear. It was sent by the Ministry of Information to the Home Office on 13 September 1939, only ten days after the start of the war: "The people must feel that they are being told the truth. Distrust breeds fear much more than knowledge of reverses. The all-important thing for publicity to achieve is the conviction that the worst is known. This can be achieved by the adoption, publication and prosecution of a policy. The people should be told that this is a civilians' war, or a People's War, and therefore they are to be taken into the Government's confidence as never before" (quoted in McLaine 1979, 28).

This assumption was borne out by the ministry's own research. The morale report on 22 May 1940 stated that "there is a continued demand for truthful news, however black it may be, particularly if it can be given out before German claims are heard" (INF 1/264, 97/15 H.I.). But the memorandum of 13 September made a careful distinction between telling people the truth and making people believe they were being told the truth. It also acknowledged that a lie can become the truth if people believe it and work to make it true: "But what is truth? We must adopt a pragmatic definition. It is what is believed to be the truth. A lie that is put across becomes the truth and may, therefore, be justified. The difficulty is to keep up lying. . . . It is simpler to tell the truth and, if a sufficient emergency arises, to tell one big, thumping lie that will then be believed" (quoted in McLaine 1979, 28).

As the ministry acknowledged, the difficulty was "to keep up lying." On 10 June 1940 it noted that "the public is becoming quick to notice and comment upon conflicting statements" (INF 1/264, 97/15 H.I.). Two months later, on 14 August, it was clear that the public's demand for knowledge represented a need for control over their lives: "Every day provides us with some further evidence of people's doubts about news: formulae repeatedly come in for criticism; any explanation which throws light on the background situation is welcomed. Technical descriptions, i.e., those which give the reader or listener some sense of control over the situation, are well-liked and eye-witness accounts, whose authenticity can be guaranteed, are approved" (INF 1/264, 97/15 H.I.). The people were not easily fooled. In order to build trust, it was necessary for a certain amount of trust to be genuine. In order for World War II to be a people's war, it was necessary that the people be given responsibility and, as much as possible, be told the truth. But first it was necessary to define who the people were.

The Need for Unity

> Dr. Paul Joseph Goebbels said recently that the nightly air raids have had a terrific effect upon the morale of the people of Britain. The good doctor is absolutely right. Today the morale of the people is higher than ever before.
>
> —Quentin Reynolds, *Britain Can Take It*

British wartime propaganda spoke to many different interests and groups of people, but its chief aim was unity, the notion that the entire country was in danger and was fighting back as one. Propaganda was designed to inspire as well as to espouse this ideal of unity, so that declarations of togetherness and support would come from the corner publican, the East End docker, and the urban housewife as well as from cabinet ministers, generals, and the king. In describing unity and holding it up as the wartime norm, propagandists attempted to encourage and bring about unified behavior. A Ministry of Information report from May 1940 proposed "action to encourage people to co-operate with their neighbours, principally by means of press, broadcast, and films, quoting examples to be collected of districts where this has been done successfully" (INF 1, 250, H. 1/1). But preaching to people was not enough. In order to gain full cooperation, the people had to be treated as partners in the enterprise of war. Their contributions had to be accepted, and their expertise and help sought. This policy required making gestures toward sectors of society that had heretofore been regarded as willing and uncritical followers. If "ordinary people" were to be the saviors of the nation, then the upper classes could no longer be the sole arbiters of public policy, opinion, or taste. The Ministry of Information, aware that the conservative, upper-class bent of BBC radio broadcasts might not be warmly received by all listeners, wrote on 4 June 1940: "It is suggested that something might be done to diminish the present predominance of the cultured voice upon the wireless. Every effort should be made to bring working class people to the microphone, and more frequent use should be made of left-wing speakers to counteract the propaganda of our enemies regarding imperialism and capitalism" (INF 1, 250, H. 1/1).

The commentary of ordinary people, with all their varying accents, did become an important part of wartime broadcasts. Announcers with more educated accents praised these ordinary people for their courage and cheerfulness and their role in keeping London going. A November 1940 broadcast from Piccadilly Circus Underground, used as an air-raid shelter during the blitz, is fairly typical: "In spite of . . . the sleeping on the platform, the discomfort, so far, I'm bound to say that I've found, in talking to them, that they're a pretty happy lot, and I'd like you to meet some of them." The announcer goes on to interview several shelterers, who sound alternately nervous, bored, or cheerful to the point of lunacy. Then, should anyone miss the point, the announcer ends his broadcast with: "They may be sheltering here until tonight, but at 6:00 tomorrow morning, they'll be workers once again, coming out of the tube into trains and buses and back on their job of helping London to carry on" (NSA ref. nos. 2730-2 and LP2716b1).

In this broadcast, the importance of workers in maintaining society is acknowledged, along with the assumption that they are doing a fine job and should keep it up. Privately, upper-class people might retain their disdain of "the lower orders," as is found in Vita Sackville-West's letter to her husband, Harold Nicolson: "I hate democracy. I hate la populace. I wish education had never been encouraged . . . I wish la populace had never been encouraged to emerge from its rightful place" (quoted in Smithies 1982, 170). But public presentations of London workers (Cockney cabdrivers who drove cheerfully through bombs, shop girls who showed up for work even if they had to walk) were wholeheartedly admiring.

Public presentations of cheery, uncomplaining workers remained at a fairly banal level, but there were more serious attempts to find out what people actually wanted. The Ministry of Information's Daily Reports on Morale, which covered London and the provinces, reported the ebb and flow of public feeling, the concerns and fears of the people, and their suggestions for future improvement. The Wartime Social Survey targeted specific issues and sent interviewers to collect opinions from a random sample of the population; among the topics covered were the influence of Ministry of Information films, whether people preferred white or brown bread, and whether they would like communal feeding centers. (The vitamin-packed "victory loaf" was neither brown nor white but a shade of gray, and communal feeding centers, dubbed "British Restaurants" by Churchill, were set up when it was found that people wanted them.) A Ministry of Information morale report from 14 August 1940 showed the popularity of these measures: "Low income people glad to be questioned, report several observers, and even express gratification that Government wants to know what they think because 'this is a people's war'" (INF 1/264, 97/15 H.I.).

Mass-Observation, originally set up in 1937 to study and document British behavior, remained an independent organization throughout the war but provided the government with a great deal of information about the wants of ordinary citizens. And rather poignant is the indication that people felt free to make their opinions known. The archives of the Ministry of Information show a letter written on 18 September 1939 by one E.B. Morgan, a city solicitor, who suggested several propaganda strategies and enclosed a mawkish draft of a speech designed for Princess Elizabeth, in which she was to tell evacuated children that "There's nothing at all to be frightened about" and "Do just what you're told." His suggestions were discarded, but a note attached to his letter advised that his suggestions be "cordially" replied to (INF 1/10). Thus the task of creating wartime propaganda became a joint, albeit unequal, project of government officials and ordinary citizens.

Such laudable attention to the wants of the little people did not flow from goodwill alone. A divided nation cannot hope to win a war. The paradox of British nationality was clear in 1939: though one of the oldest and most stable nation-states in Europe, it was simultaneously a highly stratified society. Divided by class, region, ethnicity, politics, and religion, the citizens of the United Kingdom had to be molded into some kind of unified whole. Theirs was a nation-state composed of four distinct geographic and cultural entities (England, Scotland, Wales, and Northern Ireland), each with its own languages, accents, music, food, ethnic identity, capital city, and patron saint.[6] It was a nation with a class system so strong and so entrenched that it affected everything from education and career choices to foods eaten and names given to children. It was a nation in which regional loyalties were strong and regional dialects mutually unintelligible, where city and country folk viewed one another as alien creatures. Politically, the United Kingdom ranged from the Communist Party to the British Union of Fascists. In such a divided society, unity could not be taken for granted but had to be carefully built. Kenneth Burke calls this process of building group solidarity "identification": "Identification is affirmed with earnestness precisely because there is division. Identification is compensatory to division. If men were not apart from one another, there would be no need for the rhetorician to proclaim their unity" (1962, 546). In war, it is necessary to identify oneself with a larger entity that purports to represent oneself and one's chosen comrades. In a religious war, religion is the unifying factor; in a class war, class feeling rules the day. In a war of nation-states, it is essential that citizens identify themselves with the state and feel that their compatriots are similar to them because of the fact of nationality, in a sense as interchangeable as foot soldiers. In such a way, the personal self is exchanged for the political self; the "we" of wartime is always a political "we."

Appeals to patriotism are common in wars between nation-states, but such an appeal is complex in the United Kingdom, where the nation-state does not correspond exactly with the nation. As mentioned, the United Kingdom consists of England, Scotland, Wales, and Northern Ireland—pretty much in that order.[7] Though England is the most populous and the most powerful, there was an attempt during the war to stop using England as a synecdoche for Britain, if only to gain the loyalty of the blitzed citizens of Glasgow, the out-of-work miners of South Wales. This appeal to patriotism had to deal with the fact of being British collectively as well as being English, Scottish, Welsh, or Irish individually. How was this to be done?

One technique was to mix everybody together, ignoring difference and division while stressing similarity and unity. A radio broadcast from New Year's Eve

1944 combined a reading of Tennyson's "In Memoriam" and a high-church sermon from St. Paul's with the commentary of (among others) a Worcestershire farmer, a "girl-worker" in a Manchester parachute factory, a Scottish train conductress, a Welsh transport worker, a telephone operator in Northern Ireland, and a South London housewife. As the clock struck eleven, the commentator called upon

> The men and women of the civil defence, guardians of our home and factories. Calling the men and women on the land, who have fed our people. Women workers who do men's work, so that their men may fight. The housewives of Britain who have kept the home fires burning. Factory workers who this year saw the triumph of their labours. The transport workers and all who helped to launch our armies into Europe. The dockers and shipyard workers, builders and launchers of the invasion fleets. Clerks and teachers, tradesmen, shopkeepers and a thousand more. We call the whole of Great Britain—north, south, east, and west. We call on you all—the people of Scotland, of Northern Ireland, of Wales. [NSA ref. nos. F44/214 and LP24739-40]

Another technique was to address the divisions that exist even in unity and to speak to two interests at once. One of the most remarkable expressions of this dual loyalty is in a speech given by David Lloyd George, announcing the canceling of the Welsh national eisteddfod, the famous singing contest held every year of peacetime in the first week of August. This speech was played on the BBC on 7 August 1940; thus the entire country could hear Lloyd George skillfully manipulating the ambiguities and tensions inherent in being both British and Welsh:

> For unknown centuries, our ancestors have resisted the invaders of our shores and valiantly fought for freedom from foreign domination. This is not the first time Britons have been called upon to repel even a German invasion. As a small nation which has ever fought tenaciously for its national recognition and rights, Wales has a special interest in the result of this tremendous struggle for international right and freedom. This is the day of the agony of little nations. On the continent of Europe, their national liberties and their hopes have been crushed under the terrible iron chariot of the Nazi legions. But the three smaller nations of the British Isles have been taught by their own history that although the national spirit of a people may be bruised and even temporarily broken, it never dies, for it lives on in the memories, the traditions, and the songs of their native land. [NSA ref. nos. 2619-20 and LP26122b6]

He goes on to discuss the increasing danger to Britain emanating from the Continent and concludes, "If her people are worthy of their forefathers, Britain will pass through this hurricane fearless and erect and will emerge from its rage mightier, more honoured and more powerful than ever for the good of mankind."

What exactly is Lloyd George talking about? At one level, he is pledging Welsh support to the British war effort, for the Welsh are always ready to fight oppression and defend their native land. At another level, he is reminding his audience that the Welsh understand oppression because they have known it themselves, and that if they fight for freedom abroad, they expect it at home as well. Especially ambiguous is the sentence "This is not the first time Britons have been called upon to repel even a German invasion." This statement may refer to World War I, when Germany bombed Britain but did not actually invade. But strictly speaking, the word "Briton" refers to the original inhabitants of Great Britain, who were conquered and pushed to Wales by the invading Angles and Saxons, who were, of course, Germanic. Unity may supersede division, but division is not forgotten.

There were also attempts to forge unity across time as well as space and to link the entirety of contemporary Britain with the greatness of Britain's past. British culture and British history were presented as some of the things for which the war was being fought; defeat would mean the loss of a distinctly *British* way of life. A Ministry of Information report from 1940, entitled "Report of Planning Committee on a Home Moral [*sic*] Campaign," makes the following suggestions to the BBC: "Performances of English music, readings of English poetry and stories of heroic achievements already occupy a considerable part of the programme, but might be increased without fear of tub-thumping or complacency" (INF 1, 250, H. 1/1). Wartime accounts noted people's fondness for repeating a phrase attributed to Queen Victoria: "There is no depression in this house. We refuse to listen to possibilities of defeat: they do not exist" (quoted in Woon 1941, 71; Vere Hodgson's diary, 4 January 1941). *Words for Battle,* a Crown Film Unit production from the early 1940s, further demonstrates this process of identification through space and time; it also gives a friendly nod to Britain's most powerful ex-colony and ally (INF 6/338). An unseen Laurence Olivier reads from Camden's "Britannia," Browning's "Home Thoughts from the Sea," Abraham Lincoln's "Gettysburg Address," and various patriotic works by Milton, Kipling, and Blake. The film culminates in Churchill's speech promising that "We shall defend our Island, whatever the cost may be." As Olivier speaks, the camera pans over British cities, towns, and fields, showing the places Churchill had pledged to defend. Another obvious historical parallel can be seen in a short, comedy-of-manners radio drama set during the Napoleonic Wars, in which Edith Evans and John Gielgud discuss the impossibility of Britain being defeated by "Boney" (NSA ref. no. LP37454f3, 16 May 1943).[8]

And the words of Shakespeare, that greatest of British voices, were everywhere. Showing the long-standing British love for puns, the Crown Film Unit made films entitled *Thereby Hangs a Tail* (INF 6/1813) and *Tell Me Where Is Fancy Bread* (INF 6/1810). This prevalence for quoting Shakespeare seems to have been the province of all classes: Anthony Eden's radio broadcast of 14 May 1940 urged volunteers "to make assurance doubly sure" (quoted in Calder 1969, 105); East Enders George and Helena Britton wrote in a letter to their daughter, "If an operation is necessary, 'twere well it were done quickly" (10 February 1943); while Kensington diarist Vere Hodgson related a funny story and then remarked, "Cowards die many times before their deaths!" (10 October 1940).

If Shakespeare was the greatest voice of the past, then the voice of the present belonged to Winston Churchill. A Wartime Social Survey conducted in August 1940 showed that the popularity of Churchill as a speaker far eclipsed everyone else, with Anthony Eden as a distant second (INF 1/264, 97/15 H.I., 6 September 1940). Even those who detested his politics were moved by his skill as an orator. Anne Lubin admitted being inspired by Churchill's speeches despite the fact that she "hated his guts. . . . But he had a wonderful turn of phrase, and he could inspire. But then, of course, any demagogue can do that. Hitler did, didn't he?" (personal interview, 13 March 1993). Anne was not alone in her feelings; many believe that Churchill's success came only from his skill as a wordsmith. George Wagner, a German political refugee, says:

> Churchill's political career was abysmal. And but for the war, he would have only been a little smudge in the annals of English history. A very unstable English politician who made a mess of nearly everything he touched. As home secretary before the war, he was dreadful. In the Admiralty at the beginning of the war, he was, if anything, even worse. After the war, he ruined the English currency and, but then, when Hitler came, he was from fairly early on, dead-set against him and became then *the* leader of the internal opposition in the Conservative party against Chamberlain's appeasement policy. And of course, he was a literate man, a bit besotted by the pompous Augustan style of the eighteenth century, and producing quite a bearable twentieth century version of the same. And he liked to write speeches, and he liked even more making these speeches. And the "blood, sweat, and tears"—they were very well conceived . . . but in the end, you know, like other star performances, you know the tricks, you begin to get a little bit tired of it. [personal interview, 23 April 1993]

Clearly, of course, the British population did get a bit tired of it; Churchill was voted out in the election of 1945. (Vere Hodgson, a former left-winger who became enamored of Churchill's speeches during the war, was horrified by this act of "ingratitude" and echoed Othello: "Oh, the pity of it!" [29 July 1945]). But no one knew better than Churchill how to express and foment unity. In a speech given on 19 May 1940, soon after he became prime minister, Churchill spoke of the need for unity to transcend partisan political differences:

Having received His Majesty's commission, I have formed an administration of men and women of every party and of almost every point of
view. We have differed and quarrelled in the past; but now one bond
unites us all—to wage war until victory is won, and never to surrender
ourselves to servitude and shame, whatever the cost and the agony may
be. This is one of the most awe-striking periods in the long history of
France and Britain. It is also beyond doubt the most sublime. Side by
side, unaided except by their kith and kin in the great Dominions and
by the wide Empires which rest beneath their shield—side by side, the
British and French peoples have advanced to rescue not only Europe but
mankind from the foulest and most soul-destroying tyranny which has
ever darkened and stained the pages of history. [Eade 1951, 184]

Here, the political "we" is formed not of those who agree on politics but of those
who have agreed to set political differences aside. The political "we" is framed as
though it is *above* politics; the cause of "mankind," the eradication of "tyranny,"
and the refusal to submit to "servitude and shame" are the ties that bind.

Churchill was not always so direct in the building of identification; to the
contrary, he sometimes showed an extraordinary ability to exploit the ambiguities
of language. This subtlety is apparent in a line from the same speech: "The interests of property, the hours of labour are nothing compared with the struggle for
life and honour, for right and freedom, to which we have vowed ourselves" (Eade
1951, 184). Here, the political "we" is formed by the two entities that are the standard twentieth-century justifications for war: self-defense ("the struggle for life")
and freedom ("honour, right and freedom"). But what is most interesting is the
seamless way that Churchill couples the terms "property" and "labour" and thus
unites two forces that are usually opposed to one another in class-stratified British
society. On the most obvious level, this sentence means that the war will take a
great deal of work ("hours of labour") and that it will require the use and destruction of a great deal of property ("interests of property"). This situation is lamen-
table but it cannot be helped, and it is the duty of each citizen to spare nothing in
the coming fight. But on a deeper level, this sentence asserts that "property" and
"labour" are on the same side. Both the "propertied" classes (who live by income
from their "interests") and the "labouring" classes (who live by income from "hours"
spent) must forget their differences and work together; the class struggle must be
subsumed by the war against the Axis powers.

Wartime sources show that many people accepted such identification as a
wartime necessity; unity was chosen as a pragmatic thing. For some people,
Churchill became a genuine hero; Vere Hodgson suggests "a statue in gold" as a
fitting tribute (23 December 1940). A Ministry of Information report from 6
August 1940 shows that, at the time, Churchill was actually more popular than

the government he led: "The Prime Minister's leadership is unchallenged but evidence suggests that there is no such close identification between the people and the Government as a whole" (INF 1/264, 97/15 H.I.). Churchill may not have been universally loved, but his ability to rally the population was making him universally necessary. A Ministry of Information report from 31 May 1940 describes the attitudes of working-class Londoners: "Taxi men and other manual workers' trades declare they are behind the present Government. 'We may have to fight Churchill after, but he's the man for us now.' Appreciate Bevin and Morrison in Government" (INF 1/264, 97/15 H.I.).

If Ernest Bevin, a working-class trade unionist, and Herbert Morrison, a policeman's son, could become cabinet ministers, then perhaps Britain was changing after all. In a broadcast on 14 February 1941, W.J. Brown gave a working-class, trade unionist conception of national unity, coupled with a passionate plea for a new type of Britain, a place where all have worth and value and fight equally to defend the common weal:

> I want a world where man may meet his fellow men not on the basis of the position he occupies nor the size of his bank balance nor the type of school he went to, but on the basis of his own inherent qualities of mind and spirit. Can we hope to see this? Yes, I think we can. For in the community of danger and sacrifice which this war imposes on all of us, in the fraternity of arms, in the comradeship of the Home Guard, in the fellowship of fire fighting, in a hundred ways, artificial differences are being melted in the fires of war. [NSA ref. nos. 6348-9 and LP6348]

Less optimistic were George and Helena Britton, left-wing, working-class residents of the Bethnal Green district of East London. In a letter to their daughter in California, they show a partial and pragmatic attachment to unified national goals for the duration: "We have a long and hard road to travel before the German military machine can be ground to powder. When it is, we have the task before us of beating our own capitalists and taskmasters" (11 November 1942).

One of the most common tropes in the theme of wartime unity was the notion that the blitz had turned Britain into a battleground; thus everyone—service personnel and civilians alike—was in the front lines, and Britain was referred to as the "home front." A Ministry of Information morale report from 10 September 1940 outlined this strategy, even suggesting that blitzed civilians be buried with Union Jacks during a cloth and paper shortage: "Now that they [Londoners] are beginning to feel, and are being referred to, as 'soldiers in the front line,' everything should be done to encourage this opinion of themselves. It would undoubtedly help if the public were made to feel that their friends and relatives had died for their country, in the same sense as if they were soldiers, sailors or airmen. It might be a small but extremely telling point if, for instance, the dead were buried with Union Jacks on their coffins, or if the Services were represented at their funerals" (INF 1/264, 97/15 H.I.).

The king's Christmas broadcast from 1940 followed this theme, stressing that all citizens were bound together in the comradeship of fellow soldiers. He also stressed the difference from World War I:

> In the last great War, the flower of our youth was destroyed, and the rest of the people saw but little of the battle. This time, we are all in the front lines and the danger together. . . . Remember this: if war brings separation, it brings new unity also—a unity which comes from common perils and common suffering willingly shared. . . . I have seen for myself the battered towns and cities of England, and I have seen the British people facing their ordeal. I can say to them all that they may be justly proud of their race and nation. On every side, I have seen a new and splendid spirit of good fellowship springing up in adversity—a will, a desire to share burdens and resources alike. Out of all this suffering, there is growing a harmony which we must carry forward into the days to come, when we have endured to the end and ours is the victory. [NSA ref. nos. 2831-2 and LP 2812f2]

Compared with the ringing timbres and imperial locution of Churchill, George VI was not an especially good speaker. A shy man with a speech impediment, he had not expected to be king and was made so only by his brother's marital problems and suspected fascist sympathies. Yet most felt kindly toward this gentle-voiced family man who refused to leave the capital when his country was in danger and who sent his daughters only to the English countryside, like any other evacuated children. Creina Musson, the daughter of an army officer, tells the following story about the royal family's reputation:

> Somebody said, would they send the princesses over to Canada or one of the other Dominions, as they were in those days. And the queen said (the present queen mother) said, "Oh, no." She said, "The princesses couldn't go . . . without me and I couldn't go without the king and the king would never go." And of course, the king was very, very popular. Well, they both were because they stayed in London a lot, and when Buckingham Palace was bombed the queen mother, then the queen, said, "Now I can look the East End in the face." Because they used to go down to the East End on the days after the worst raids, you know. Pick their way among the rubble and so on. And they were very much loved. [personal interview, 28 July 1993]

Though the king spoke of visiting "the battered towns and cities of England" (not Britain), it was in London that this image of a home front battleground was the strongest. During the blitz, the *News Chronicle* spoke not of Britons but of Londoners as "front-line soldiers" (quoted in Woon 1941, 82), and many asserted that there were no civilians in London. S.H., whose father was a career navy man, said that during the early part of the war, it was Londoners rather than service people who were inured to bombs and air raids (personal interview, 22 March 1993). And on 6 November 1940, George and Helena Britton read in the paper that fourteen thousand civilians had been killed and twenty thousand injured (with four-fifths of the casualties occurring in London), as opposed to three hundred deaths and five hundred injuries among soldiers.[9]

London was a central focus of wartime propaganda for both practical and symbolic reasons. The London blitz was harsher and more sustained than similar attacks on the provinces, lasting from September 1940 to May 1941. In addition to bearing the brunt of wartime dangers, many Londoners suffered more acutely from wartime privations: Londoners did not have gardens or farm animals on the scale that country people did and thus could supplement their rations less successfully. London was the political, commercial, financial, and artistic center of the country, its major port, and the largest city in the world. London was where wartime decisions were made, where much wartime propaganda was created. It was also the headquarters of many European governments in exile and, after Dunkirk, the only major European city outside of the USSR at war with the Axis powers. If London fell, the Allies fell—or so it seemed at the time.

It was necessary, therefore, for Londoners to understand their importance, both as residents of a strategically important city and as the people who made the city work—or could make it stop working. Londoners were valiant soldiers in the battleground that was London. Churchill, commenting on the blitz in a speech to the London County Council in July 1941, praised Londoners by saying, "The courage, the unfaltering, unconquerable grit and stamina of the Londoners showed itself from the very outset" (NSA ref. nos. 3843-5 and T3843b1). A film entitled *Ordinary People,* made by the Crown Film Unit in 1940 and 1941, also praised the common foot soldier who was the London civilian. In the prologue to the film, R.G. Menzies, then prime minister of Australia, praised the ordinary folk who were doing extraordinary things:

> [The film] is made by the people of London, about the people of London—the plain people—the true people. I have recently been seeing something of them and I now know what it is like to be in a city that's being bombed.
>
> Great things are happening in Britain, but perhaps the greatest is the display of neighbourliness, of kindness, of cheerfulness, of uncomplaining suffering that is being given by ordinary people who secure no fame and have no place in the headlines.

In this picture, you will catch a glimpse of that spirit which is the surest bulwark of Britain against senseless and indiscriminate bombing by the half-civilised Hun. In brief, in this picture you will see why Hitler cannot win. [INF 6/330]

Often, the "cheerful Cockneys" were singled out for special tribute. Basil Woon's comments on the East End, written in 1940 and published in 1941, are typical in that regard: "The East End. Taking it on the chin, as it always has taken whatever has come to it during its dark, hopeless history. The East End, which knows how to suffer—and to hate. . . . The East End, which can look at the ruins of its homes and the bodies of its families and shake its fist and cry, 'Thinks 'e's got us darn! 'E's got another think comin'!' Grubby, glorious East End" (1941, 23).

As Gareth Stedman Jones remarks in his study of "The Cockney," this stereotypical image valorized members of the urban working class, even while presenting them as inured to hardship, ready to greet trouble with a joke rather than a riot or an organized picket line (1989, 314). As Jones points out, this valorization crossed political boundaries, replacing the Conservative rural ideal with the ideal of a contented working class, giving Labour the iconography of a mass working-class hero.

Other sources stressed the unity of all classes and groups of people, a unity heretofore unknown in British society. In a letter to a Canadian friend, a London air-raid warden described his fellows: "We're nearly all voluntary workers, and its [sic] been astonishing to find men and women coming down after a day's work and cheerfully doing night duty, ready to do anything, or go anywhere. And we're all sorts and kinds—barristers and journalists and secretaries and shopkeepers and lorry drivers and manufacturers—and we get on famously. And we've no rights and no authority and a lot of work and responsibility and no discipline except what we make for ourselves. And it works!" (quoted in Lambert 1940, 38). Others stressed the unity that came from a sense of common purpose. A particularly moving account of this sentiment was given by J.B. Priestley in a retrospective broadcast on 11 May 1945:

> In that magnificent summer of 1940, when I spent my days collecting information and my nights broadcasting it to the world beyond the ring of steel round us, I think I felt better than ever before or since. We lived at last in a community with a noble, common purpose. And the experience was not only novel, but exhilarating. We had a glimpse then of what life might be if men and women freely dedicated themselves not to their appetites and prejudices, their vanities and fears, but to some great communal task. And not even the brute threat of war, the menace of the very skies, could remove from that glimpse a faint radiance of some far-off promised land. [NSA ref. nos. 8018-9 and MT8018]

No image was more prevalent during the war than that of the unified London populace, and no image has been more attacked by postwar scholars. Tom Harrisson writes: "Much has been made . . . of the drawing together of strangers. . . . But it would be a mistake to make too much of these temporary associations. There were few signs of any keen urge to share once an immediate threat was past. There were as many fresh disputes and frictions as new fellowships" (1990, 311). Similarly, Angus Calder suggests that the forging of new unities often required the strengthening of new divisions: "Clearly, evacuation, like other wartime phenomena such as the direction of labour and conscription into the forces, did help to mix people in Britain together as never before and gave a basis for a new degree of mutual respect and understanding, where those people were disposed to be kindly and tolerant. . . . But heightened social awareness among some sections of the middle classes clearly did not exclude the sharpening of prejudice in others" (1991, 63).

Both Harrisson and Calder show an ambiguity in their attitudes toward the notion of wartime unity: it was there and not there at the same time. A similar ambiguity is found in oral history interviews. Many of my interviewees remember the famed unity of wartime, while others remember incidents of pettiness and selfishness as well. One of those to whom the image of wartime unity rang true was Geordie, an engineer from the north of England who was stationed in London during the war. Geordie responded to my question about unity with a quotation from Milton, then a description of the hardships visited upon wartime London. He spoke with great admiration of the Londoners and mentioned, as did Creina Musson, the morale boost provided by the royal family. After describing the blitz and the V2 raids, he wrote: "Whilst all this was going on the morale was superb, the fact that [the king and queen] were resident in Buckingham Palace, which was itself bombed, had much to do with it, each day they visited bombed areas and mixed with the Londoners to share their troubles. Never belittle the ordinary Londoners, they just wouldn't give in, their behaviour and wit was exemplary, they all deserved a medal, believe me, I was there!" (personal letter, 19 January 1993).

Whereas Geordie stresses the courage of Londoners, others focused on their cheerfulness and friendliness. Many people mentioned, with delight, an important change that wartime had wrought in British social behavior: people talked to one another. Angus Calder remarked: "During the first weeks of war, observers were impressed with a bizarre phenomenon. In the buses, the trains and the pubs of Britain, strangers were speaking to one another" (1969, 34). Several of my interviewees remarked that people would tell one another if a local shop had scarce items such as bananas; people with cars gave rides to strangers; and people whose gas had been cut off by bomb damage boiled kettles in their neighbor's homes.

Basil Woon discusses meeting his neighbors: "And I reflect what grand people they all are, and how glad I am to know them—and then I reflect that, but for the Blitz, we'd all be strangers still" (1941, 169). Ettie Gontarsky, from a working-class Jewish home in central London, remembers her parents' kindness to a family who had been bombed out: "I can remember one particular family who were Orthodox Jewish, and my parents said to them, 'Look, Friday night, you come up into our kitchen and you light your Sabbath candles. Regard it as your home.' And this was the kind of atmosphere . . . that went on" (personal interview, 4 April 1993).

I.E.W., from a working-class family in south London, also mentions that people spoke to one another without introduction, bombs being a great icebreaker: "You had a common aim, and you were not fragmented because of this common aim, that you were going to win this blooming war, that you were all concerned about that and helped each other in order to win the war. This was probably the reason for it. And the fact that you could walk out in the blackout and you wouldn't be molested or anything like that, young girls walking around in the blackout" (personal interview, 7 May 1993). There was no fear of other British people; danger came only from one's national enemies. Poppy Morris gives a pragmatic reason for the unity of wartime: "We wanted to win the war and we wanted to survive and to survive you had to hang together, didn't you? That is survival, isn't it?" (personal interview, 1 July 1993). Albert Fredericks, whose family owned a small business in north London, spoke of war's role as a great leveler: "Everybody helped one another. Didn't matter what walk of life, whether you were rich or poor, you were all in the same boat. You could have been killed the next night or the next day the same as anybody else. And everybody had that great spirit that helped one another" (personal interview, 6 May 1993).

Yet others showed the cracks in the varnish. Harold Melville Lowry was in the Friends Ambulance Unit at the beginning of the war and the British army at the end. When asked about the notion of London unity, he replied: "I think that's true generally, I mean, it's not universal. There were some people who made a good thing out of the war. We did have a black market, but it wasn't very big. Generally speaking, people respected regulations and they were content with their rations; they didn't try and get things under the counter" (personal interview, 21 January 1993). Others, however, spoke bitterly of the favored few for whom the butcher would keep choice cuts of meat or who could bribe the greengrocer for a banana or a lemon. Discussions of unity, like discussions of other aspects of wartime life, are filled with contradictions. Sylvia Gordon said that people were very kind and they shared everything, but she also has memories of the rude and unhelpful treatment she received from a London housing authority (personal interview, 18 June 1993). The records of the Tilbury Shelter in the East End show a diverse group of thousands forming a community with its own newspaper, youth clubs, concerts, and religious services. The records also show complaints of badly behaved children, people who left verminous bedding in other people's bunks, and a drunk who, when refused admittance because he did not have the appropriate ticket, shouted at the warden: "I'm an Englishman and you're a so-and-so Jew; wait till Hitler comes!" (private papers).

G.H.R., from a working-class family in north London, worked in a textile mill until his call-up into the army. His comments show the various contradictions that abound in the notion of wartime unity:

> War naturally cuts down the amount of social intercourse which people had. In the phony war people carried on as before and the war itself made people aware of being "us" on a little island and there was "them" especially "him."
>
> As to fellow feeling, the story went around in the press and on radio but I cannot really say that one actually experienced it much due as I said.
>
> However once the bombs came down it was different . . . we seemed to split into protectors and protected. In other words there were more opportunities for asserting one's helpfulness—in shelters a sort of natural core group emerged—fairly constant—they organised anything going from sing-song to cups of tea. . . .
>
> My own belief is that we reacted according to the psychological principle that an external enemy consolidates a group and gives them identity. This being so all us British were in, everyone else was out until Russia was invaded and then there was a feeling that they were like us.[10] [personal letter]

Marjorie Newton, a schoolgirl from a working-class family, spent most of the war in London, with brief evacuations to Essex and Leicester. She also expresses the view that wartime unity was partly a creation of government propaganda that sometimes did and sometimes did not correspond to the lived reality: "To some extent there was a sense of 'all being in it together' but there was an element of official mythmaking. I have mentioned two examples of lack of fellow feeling where my friend was badly treated by a farmer when she was evacuated and also the looting that took place after raids. I also noticed when I left London in 1944 and went to Leicester that rationing was nothing like as severe as it was in London" (personal letter).

Interestingly, those who were children, and particularly evacuees, during the war seemed less apt to have strong memories of wartime unity. There are probably many reasons for this: memories of childhood tend to be vaguer than those of adulthood; the distrust that some foster families felt for the city children billeted on them (some called the evacuees "refugees") did not lend itself to a spirit of oneness; the tension of evacuation itself may have superseded other emotions; and unity was most strongly claimed in London itself, where the bombs and sense of national importance fostered both pride and purpose. But praise of the ordinary Londoners was essentially limited to adults. Perhaps wartime children do not have strong memories of unity because their place in this unified populace was considered tangential and unimportant: they were simply supposed to get out of the cities and let the adults get on with the serious business of winning the war.[11] Very young children probably would not have been aware of the official mythmaking at all and thus would have been unable or at least unlikely to canalize their memories along these lines.

J.D., from a working-class family in central London, was a schoolgirl of sixteen when she was evacuated. Most working-class children began work at fourteen in those days, and her foster family commented derisively on her continued study: "'[We] cannot understand what a girl of your class is doing studying at your age. You should be at work'" (personal interview, 15 January 1993). She dismisses notions of wartime unity as: "Propaganda. . . . I mean, there was a flourishing black market, rich people didn't go hungry. But there was a very good rationing system which didn't exist in the First World War, I gather. . . . But, no, it wasn't true. It wasn't true at all. They didn't all pull together, it was everybody out for themselves. . . . I think there was a much more intense patriotism about then, you know, 'We're British, nobody's going to get us down'" (personal interview, 26 April 1993). Yet even her critical comments are ambiguous; she mentions a widely expressed patriotism and the system of rationing which ensured that everyone got basic nutrition, if not the delicacies to be had on the black market or the expensive food still available in restaurants.

The image of wartime unity, particularly unity during the blitz, has been criticized by scholars such as Tom Harrisson, Clive Ponting, Paul Fussell, and Angus Calder. All make valuable points, yet I believe their mistake lies in dismissing the notion of wartime unity because it did not exist at all times and for all persons. Arthur Marwick says: "It does no good to glorify the Second World War, or to minimize the grinding boredom, the real grievances and the terrible suffering. But it does no good either to deny the exaltation, the sense of achievement and the heightening of consciousness" (1976, 181). Unity is not a thing that one can easily quantify or measure. It was an emotional and ideological state that people tried to create during the war, and in such striving many felt that they had succeeded.

Whether national unity was strong or weak, a governmental imposition or the spirit of a great people, most agree that it was a wartime phenomenon. Irene Wagner, a German Jewish refugee, comments on her adopted homeland: "The common tragedy welded people together. The Brits are that sort of type of people that will have a stiff upper lip and 'My house is my castle' type of thing, but come not only tragedy, but come any disaster, and they will huddle together. And therefore, the huddle together means also contact" (personal interview, 4 March 1994). During the blitz, the residents of her apartment building got to know one another. Their doors opened, and they offered one another cups of tea. But when they no longer needed each other's aid or companionship, such friendliness faded away. "The war ended," says Irene. "The doors shut" (personal interview, 4 March 1994).

The Need for Humor

Humor may not be an obvious concomitant of war, but in wartime Britain it was considered an essential morale booster. Humor was prized not only for the escapist relief it provided, but for its ability to render the terrifying ridiculous and therefore manageable. M.M. Bakhtin writes:

> Laughter has the remarkable power of making an object come up close, of drawing it into a zone of crude contact where one can finger it familiarly on all sides, turn it upside down, inside out, peer at it from above and below, break open its external shell, look into its center, doubt it, take it apart, dismember it, lay it bare and expose it, examine it freely and experiment with it. Laughter demolishes fear and piety before an object, before a world, making of it an object of familiar contact and thus clearing the ground for an absolutely free investigation of it. Laughter is a vital factor in laying down that prerequisite for fearlessness without which it would be impossible to approach the world realistically. [1981, 23]

Laughter renders the world manageable, perhaps controllable, and at least bearable. Laughter turns objects and situations on their heads, presenting them as their opposites, so that a terrifying situation has great potential for comic representation. Laughter is especially useful in dealing with the unknown: to laugh at a death is callous, but to laugh at the potential for death is brave.

Even before the blitz, laughter was sought as a relief from the grimness and uncertainty of the war. A Ministry of Information morale report from 27 May 1940 remarked, "Cinema audiences thin. Comedies and musicals preferred to serious and war pictures" (INF 1/264, 97/15 H.I.). But it was during the blitz that the image of the fearless and defiant Londoner, laughing while bombs fell, came into its own as a rhetorical trope. London did not just take it; London took it with style. The construction and valorization of this image specified the behavior most likely to render wartime conditions bearable. Richard Fawkes writes: "The Blitz was a deliberate attempt to destroy civilian morale and became a part of folklore before it was over. The tales of heroism and courage, the stories of the night before (the 'bomb' story became the latest way to bore your friends) and accounts of the humour of London's citizens became part of legend as did the myth that every Cockney dug from the rubble came up with a wise-crack on his or her lips" (1978, 65).

The Cockney image, that idealized portrayal of the quintessential Londoner, embodied the ideal of humor. These cheerful, uncomplaining types lived in the parts of London where bombs fell most heavily, so it was well that they were cheerful and uncomplaining. The film *Ordinary People* shows an example of this Cockney spirit in its representation of two young working-class men who are caught outside in an air raid. When the raid is over, one looks around for his friend and upon finding him says, "Blimey, I thought they'd got you." His friend grins and holds up his hand. "Me?" he says. "Naw, I'd got my fingers crossed" (INF 6/330). Gareth Stedman Jones describes how the Cockney image combined patriotism with humor in a distinctly urban way: "The late-Victorian cockney archetype had gathered together many of the ingredients of a populist and city-based conception of the nation and had projected the fantasy of a metropolitan community grounded in the good-humoured, if sometimes ironic, acceptance of social difference and subordination. During the Second World War, it was Labour which proved to possess a more certain sense of the patriotism of the urban nation. The Labour press did not turn its back upon the 'cockney' stereotype, but subtly transformed it" (1989, 314). Both Conservative and Labour supporters could rejoice in the "cheerful Cockney." Labour supporters could stress the accomplishments and contributions of an urban, working-class hero, while Conservatives could be pleased with the notion of the contented lower orders, happy with their jokes and foolery, never straying from their appointed place in the social hierarchy.

The Cockney archetype may have lived more in the minds of Whitehall propagandists than in the real streets of Lambeth and Poplar, but the actual use of humor among the London populace was too widespread to be denied. Virtually every contemporary account of wartime London speaks of the jokes, wordplay, and puns that have long been part of British culture. A Ministry of Information morale report from 28 June 1940 shows the combination of work, humor, patriotism, and dedication to the war effort that the government was trying to encourage: "Cowley Estate, Stockwell reports tenants busy making shelters comfortable with carpets to sleep on, furniture, beds for children, pictures of King and Queen, artificial flowers, Union Jacks, etc. Women scrubbing floors and laughing, 'wish Hitler could see us now!'" (INF 1/264, 97/15 H.I.). Joking was an index of patriotism; therefore, many jokes emanated from governmental institutions. The witty "Be like Dad—keep Mum" slogan indicated that even the need for silence could be expressed with humor.

Shopkeepers were fond of placing signs on what remained of their bombed-out storefronts; this was a way to speak directly to other Londoners and to show the ability to carry on, quietly and with words of humor. Anne Lubin remembers the mornings after air raids: "You'd be going along, and there're all these shop fronts all smashed open. People were—they immediately, straight away had put notice in, 'Open for Business.' And, of course, that was a lovely pun as well, because there was no window there" (personal interview, 21 January 1993). "More Open Than Usual" was another variation on this theme. Stores were open because shopkeepers refused to be cowed; they were also open in a literal sense because of their lack of windows. The kind of shop might affect the sign that hung in its window. Janet remembers a sign on a fishmonger's shop that made a rhyme out of food shortages: "Owing to Hitler, the fish is littler" (personal interview, 30 January 1993). Basil Woon reports a sign in a barber shop that read: "Open as Usual. Close Shaves a Specialty" (1941, 27). Woon also reports a sign that surely takes the prize for turning the tables on the enemy: "We were going to build a new building anyway. This saves us £11,000 for demolition. Thanks, Goering!" (173).

Popular entertainment was an obvious avenue for humor. Comedians such as Flanagan and Allen, the Western brothers, and Arthur Askey were widely enjoyed. The popular *Hi, Gang!* radio program, with the Americans Ben Lyon and Bebe Daniels, combined humor with music, as did venerable British traditions such as the music hall and variety programs, which also found their way to the radio. (A BBC catalogue for 4 December 1944 lists a Punch and Judy show—in Arabic.) The government continued its practice of finding out what people wanted and trying to provide it as much as possible, particularly in little things. A Ministry of Information morale report from 30 May 1940 stated: "A . . . survey made to ascertain reactions to variety programmes on the wireless showed an overwhelming majority in favour of continuing them even under emergency conditions. Many say they will be more necessary than ever" (INF 1/264, 97/15 H.I.).

Almost everyone listened to the radio (usually called "the wireless" in those days) for both information and entertainment. The blackout and the blitz made travel of any kind difficult and potentially dangerous, so going to the theater, the cinema, or a restaurant was fraught with problems. The radio, on the other hand, provided at-home amusement and beckoned wartime Londoners to stay by their own firesides. The radio was both companion and teacher, the voice of authority and the comfort of a friend. On 4 July 1940 Vere Hodgson wrote, "My wireless continues to be my greatest joy." On 6 September 1942 she described a skit done by the Western brothers on the wartime slogan "Is Your Journey Really Necessary?" The slogan was designed to cut down on wartime travel so that fuel might be saved and trains carrying troops and military supplies might travel without difficulty. Wartime train travel was crowded, uncomfortable, and uncertain—signs had been removed from stations in case of invasion, so one had to be especially careful to get out at the right place, not the easiest task when traveling in the blackout. The skit parodied wartime travel and asked the old question in a new way: "We listened to the Western brothers in a skit on: Is your journey really necessary? It was really funny. . . . One verse was about the feeling of an unfortunate traveller who found himself one of 20 in the carriage with 140 in the corridor, and the door opened to admit the British Army with Geraldo and his Band. . . . It finished up with a scene at Hitler's birth, and the doctor asking the new born infant the same question."

Without doubt, the most popular radio program, the one most often remembered by my interviewees, was *ITMA,* short for *It's That Man Again,* an incredibly zany, self-reflexive, and densely packed bit of wordplay. According to Angus Calder, more than sixteen million people listened to the program every week (1969, 362). The main character, played by the British comedian Tommy Handley, was head of the fictional Ministry of Aggravation and Mysteries, housed in the Office of Twerps. Later, he became mayor of the seaside resort of Foaming-at-the-Mouth, a name similar to many genuine English villages. Everything was pilloried in *ITMA* and presented in familiar stereotypes: the decrepit and rather stupid British upper class, the bumbling and overeager middle class, the vulgar and uncouth working class, the crass and violent Germans, the scheming and incompetent Italians, and the incomprehensible, golf-playing Scots. *ITMA* provided its own cast of stock characters; they included the German spy Funf, the Italian "foreign secretary" Signor So-So, the charwoman Mrs. Mopp, and the cheery commercial traveler, who tried to sell everything from makeup to taxes. The dizzying wordplay is everywhere, even in an aside of Tommy's, from a program of 26 September 1941: "Now, what's on the agenda? [Yowl of cat] Oh, the cat's sitting on it. Get off it; it's not a catalogue. You've gone and purred all the print off the pages. That's the worst of having everything tabulated" (NSA ref. nos. F41/102 and T28071b1).

Wordplay is, in fact, the hallmark of *ITMA.* Its producer, Francis Worsley, discusses the importance of words and sound to the creator of radio programs: "He has to rely on sound alone so that most of the means by which stage comedians have been getting laughs for years are denied him—no funny falls—no business with comic hats or makeup—just plain sound. This boils down to funny lines and funny noises. . . . The radio script writer is confined then to character study, that is getting laughs out of the peculiarities of manner and speech of his puppets, 'situation' comedy which without visual help presents all sorts of technical difficulties, or pure verbal word play" (1946, 51). Each character has his or her identifying speech style. For Tommy's "foreign secretary," Signor So-So, it is malapropism. As Tommy says of him, "He's always monkeying about with the language. I think he talks King Kong's English" (NSA ref. nos. 22230-3 and T22226b2, 28 October 1943). Sometimes So-So's malapropisms provide the opportunity for political commentary, as when he discusses advertising a show:

So-So: In all the shops I hung up great big blackguards.
Tommy: (laughs) Well, it's time some of them were hung up. I can
name three for a start. Oh, you mean placards, do you? [NSA ref.
nos. F41/102 and T28071b1]

For Tommy's American assistant, Sam, it is alliteration. Sam is a very nervous lad
who starts every conversation with "Boss, something terrible's happened." As
Tommy and company get ready for the show, Sam gives the dread tidings: "The
stage manager says the slap-up special safety curtain simply sags because somebody snappled the screws out of the side of the stage" (NSA ref. nos. F41/102 and
T28071b1).

Funf, the German spy, usually speaks on the telephone, and he speaks badly.
In a verbal duel with Tommy, Funf always loses. As Tommy and his friends await
the arrival of the actors by train, Funf threatens this outcome. Tommy, reflexive as
always, replies with the name of an *ITMA* actor, Jack Train:

Funf: There will be no train.
Tommy: What, not even Jack Train?
Funf: There will be no show, either. Funf has spoken.
Tommy: . . . [Slams down phone] I'd like to see him stop the show. He
can't even stop his retreat. (NSA ref. nos. F41/102 and T28071b1)

Francis Worsley describes the necessity of making the German spy funny and con-
nects this comic villain to similar figures in British folklore and popular culture:

"Funf" was the epitome of Bogeyman, his name taken from the German numeral *funf* [*sic*] but pronounced, with British contempt for foreign languages, *Foonf*. People were really a little scared—the might of
Germany *was* recognized—witness the flight from London at the out-
break of war—and this comic spy provided a safety valve. . . . Almost
everyone who had a telephone had also a humorous friend who never
failed to open the proceedings with "This is Funf speaking." Tommy
had thousands of calls from practical jokers, children began to play "Funf"
games and the Pantomimes that year—1939—rang with his name. Yes,
Funf was the Fairy Queen as well as the Demon King of this first Itma
series. He was, of course, in the tradition of all British comic villains
stretching right back to the Beelzebub of the Miracle plays—the power
of evil made funny to rob it of fear. [1946, 46; emphasis in original]

Foreigners were not the only ones subject to verbal parody. The British working class provided Mrs. Mopp, the charwoman, who is always experimenting with
wartime recipes and whose verbal wit is equal to Tommy's own. Her speech style
is sexual innuendo, and she always begins conversations in the same way:

Mrs. Mopp: Can I do you now, sir?
Tommy: Go away, Mrs. Mopp. Can't you see I'm dressing? Come back
when I'm covered.
Mrs. Mopp: Can't I darn your dickey, sir?
Tommy: It doesn't want darning. That's a spider's web on it.
Mrs. Mopp: Couldn't I empty your chest, sir?
Tommy: Empty me chest? No. You can't even take a stitch out of me
side. [NSA ref. nos. F41/102 and T28071b1]

The British upper class is not always portrayed so sympathetically. Their stereotypical locutions and dropped final g's give many opportunities for comedy. In one
episode, Tommy is in a house when hunters arrive, wanting their hunt breakfast,
which is not there:

Tommy: Anyway, it's nearly tea time.
Upper-class voice 1: Oh, bad show, dashed bad show.
Upper-class voice 2: My dear sir, breakfast is always served about this
time in huntin' circles.
Tommy: Well, I never hunt in circles. It makes me dizzy.
Upper-class voice 1: Bad show, dashed bad show.
Tommy: This fellow must be a radio critic. [13 January 1944]

ITMA existed for awhile after the war, but "victory *ITMA*" seemed somewhat lack-
luster compared with the verbal skirmishes of the war years. Tommy (by a happy
coincidence, the typical name of the British soldier) had triumphed and therefore
was no longer needed. Nonetheless, when Tommy Handley died, Ettie Gontarsky
remembers a sense of personal loss: "It was literally a day of mourning; we felt we'd
lost a personal friend. Oh yeah, we were so cut up—we'd never seen this person,
it was a character on the wireless. The wireless was very important at that time.
Most important. Not only about the news, naturally, but also about these programs. . . . Which I think were brilliant" (personal interview, 4 April 1993).

Creative humor was not always the product of official agencies or mass culture; the much praised "ordinary people" laughed at their own targets. The enemy, of course, was a primary target, but so were governmental foolishness and
ineptitude. Soon after VE Day, Vere Hodgson chuckled over wartime requirements
for laughter: "I was very amused at the rescinding of the Bill against Gloom and
Despondency. Now it is not against the law to be gloomy or despondent! So great
was our danger in certain years that we were forbidden to look miserable. Now we
can be as unhappy as we please! Freedom is returning" (16 May 1945). More caustic
were George and Helena Britton, who were unimpressed by wartime propaganda
and wrote on 14 April 1940: "The stuff they dish out over the wireless these days
makes one sick." In a letter to their daughter written on 28 August 1940, they

show that East End humor can be sharper and more biting than the "Cockney" palaver beloved by Whitehall: "Don't forget that a Cabinet Minister has said that shabbiness will be the mark of patriotism. Surely he must appreciate the fact that a very large proportion of the population continually flaunt their patriotism in that way."

A diary entry from William Bernard Regan, a bricklayer from the East End neighborhood called the Isle of Dogs, parodies the image of the gallant RAF pilot and the unflinching support that the fearless Londoners gave him. During a V1 raid, Regan and his friends watched the pilotless aircraft being shot down: "They seemed to be small fast fighters, with an apparently outsize bombload. Just about here, Martin who had varnished his tonsils with his usual double scotches, got very talkative, and tried to bolster himself with loud talk. 'I'm with you, lads, first to go out, I'll be there,' etc. etc. Before he could impress us, another one came over, passed, went silent, dropped, same white flash, pause—red flash, bang" (15 June 1944). Regan was also able to target the enemy—with a parrot story: "[The parrot] was well educated, and after preening itself, it gave a most wonderful recital of obscene language I have ever heard, and the building trade wants some beating. It finished off with two words, repeated very rapidly, 'F—— Hitler, F—— Hitler, F—— Hitler,' my sentiments exactly" (13 September 1940). Sometimes the oddities of war provided their own opportunities for humor. Janet, who had come to London from Ireland in the late 1930s, worked as a nurse during the war. She remembers a patient's reaction during a bad air raid near the hospital where she worked: "We were having rather a bad raid one day, one evening, and I was in this, working this men's ward. 'Oh,' I said, 'pretty awful, isn't it?' He said, 'You don't need to worry. You're neutral. What are you worrying about, you're neutral. You come from Ireland.' I said, 'Thank you very much. I don't think I've got anything on me to show that.' That kind of humour you'd get" (personal interview, 30 January 1993).

Silent repression and unified patriotism are always encouraged in wartime; why was humor so equally important? I suggest that humor was emphasized in part because it was a pleasure that could not be rationed. While eating and drinking were restricted and expensive, one could still be merry. Humor was cheap, readily accessible, and one could make it oneself. Second, as noted, humor was a kind of defiance, an act of ridicule that could remove terror. If the Fifth Column were no more dangerous than the incompetent spy Funf (who could always be bested by Tommy Handley), if the most notorious British traitor could be reduced to the jeering appellation Lord Haw-Haw, then the world seemed a little more orderly, a little less threatening. It would have been disastrous if these representations had been taken literally. But even if they were not believed, they allowed people the illusion of some measure of control. Similarly, the image of a cheerful, wisecracking population was comforting; he who laughs alone may be mad, but he who laughs in company has friends and allies.

"The British are very good at taking the Mickey out of themselves," says J.D. (personal interview, 26 April 1993). They could also "take the Mickey" out of their government and their enemies. By reducing both themselves and their adversaries to objects of humor, the world seemed to shrink to a manageable size. Then people could perform that most necessary of wartime tasks: "just getting on with it." Since this was a "people's war," it was the people's laughter that was valorized. Light opera, Restoration comedy, and Oscar Wilde may have had their place in wartime Britain, but this place is not well remembered. It was the music hall and the radio comedian, the Cockney joke and ironic way of speaking that represent British wartime laughter. These democratic, easily accessible forms, what Bakhtin calls "the common people's creative culture of laughter" (1981, 20), showed a common people loyal to their country and a country devoted to the welfare of all its people. And who knew who would have the last laugh?

The Need to Talk about the Future

> I will not cease from Mental Fight,
> Nor shall my Sword sleep in my hand
> Till we have built Jerusalem
> In England's green and pleasant land.
>
> —William Blake, "Jerusalem"

Wars are usually considered temporary measures designed to achieve a common end. Though some may agree to fight in a blind excess of patriotism and others go to battle for the mere love of fighting, most people need a sense of something to fight *for* or, at the very least, to fight *against*. A "total war" such as World War II, in which civilians as well as soldiers are required to make sacrifices and endure dangers, makes discussions of the future—a future unlike the pain-racked present— especially important. Professor Bartlett, writing from the Psychology Laboratory at Cambridge, gave sound advice to the Ministry of Information: "Within a few months . . . your publicity will have to go out to masses of people who are over-tired, over-strained, irritable and in consequence a great deal more negatively critical than usual. . . . You can't permanently allay public irritation by words, however cunningly they are arranged and distributed, but it may be that the only thing to do is to foresee this prospective state of the public and have some sort of palliative publicity ready (INF 1/318, H.P. 345). Bartlett's advice was taken to heart. On 18 May 1940, for many people the low point of the war, the ministry also suggested that fine words were not enough: "Even at the eleventh hour people are seeking and needing a *positive purpose,* something aggressive, dynamic, beyond themselves, worth dying for, not just survival or 'blood, sweat, and tears'" (INF 1/ 264, 97/15 H.I., emphasis in original).

Words may have been insufficient unto themselves, but they remained necessary. Words were the means by which future goals could be discussed, negotiated, and publicized. Words continued to be the quintessential propaganda tool, for they are the only way we have to describe what lies ahead. Different sectors of the population were targeted as requiring an articulation of future goals. In May 1940 the Ministry of Information suggested that "some fundamental statement on a post-war social policy coming from the 'the new Government' would have an effect in rallying the extreme Left-Wing section of youth organisations" (INF 1/264, 97/ 15 H.I., 19 and 20 May 1940). On 5 August 1940 demands about war aims came from "the more thinking section of the population" (INF 1/264, 97/15 H.I.). Here, the ministry implied that left-wing and intellectual views were to be incorporated into government policy—and no doubt modified—but not quashed or summarily dismissed. On 15 August 1940 the ministry began to notice some pleasing results of its efforts:

> It is of great importance that people should realise that in this war they are fighting *for* something—not merely against something. In reply to a question on our war aims, no less than 68% of people said we were fighting for liberty or freedom, 10% said we were fighting to save our lives or our country, 7% said to destroy the rule of force and Hitlerism, and 6% to save civilisation. Only about 2% expressed cynical views about our war aims. This shows a most satisfactory state of affairs. The people of Britain are fully alive to the positive aspects of the struggle in which we are engaged. [INF 1/263, H.I. 85; emphasis in original]

A similar complacency was apparent on 5 September 1940, when a morale report noted that "while various small intellectual groups are still asking for a definition of war aims, there is evidence that the great bulk of the population are satisfied with the present situation and are prepared to leave this matter until victory is in sight or attained" (INF 1/264, 97/15 H.I.).

Yet such complacency did not eliminate discussions of the future, which remained an indispensable part of wartime rhetoric. Particularly at the beginning of the war, governmental support was not automatic in a highly stratified country emerging uneasily from the Great Depression. Lurking behind the reluctance of most normal people to go to war, even for the noblest of purposes, was the specter of the World War I soldier or veteran—maimed, gassed, or dead. Well and bitterly remembered was David Lloyd George's promise that soldiers of the Great War would return to a "land fit for heroes." Instead, the veterans of the First World War found unemployment and inadequate social services and medical treatment, and were left to shift for themselves, to depend upon family or charity, or, in the worst of cases, to beg in the streets. Having served their country, their country showed no inclination to serve them. During the Second World War, there was a determination that this state of affairs should not happen again. This mood is well expressed by Harold Melville Lowry:

> One of the things which grew up during the war was a determination that the world after the war, supposing we won it, and I suppose we really never thought that we would lose except in those early days before Russia and America were involved. But after that, I think we always felt that we would eventually win. And we wanted, in the words of Lloyd George after or during the First World War, 'a land fit for heroes.' Certainly there was this determination that all the things that were wrong with the old prewar society would be put right. [personal interview, 21 January 1993]

George Wagner analyzes the process of hegemony as flowing from two main sources: the need for the government to convince people that they would not be duped and forgotten as they had been after World War I, and a "collective bad conscience" on the part of Conservative politicians for neglecting the veterans, appeasing Hitler, and doing nothing to ease the economic misery of the 1930s. He also mentions Lloyd George's "land fit for heroes" speech:

> And the wonderful speeches of Lloyd George during World War I, "When the war is over, you'll have a fatherland worthy of the returning heroes." And what came? Unemployment, misery, and so on, and so forth. Now that was a thing which people kept on quoting, kept on talking about, "God, are they going to do us again after we've done our duty?" And that is where this war was different because already, certainly from the moment on that there was a coalition and Labour was in the government, from May–June 1940, there was a continuous flow of statements: "This time, you'll not be done again. This time we'll make sure that you get your reward, and this time, we'll think of all the social and so on misdeeds." And somehow among Conservatives . . . there was a bit of a collective bad conscience: if we hadn't allowed the world to go to pot economically, all these things wouldn't have happened. And we really were very ruthless, and we cosseted Hitler. . . . By the time the change back from Attlee to Churchill came . . . the difference between the Labour government and the Conservative government was one of degree but not of principle. [personal interview, 7 April 1993]

Clement Attlee, who became Labour prime minister in the 1945 election, offers a similar analysis of the wartime consensus between the major political parties: "I can remember no case where differences arose between Conservatives, Labour and Liberals along party lines. Certainly not in the War Cabinet. Certainly not in the big things. . . . When one came to work out solutions they were often socialist ones, because one had to have organization, and planning, and disregard vested interests. But there was no opposition from Conservative ministers. They accepted the practical solution whatever it was" (quoted in A. Calder 1969, 99).

Looking toward the postwar future and implementing wartime social programs went hand in hand. Social programs were one way to rectify the neglect of the interwar years and to reward the fighters of the forces and the home front. The usefulness, even the necessity, of wartime social programs made them respectable; there seemed no reason why, once implemented, they should not continue when the war was over. An enormous amount of discussion about wartime programs and postwar society existed: on the airwaves, in private conversation, and in secret documents. The Ministry of Information was involved in this discussion from the beginning. A remarkable document entitled "Post War Aims" was drafted by the ministry between December 1939 and August 1940; it discussed both wartime and postwar policy. In a section entitled "Social Reconstruction at Home," the document proclaimed that a modified socialism would benefit wartime capitalism and accepted somewhat uneasily the concomitant rise of the middle and working classes that such a change would entail: "The replacement of *laisser-faire* by a rationally planned system would permit an enormously increased war production; and the rise of the propertyless but vigorous social class, typified by the airmen and technicians drawn from state schools, would revitalise our society and provide a new source of leadership" (INF 1/862).

But the document goes much farther and adds a moral imperative to the aforementioned economic one. The path is prepared for the Ministry of Information, in accord with the people it discusses, to build Jerusalem on England's green and pleasant land:

> The primary aim must be to create a society founded on elementary conceptions of human dignity, and on the idea of participation in shared enterprise. It must provide a decent living for all, based on the standard of physiological health which modern science has enabled us to set up. War-time conditions have already compelled us to make sure, not only that the rich do not consume too much, but that others get enough. The needs of war production call for new measures for improving the housing, welfare and transport of workers. The evacuation scheme should give the impetus to radical improvements in our educational system and social services. The war-time measures to protect the standard of living point the way to a planned population policy. The mobilisation of manpower should spell the end of mass unemployment and those who are unavoidably out of work must be regarded as citizens serving in a reserve labour force. War measures for rationalising the distribution of various products should lead to a remodelling of distribution as a whole, so as to

transform increased productivity into increased consumption on a higher standard. At the moment the claims of armament and supply prevent these measures from being used to effect the social transformation out of which a healthy and well-planned Britain would emerge. *But it is vital that they should at once be publicly proclaimed as the basis for a new and thoroughgoing social policy.* [INF 1/862; emphasis added]

Thus, one of the most important attributes of wartime propaganda was its orientation toward the future. Rather than dwelling on the exigencies of the present (bombing, rationing, the possibility of a German victory), wartime was treated as a societal baptism by fire, a difficult but ennobling transition period to a just, peaceful, and free society. It was not enough to implement emergency social programs; it was important to proclaim that such measures were both reward and reason for the war itself. The necessities of war had wrought enormous changes on the British social landscape, and the government loudly proclaimed its intent to turn these changes to positive advantage. If evacuation had forced the well-to-do to see how poor children lived, then it was inexcusable to allow them to live so poorly any longer. If those of the "propertyless but vigorous social class" had risen to prominence because ability counts more than pedigree in an emergency, then class positions lost any moral or rational justification. If rationing had enabled a more just allocation of resources, then what could excuse returning to a world in which the rich feasted while the poor went hungry?

The government was not always sanguine in its belief that the postwar world would usher in the New Jerusalem or that the people trusted in the government's ultimate benevolence. On 9 October 1942, when the thrills and danger of the blitz were long over, the ministry wrote in a secret memorandum: "Post-war conditions seem to be more a cause of anxiety as to what they may bring to the individual in the shape of unemployment and distress than of hope for the blessings that they may bring to the nation at large" (INF 1/284, H.I. 1013/3). Such sentiments had, of course, to remain secret. (This document, like many others, was not available to the public until 1972.) Public discussions of the postwar world focused on the beneficial changes that war had wrought and the fact that peace could continue these changes without danger or suffering. Ritchie Calder's book *Carry On, London* is a paean to the new world order arising from the ashes of the old. Being a Scot, he quotes Burns rather than Kipling, Milton, or Shakespeare; being a Briton, he cherishes London:

In a thousand ways, for a thousand common objects, people have learned to work together, to appreciate each other's values, and to realise, as Burns said, "The rank is but the guinea's stamp; The man's the gowd for a' that." New democratic institutions have sprung into being. Men, and women, have discovered latent qualities of leadership. . . .

We are a nation galvanised by a new sense of purpose. At the moment that purpose is directed to settling this war, to ridding the world of a tyranny which would seek to crush that individuality which has roused itself to defeat it. We must never again lapse into torpor, indifference, and sluggishness which threatened to make democracy a sham. We must harness this new dynamic energy to the constructive purposes of peace, to the regeneration of the world. London, because it showed so emphatically by the character and the courage of its people, that a free people cannot be bludgeoned by force and that free men and women can rise to almost any demand made upon them, their spirit, their hearts, and their minds, has become to the world the symbol of a new awakening and a new hope. [1941, 159–60]

This orientation to the future was not always cloaked in such noble and ambiguous language. John Hargrave Wells Gardner sharply criticized governmental propagandists for their inefficiency and their inattention to certain controversial economic solutions: "Truth needs a trumpet no less than lies. . . . Where is that trumpet and that trumpeter? They are not in the Ministry of Information. Nor can they be, until we have the courage . . . to place in the very forefront of our war-objectives, not merely the ending of Hitlerism, but *the technique of the Economics of Abundance*" (1940, 146; emphasis in original).[12]

Books such as Calder's and Gardner's, however wide their circulation, reached fewer people than the BBC. Radio broadcasts show the same tendencies as do these writers: vague but stirring praise of wartime spirit and its potential for change in the postwar world coupled with discussions of specific social programs to be implemented during or after the war. Though left and right cooperate in the former tendency, the voices of the left are stronger and more fervent in the latter. The former tendency can be seen in King George's Christmas broadcast of 1940: "Out of all this suffering, there is growing a harmony which we must carry forward into the days to come, when we have endured to the end and ours is the victory. Then, when Christmas days are happy again and good will has come back to the world, we must hold fast to the spirit which binds us all together now" (NSA ref. nos. 2831-2 and LP2812f2). The trade unionist W.J. Brown expressed similar sentiments in a broadcast on 14 February 1941. Brown's words were designed to appeal to a broad base, but they are not as ambiguous as the king's; Brown mentions political and economic institutions that need changing. He even refers to the model society as "the good republic," a form of government that, in the modern world, would obliterate kings: "We are beginning to think of each other for what we are worth as human beings and not merely for what we have. Peace, economic security, fellowship—these are the main elements of the good republic, the dream of which has haunted man's mind for centuries. It may be that only out of the crucible of such ordeals as we are now experiencing that the golden metal of these things could come" (NSA ref. nos. 6348-9 and LP6348).

The theme that "things will be different this time" was important in many radio broadcasts. "Women of Britain," fourth in a series called *An American in England*, is a good example of this theme. "Women of Britain" was a CBS presentation that aired on the BBC on 5 September 1942. It was written and directed by the progressive American writer Norman Corwin, produced by the liberal American journalist Edward R. Murrow, with music composed by the British pacifist Benjamin Britten. In "Women of Britain," a sympathetic American (in the hardboiled journalist mold) walks the blacked-out streets of London, overcome with admiration for the activities of women: "The widowed and bereaved left behind to mourn. That's the way it's been with women since war immemorial, hasn't it? Until this war. Something new has been added to this one. They don't stay at home and mourn anymore. Every home in Britain is a front line. . . . Yes sir, it's different this time" (NSA ref. nos. 5661-5 and T5661). He is unimpressed by the rich women who dine in evening dress in the big hotels, but full of admiration for the women factory workers, the bus conductresses, the women in uniform, the left-wing Member of Parliament Ellen Wilkinson. He discusses future goals with a middle-aged woman who is working as a chambermaid because the regular chambermaid has been called up:

> *Chambermaid*: Why, you know what a woman said to my sister last week, she said, "I'm having such trouble getting a maid because all my maids keep getting called up. So I'll be glad when this war's over, she said, because after the war, there'll be lots of unemployment and good maids'll be plentiful and cheap."
>
> *Narrator*: What did your sister tell that woman?
>
> *Chambermaid*: Well, my sister said to her, "You have another guess coming, ma'am." That's what she said, right to her face.
>
> *Narrator*: Hmm. What else did she say?
>
> *Chambermaid*: She said, "This war ain't being fought to make maids plentiful and cheap," she said. "This war ain't being fought to make the world safe for unemployment. Just the opposite." She talked right up, she did. Oh, my sister can be a terror, you know. 'Course she's younger than me. [NSA ref. nos. 5661-5 and T5661]

The narrator, however, thinks this terror of a woman is "dead right." At a mixed ack-ack battery, he watches women learning to shoot and discusses with the captain the future education and emancipation of women who, prior to the war, had "lived in a pretty narrow world." The narrator ends by saying: "These girls, these women of Britain, so keen, so concentrated on their work, have got their eyes fixed on more than one target. Perhaps they're training their guns on an objective greater than they know" (NSA ref. nos. 5661-5 and T5661). This mixture of admiration and condescension was common in wartime treatments of women's achievements. Yet the fact that women's contributions were sought and women's work was respectable represents a fairly momentous change.

Working-class men also expressed their views on the radio, complete with non-standard accents and left-wing ideas. On 22 May 1942 a group of Welsh trade unionists debated the question "What shall we do with our future?" This detailed, politically sophisticated discussion assumed left-wing solutions to economic problems, and one man affirmed his "socialist faith" with a tenderness that Churchill (among others) must have found unnerving (NSA ref. nos. 4621-3 and T4621b1). On 5 February 1943 two doctors debated the topic of "State Organised Medicine," with one doctor arguing for a continuation of private practice and one arguing that doctors should be salaried members of the civil service (NSA ref. nos. 5932-4 and T5932b1). The question of national health insurance was common on the popular *Brains Trust* program as well. On 2 December 1942 Sir William Beveridge spoke on the BBC and described several highlights from the Beveridge Report, which laid the foundations for the postwar welfare state. Among the social programs that Beveridge described were children's allowances, old-age pensions, and medical insurance of everything for everybody (NSA ref. nos. 4936-8 and LP4936f1).

My interviewees held a wide range of opinions on the reasons for World War II. Some believed literally in the pledge to defend Poland, while others accepted their country's call to arms simply as a patriotic duty. Many, particularly those who had had less than their share of the pie before the war, believed that they were fighting for a better world. Ettie Gontarsky says: "A lot more equality was on the agenda. There was a great levelling of the class system. . . . I feel that the ordinary serving soldier, sailor, airman felt, 'Well, it's our turn now. We're going to have something to say. We fought for our country; we're going to have something to say about it.' Now, those are my words, but I think this could sum up the feeling of a lot of people at the time" (personal interview, 19 April 1993). Similarly, Anne Lubin remembers: "I thought that that was what the war was about, for a more just society. And of course we were absolutely delighted when there was a land-slide, and a Labour government came in, and we thought this was the beginning of El Dorado" (personal interview, 13 March 1993).

These are two examples of the "ordinary people" beloved by wartime propaganda, the gallant soldiers of the home front, those who made the planes and kept the home fires burning. In the "People's War," they had done their duty. As Jews and antifascists, they were devoted to the defeat of Hitler; as British citizens, they expected a bit of their own back. If all Britons were soldiers and all soldiers were heroes, then it was time to build a land fit for heroes. As working-class people, they were the eternal foot soldiers; as women, their position had always been undervalued. But things were changing rapidly in every way. They could see the changes with their own eyes—fires and bombs, rationing and day nurseries—and they heard what the government had to say. The future would bring a change for the better, just as soon as the war was over. And this promise was easy to keep, for the future would be better if only because the war was over. Who could tell what else would happen? Would El Dorado emerge? Would the New Jerusalem be built?

Foot soldiers, like policemen, have an ambiguous position—they guard the status quo but are not acceptable in the "Best Society." Rudyard Kipling described this attitude in "Tommy":

> For it's Tommy this, an' Tommy that, an' "Chuck him out, the brute!"
> But it's "Savior of 'is country" when the guns begin to shoot;
> An' it's Tommy this, an' Tommy that, an' anything you please;
> An' Tommy ain't a bloomin' fool—you bet that Tommy sees!

After the war, Tommy saw. In the 1945 election, in a much-debated precedent, an overseas Tommy could vote. If blitzed civilians were treated as honorary soldiers, then suddenly the nation was full of Tommies. And the nation waited to see how the general and milord would treat this change in their ranks, and whether Tommy would ape his former betters or share his place with Mrs. Atkins and Judy.

4

Time Long Past
Narratives of Wartime London

Like the ghost of a dear friend dead
 Is Time long past.
A tone which is now forever fled,
A hope which is now forever past,
A love so sweet it could not last,
 Was Time long past.
 —Percy Bysshe Shelley, "Time Long Past"

Stories about wartime London are to this day an important component of British cultural and national identity. Told with relish to tourists, scholars, and bored or fascinated grandchildren, these stories are ways of keeping the past alive and of asserting one's own place in a crucial historical epoch. They are also the precious cultural capital of the generation that experienced the war. The many small stories told by the much-touted "ordinary people" of wartime London flow into the master narratives of European history, enriching them, enlivening them, and occasionally colliding with them. Even before the war's end, people realized how important stories about wartime would be. Shortly after VE Day, Kensington diarist Vere Hodgson wrote: "How the bombs will be multiplied in reminiscence during these years in stories, and people who never heard one, will think they were in the heart of the Blitz. Never mind, I have recorded my sufferings and I shall be able to refer back" (22 May 1945).

No cultural product about the war is easier to find than these wartime narratives, yet none is harder to assess. It is possible and perhaps even likely that many people do, as Vere Hodgson suggests, multiply the bombs in memory that they never heard in reality. Yet the war was filled with enough drama to make such embellishments unnecessary in many cases. None of the incidents described by my interviewees was either impossible or unlikely. Like other reconstructions of the past, retrospective narratives must be viewed both as cultural constructs and as sources of historical information, though their accuracy cannot always be realistically assessed, even when compared with written testimony. Stories built of memory are always subject to the ravages of time, which can erase some details while inscribing others. My interviewees were well aware of the dangers and value of personal memories. After telling me several fascinating stories, Ettie Gontarsky remarked, "I'm afraid it's all rather waffley, this, 'cause it's memory, and you know, one's memory after all these years, it's not exactly very clear" (personal interview, 4 April 1993). However, even when the historical accuracy of wartime narratives is uncertain, they yield another kind of information, for they tell us about the ways that people make use of stories about the past. Wartime Londoners were well aware of their status as makers of history, and they were not about to let future generations forget either the large narratives that we call history or the smaller stories that are our own.

At present there is great interest in narrative among scholars of many different disciplines, including history, folklore, literature, and anthropology. The discipline of history takes as a central charter the creation of narrative reconstructions of the past; in the words of Hayden White, a historical work is "a verbal structure in the form of a narrative prose discourse that purports to be a model, or icon, of past structures and processes in the interest of *explaining what they were by representing* them" (1973, 2; emphasis in original). The words "history" and "story" were used interchangeably in English as late as the nineteenth century; in many languages, only one such word exists (*Geschichte* in German, *histoire* in French, *storia* in Italian). Since much human thinking, at least in the West, is based on ideas of chronology and temporality, narrative achieves an importance even in disciplines that do not choose it as a prime concern. Walter J. Ong writes: "In a sense narrative is paramount among all verbal art forms because of the way it underlies so many other art forms, often even the most abstract. Human knowledge comes out of time. Behind even the abstractions of science, there lies narrative of the observations on the basis of which the abstractions have been formulated" (1982, 140).

Historical narratives—purportedly true stories about the past—present special theoretical and methodological concerns. Classic historiography, particularly as exemplified by its nineteenth-century masters, treated narrative as a virtually transparent mode of representation within which the past could be most properly situated.[1] Such historiographic narratives are so broad-based that their narrative elements are muted, their emphasis focused on documented information, rational explanation, and claims to historical truth. In accord with Ranke's dictum to portray the past "as it really was," such narrative structures appear to be wholly natural because no character has been invented, no event fabricated (White 1973, 6). In the twentieth century, this naïve faith in the transparence and naturalness of historical narrative has been criticized by scholars such as Walter Benjamin, Hayden White, and Paul Ricoeur. Yet, as Ricoeur points out, even the most self-consciously analytical history depends upon a conception of historical time that is essentially narrative in nature (1984a, 91). In other words, history that is completely divorced from narrative ceases to be history.

In the twentieth century, historians are less sanguine about the reliability of written documents; some are inclined to pay attention to oral artifacts as well. Allan Nevins (1984), who first proposed the idea of oral history in 1938, believed that new developments in technology made oral history both possible and inevitable: the telephone, the telegraph, and rapid intercity transportation were depriving historians of their traditional fund of documents. At the same time, historians recognized that written documents are not indisputable sources of "truth" but are contextually anchored, potentially inaccurate personal accounts that have the great virtue of never changing. Scholars of wartime Britain are able to draw upon a fantastically rich fund of written and oral documents, from history books, archives, libraries, films, radio programs, records, and personal interviews. All of these sources indicate the importance of narrative in discussing the past and in surviving the present.

A distinction should be made between narratives told during the war and narratives told about the war. Stories told during the war were used, like other art forms, to promote unity and to create the ideology necessary for successful prosecution of the war effort. As such, they were subject to wartime censorship and were limited in terms of structure and theme. Postwar stories are subject to no such restrictions and exist in counterpoint to wartime material. Consider, for example, two different descriptions—one wartime, one postwar—of people's reactions to air raids. The wartime story is taken from the diary of Vere Hodgson, a middle-aged, middle-class Kensington woman who began keeping a detailed diary during the summer of 1940 and continued it until the end of the war. On 6 December 1942 she paraphrased a story she had read in a book entitled *The Front Line*: "I like the story of the little boy in a Welsh town who was dug out by rescue men. He was found because he could be heard singing GOD SAVE THE KING over and over again beneath the wreckage. He was only six, and it took six hours to release him. He sang all the time. When asked why he said his father was a collier and had told him that the men always sang when they were trapped underground, and he thought he had better do the same thing." The Welsh coal mining areas were well known for political radicalism and for occasional bursts of Welsh nationalism. The links to England, though institutionally much more solid than the ties between England and Scotland, were culturally and politically uneasy. The English suppression of the Welsh language was bitterly remembered; Wales was, in a sense, a country that England had conquered and annexed centuries before. Yet in the story, a child of this radical milieu declares his loyalty to the British monarchy and his affinity with all of Britain by singing—over and again—the British national anthem. Such a story published in wartime fostered the popular notion of cross-class, cross-ethnic British unity, and its citing in Vere Hodgson's diary—which was written to describe the war to non-British friends—fostered it yet more.

Postwar storytellers are aware of the famous image of wartime unity and must come to terms with it; at the same time, postwar stories allow us to see the deficiencies that wartime storytellers could not discuss. George Wagner, a German political refugee who came to London shortly before the war, told the following story about less-than-exemplary behavior following an air raid: "Now, there were all sorts of people lying around the road, some simply stunned, and there was one woman who worked with us, who said, 'I wasn't hurt, but I was lying there, and somebody was pulling at my golden earrings.' So that existed here, too" (personal interview, 23 April 1993). Such a story would not have been published and probably would not have been told during the war. Yet the context of the telling is important; this story was told in response to my question about whether there was, in fact, unity and camaraderie in wartime London. If we listen to George Wagner's commentary on his story, we see that he is positing it as an exception: "So that existed here, too. But nothing like as bad as anywhere else. . . . By and large, the— I mean, these tales about how wonderful they stood up to it, so on, so on, what a grand old race, the usual thing, 'Land of Hope and Glory,' toot, toot, toot, toot, they're always a bit overdone. But there is a solid kernel of fact" (personal interview, 23 April 1993).

In oral history interviews and in printed and archival material about wartime London, I found roughly three kinds of narratives. I refer to them as anecdotal narratives, historical narratives, and epochal narratives. Like the anthropological distinction of folktale, legend, and myth, these narratives work at the level of the personal quotidian, the communal historical, and the universal symbolic. Anecdotal narratives tell of small-scale events that affected few people. (Though, as we have seen in the story quoted by Vere Hodgson, the telling of such a tale may have political and propagandistic importance beyond the event itself.) Most anecdotal stories that I found were narratives in which the teller of the tale was also the protagonist, but some people told stories about friends and family as well. The stories that I call historical narratives describe events that the teller believed to be of historical importance but in which the teller was not necessarily a participant. These events were typically small-scale and of short duration, but they were deemed to have historical significance that went beyond the participants.

The epochal narratives, by contrast, deal with the course of the war itself and indicate the teller's own interpretation of a large-scale world crisis. Some historians, such as Angus Calder and Clive Ponting, have used the word "myth" in discussing this level of discourse, and it is at this level that the wartime London debates typically occur. In general, my interviewees did not relate full-blown epochal narratives, perhaps believing them too obvious to bear repeating, but commented instead on aspects of this well-known story. The standard British narrative of World War II tells of a time when civilization was threatened but not conquered, when free men and women banded together to defeat the forces of evil. In this narrative, Britain stood, brave and united, fighting alone until joined by the Allies, never defeated, never down-hearted. London appears as a communal protagonist in this narrative, the chief actor in the fight against Nazism. Whereas few people disagreed with the basic structure of this narrative, all highlighted the strands that they felt were most important and criticized aspects that they believed were facile or simplistic.

To treat history as a narrative is not to suggest that writing history is the same as writing fiction or that, completeness being impossible, scholarly standards may be abandoned. To the contrary, such an approach may involve the tightening of scholarly standards. In recognizing that all history is selective, we can accept no document, written or oral, without considering it in context and without seeking corroborating evidence. Such methodological stringency does not preclude the reconstruction and understanding of the past; we can still amass different kinds of evidence and assemble a fairly good idea of what has happened, in certain times and places and to certain people. Nonetheless, we cannot ignore the ideological implications embedded in the narrative structures that historians use to represent the past. Hayden White's study of the great nineteenth-century historians articulates this premise:

> Considered purely as verbal structures, the works they produced appear to have radically different formal characteristics and to dispose the conceptual apparatus used to explain the same sets of data in fundamentally different ways. On the most superficial level, for example, the work of one historian may be diachronic or processionary in nature (stressing the fact of change and transformation in the historical process), while that of another may be synchronic and static in form (stressing the fact of structural continuity). Again, where one historian may take it as his task to reinvoke, in a lyrical or poetic manner, the "spirit" of a past age, another may take it as his task to penetrate behind the events in order to disclose the "laws" or "principles" of which a particular age's "spirit" is only a manifestation or phenomenal form. [1973, 4]

White, like many pioneers, goes too far. His emphasis on the implications and potentialities of narrative structure threatens to subsume the entirety of the historical task. His unrelenting formalism and stress on what he terms the "protoscientific" character of history seem to leave the selection of data and emplotment to the chance whimsy (or deliberate ideological bias) of the historian. An important critique is supplied by Paul Ricoeur who, like myself, finds much to value in White's analysis:

A certain tropological arbitrariness must not make us forget the kind of constraint that the past exerted on historical discourse through known documents, by demanding an endless *rectification* on its part. . . . Of course, we must combat the prejudice that the historian's language could be made entirely transparent, so that the facts would speak for themselves; as if it were enough to get rid of the *ornaments of prose* in order to do away with the *figures of poetry*. But we would be unable to combat this first prejudice if we did not at the same time combat the second, according to which the literature of imagination, because it constantly makes use of fiction, can have no hold on reality. [1984b, 34–35; emphasis in original]

To perceive history as a narrative is to emphasize both its completeness and its incompleteness. A narrative is a complete, bounded entity with a beginning, a middle, and an end. Yet because it is bounded, it ignores events and people that exist outside its boundaries. One of the most succinct historical narratives is Julius Caesar's description of his victory at Zela: "*Veni, vidi, vici*" ("I came, I saw, I conquered"). In three Latin words, Caesar tells an entire story of war, triumph, and conquest. In "Questions of a Worker Who Reads," Bertolt Brecht suggests that Caesar's descriptions of events and dramatis personae might be a bit limited: "Caesar beat the Gauls. Didn't he even have a cook with him?" Brecht's worker both accepts the historical parameters that Caesar has set and radically transforms them: Caesar's stories remain reports of triumph and victory, but Caesar's position is much more equivocal (Brecht 1961: 45–46). Brecht forces us to ask: Did Caesar control the legions or depend upon their cooperation? Was it Caesar's genius or the army's strength that conquered Gaul? What of the cook he had in his army?[2]

Brecht's worker transforms Caesar's narrative but does not discard it. Though he wonders about the people over whom Caesar triumphed, he does not tell the tale from the defeated point of view. Other historical narratives have been completely rejected by those who disagree with their premises; thus, parallel narratives exist, each describing the same occurrences in very different ways. For example, the story of Columbus discovering America, taught to every American schoolchild, has been inverted by Native Americans and others concerned with human rights, who tell it as a tale of Columbus *invading* America. The familiar story of success, courage, and adventure becomes a story of defeat, victimization, and tragedy.

Likewise, Rachelle Hope Saltzman (1988) shows that the British General Strike of 1926 is remembered and described quite differently by strikers and strikebreakers. To strikers and their supporters, the strike is a story of working-class courage and unity defeated by the superior strength and power of the capitalist class. To the strikebreakers (or "volunteers," as they preferred to call themselves), the strike was a time when middle-class and upper-class people rallied together and successfully defeated the threat of a potentially revolutionary working class. The "event" of the strike, the bare bones of the narrative, is essentially the same in stories of both types. There is little debate about what happened during the General Strike or what the salient parts of the story are. The interpretation of these accepted facts, however, makes all the difference. Were the workers or the capitalists the dangerous ones? Were the strikers heroes or nascent thugs? Were the strikebreakers heroes or despots? These are the questions that must be answered before the story has much meaning. Thus the creation of a meaningful historical narrative can be divided into three parts: data collection, or amassing the evidence; weaving the data, the facts, into a coherent story; and supplying a meaning to this story within the light of a larger story, perhaps one of British history, perhaps one of Western civilization, perhaps one of humanity. In the themes and story lines of these narratives, we can find important symbols and key metaphors for remembering, understanding, and representing past experience.

Anecdotal Narratives

Narratives are a means of placing one's experiences within history and of showing one's part in a larger scheme of events. Narratives gleaned from personal interviews are especially interesting because they exist in the present while simultaneously describing the past. In so doing, they refract the past through the lens of the present and comment upon both time periods by reference to one another. Richard Bauman describes the special qualities of oral narrative with reference to Roman Jakobson's distinction between narrated events and narrative events: "Oral narrative provides an especially rich focus for the investigation of the relationship between oral literature and social life because part of the special nature of narrative is to be doubly anchored in human events. That is, narratives are keyed both to the events in which they are told and to the events that they recount, toward narrative events and narrated events" (1986, 2). Written retrospective narratives can also perform this double function; they exist within the culture of the present even as they comment upon the past. In looking at the patterns that emerge from these narratives, we can see not only what has happened in the past, but why the past must be remembered.

Retrospective narratives are highly selective entities, carefully and often lovingly constructed out of the raw material of memory. As memory is fashioned into story, certain facts are chosen to represent the experience of the past. Once the story has been set and as more time passes, specific narrative threads are highlighted while others are cast in shadow. This process need imply no actual forgetting—the facts of the story may remain the same—but the teller's present point of view will determine the facts that will be emphasized, the facts that will be told at all. The counterpoint to these retrospective narratives is provided by narratives actually told during the war, which we can glean from written wartime documents. In examining both oral and written narratives, as well as the tension between them, we can add valuable information to current debates about the nature of wartime London. We can also see the ways in which past concerns remain present ones.

Both wartime and postwar stories are shot through with contradictions: the wartime rhetorical emphasis on humor and normality contrasted sharply with the lived reality of horror and abnormality. During wartime this contradiction was downplayed, the horror muted, while stoical courage and bold jests were highlighted. Ritchie Calder's description of people sheltering in the vault of a church is one example of a story that emphasizes the refusal to relinquish humor and normality. Calder is aware of the contradictions, but his subjects appear not to be; these "cheerful Cockneys" carry on their ordinary activities unafraid of German bombs or British revenants, apparently ignorant of the irony that Calder highlights: "In a corner, by the light of trembling candle flames, a little group was playing cards, quite undeterred by the creepy unnaturalness, or the grim humour of using the dead as a card-table. They treated the whole thing as so commonplace and with so little sense of the superstitious that if the spirits of the dead, disturbed by this strange intrusion, had decided to walk, those East Enders would probably have asked them to take a hand at cards!" (1941, 37).

Many postwar narratives are in a similar vein, emphasizing a strange mix of humor and horror, of ordinary people caught in extraordinary circumstances. In postwar narratives, we also can see a kind of tale forbidden in wartime: stories of unrelieved horror and bitterness, with no sense of purpose or irony. Occasionally, I heard such stories from people who had been evacuated children, particularly those who had been very young at the time of evacuation. Unaffected by wartime rhetoric, too young to understand the purpose of separation from their families, evacuees were unable to canalize their emotions in ways that their parents could. Shirley was from a middle-class, Jewish family in East London (her father was a doctor) and was only six years old during the time of her first evacuation, at the beginning of the war. As an evacuee, she found herself the target of anti-Semitism ("It's because of you Jews there's a war!") and neglect. During her last evacuation, she was forced to play outside in the snow when she had a heavy cold. As a result, she developed double pneumonia, and her parents brought her back to London the night the docks were on fire:

> I can remember this train breaking down outside Liverpool Street station, stopping. And the whole of London was alight; there were just bombs dropping and you could see buildings, outlines of St. Paul's. . . . I remember the fear. Obviously I felt ill because I had this double pneumonia. And there were some Americans in the carriage; one of them, I think, dropped a helmet nearly on top of my head. It was very frightening. I

mean, if you're sitting in a train in the open when most people are sheltering, you expect a bomb to sort of drop onto the train. I can still see it;
I mean, it's very vivid in my mind. The searchlights and the fires and,
oh, it was horrible. [personal interview, 22 January 1993]

These examples—from the matter-of-fact courage of the card players in the
crypt to the terror of the sick child—will give some idea of the range of tales told
about wartime London. I have chosen to concentrate in this section on four kinds
of anecdotal narratives that I found to be especially prevalent: humorous stories,
love stories, horror stories, and near-miss stories.[3] These stories correspond roughly
to the dramatic conventions of comedy (humorous stories), romance (love stories),
and melodrama (horror and near-miss stories). I do not believe that any of them
represent tragedy in the classical or Shakespearean sense. This is not to suggest that
people told no stories of sadness and loss; such stories are inevitable when one is
discussing war. But in all the wartime stories and in most of the postwar interviews, there is a sense that this sadness and loss was not purposeless, that the ultimate outcome of the war was right. Even those who felt most bitter about the
stupidity and violence of war did not say that the war should never have been fought
or that the wrong side had won. Such opinions may be held, but those who hold
them are unlikely to say so into a fieldworker's tape recorder; their memories are
either too painful or too far removed from the political mainstream to allow an
interviewer to get near them. Such opinions are so completely at odds with the
national imagery of wartime and so inimical to most contemporary British political stripes that they are unlikely to surface unless one is specifically looking for them.

Humorous Stories

> Nothing is funnier than unhappiness.
>
> —Samuel Beckett, *Endgame*

If the essence of humor is inappropriateness, then wartime London was a fertile
seedbed for comedy. Anne Lubin remarks, "You . . . saw these peculiar sights of
the whole front of a house away, half the floors gone, and sitting on a mantelpiece,
a teddy bear or something like that that had been untouched" (personal interview,
21 January 1993). As noted, humor was an essential part of wartime rhetoric, a
way of belittling danger and rendering it more manageable. The bizarre occurrences
and grotesque juxtapositions of wartime were exploited for all their comic potential. Londoners, like medieval fools, were proud of their ability to find humor in
the grimmest situation and to twist words until they made one laugh. Geordie, a
young engineer at the time, remembers the aftermath of a V2 attack on New Cross
as follows: "Two doors from me the husband and wife were at their gate laughing,
she had just put a plate of sausage, bacon and egg on the table when the rocket

went off, the plate exited with the window and landed instead on the garden hedge. True, honestly, and it was considered a great joke at the time" (personal letter, 18 February 1993).

While couples watched their lunches disappear into hedges, popular entertainment was replete with zany and implausible humor. Tommy Handley and his radio program *ITMA* kept up a dizzying series of jokes: Mayor Tom shows a film of his bogus trip around the empire and says, "This is the accident I had in the Occident" (NSA ref. nos. 2684-R, F42/3 and T28071b2, 9 January 1942); Tommy casts himself as "Sweeney Tom, the Demon Blubberer of Fleet Street" (NSA ref. nos. F41/102 and T28071b1, 26 September 1941); and Tommy visits a school and suggests writing a Christmas song called "I'm Dreaming of a White Blackboard" (NSA ref. nos. 22230-3 and T22226b2, 28 October 1943). Francis Worsley, who produced *ITMA*, described Handley's character as a "swashbuckling, plausible, quick-witted rogue—a racketeer, slick but not very successful—all his grandiose schemes go crazily wrong. There is something Elizabethan in his reckless attitude to life and his zest for the colourful—something very British in his refusal to admit defeat—something very admirable in his contempt of humbug and bumbledom" (Worsley 1946, 45).

In 1940 there was very little to laugh about, and the government was concerned about morale in the East End, where the raids were heaviest and the residents had few resources with which to make things palatable. Fearing defeatism or open revolution, the government worked (albeit slowly and somewhat capriciously) to improve shelters and provide services for those rendered homeless. At the same time, it turned the tables on those who were seen as potential threats and marked them as targets of official praise. Angus Calder writes: "Fairly or unfairly, the reaction of the East Enders to the failure of the authorities to plan for the real nature of the blitz was first bewilderment, then anger. Yet they did not revolt nor, truly speaking, panic. Explaining this phenomenon, some journalists of the period created a myth of the Cockney wisecracking over the ruins of his world, which is as famous as the myth of the Few soaring into battle with laughter on their lips, and equally misleading" (1969, 165–66).

The Cockney was a folk character ripe for the plucking. Like the timeless peasants beloved by nineteenth-century antiquarians and nation-builders, the Cockney is always in danger of disappearing (Jones 1989). Like those selfsame peasants, Cockneys are poor but contented and represent an essential heart of the national character. Unlike peasants, however, prewar Cockneys were not particularly admirable characters. The urban milieu had rendered rural virtues obsolete: the Cockney was clever rather than wise, canny rather than generous, a bit of a rogue and a huckster, the kind of person who could pick your pocket so cleverly he would make you laugh and admit it was probably a good thing. As Gareth Stedman Jones points out, the Cockney character has a long history and is open to many interpretations, but a popular twentieth-century conception includes a "picturesque cheerfulness and wit embedded in characteristic turns of phrase, a mildly irreverent attitude to law and authority, a comic particularism, a stubborn and often illogical ethical code, combined with a good-hearted patriotism. To invoke this 'cockney' is also to invoke a particular notion of an urban community: a community of the poor, but of a distinctly conservative and indigenous kind. There is no place in a 'cockney' typology for the spiv, the teddy boy, the punk . . . nor . . . for the West Indian, the Bangladeshi, or the Cypriot" (1989, 278). Cockneys had their traditional occupations, and the Cockney costermonger was a classic example. A perfect exemplification of this notion of the Cockney is described by Vere Hodgson, after listening to a radio program on 20 June 1943: "The Postscript to-night was by three men who love their country—a Scots farmer, a Welsh trade Unionist and a London costermonger. They were all excellent, but the costermonger was the best of the lot. When he gets to heaven the first thing he is going to ask St. Peter for is a barrow."

Yet this conservative, nonethnic rendering of the Cockney, as Jones readily points out, does not exploit all of its potentialities. During World War II, such an interpretation may have been most acceptable to the ruling powers, but praise of an urban, working-class milieu opens doors that may not easily be slammed shut. After all, Cockneys, like peasants, actually exist, and they are liable to define themselves if one is not careful. One woman I interviewed, a Jew and a socialist, described herself as a Cockney because she had been born within the sound of the bells of Bow; and indeed, this is the conventional definition of the Cockney today. Harry Geduld, who grew up in the Jewish East End, describes the color and diversity of his Cockney neighborhood:

> Like my mother before me I am a Cockney. I was born in the London Hospital, Whitechapel Road. In my childhood, the area was a bustling, working-class Jewish neighborhood like the Lower East of New York at the turn of the century. It is a locale with many historic associations. For example: Chaucer and Harold Pinter were born in the vicinity. . . . In 1381, at the Mile End, the eastern extension of Whitechapel Road, Richard II was forced to put an end to serfdom. It was in this district that Jews first settled when Cromwell readmitted them into England in 1657, where Captain Cook's home was located, and where William Booth established the Salvation Army in 1868. In the late Victorian period, the London Hospital, my birthplace, housed the Elephant Man. Opposite the hospital, in Buck's Row, Jack the Ripper committed one of his grisly murders in the fall of 1888. And close by, some twenty-three years later, occurred the Sidney Street Siege, in which soldiers and police battled a group of Jewish anarchists. Quite a neighborhood!

> To be a Cockney one must be born within the sound of the bells of Stratford-atte-Bow Church. In a literal sense, I suppose I am one of the last of the breed since no one has heard those bells since the church was destroyed in 1942. (Geduld 1995: 48)

Cockneys, whatever their presumed virtues or politics, are actual people; and whatever else they may be, they are inescapably Londoners and inescapably East Enders, probably poor (though not destitute) and of either the working class or the lower middle class. In other words, they exist in the milieu most likely to be radical and multi-ethnic, which explains why a conservative, Anglo-Saxon view of them might be desired by a conservative ruling class. Thus, praising the humor and the valor of this milieu, making it a model for the entirety of London and indeed of Britain, may result in getting more than one has bargained for—one may keep people in their places while bombs are falling but be voted out of office once peace returns.

In discussing humor in wartime London, it must be remembered that humor was not always of the mindlessly patriotic kind and had many important functions in the making and remembering of wartime London. G.H.R., from a working-class family in north London (i.e., not a Cockney), was not taken in by the sudden praise of his class. He writes:

> One odd thing about the war was the change of attitude by our betters when war came. Whereas previously we had been hands, perhaps on one hour's notice, we suddenly became the salt of the earth. When the conscript army was gathered, the government in its wisdom thought that if we were to be enthusiastic we should be informed—preferably thinking the right thoughts. (1945 showed how mistaken they were.) Anyway they ordered that we should all attend groups where we were lectured from supplied papers. Unfortunately this did not always follow and more often than not the meeting became a discussion which occasionally worried the brain. [personal letter]

Though G.H.R. was neither a cheerful Cockney nor an unthinking jingoist, his memories are filled with the humor that the grotesqueries of war can create, the nervous relief that comes when one has stopped holding one's breath and realized that fear was pointless this time, and of the wit and wordplay that remain a part of this language-loving culture. He tells the following story about his experience as an air-raid warden: "On one occasion, we (we went in pairs) went to where a bomb had fallen, the house front was damaged. I walked through into the house calling and had an answer. In a back room, a man was sleeping in a made up bed on the floor. He blinked at my torch and said, 'How did you get in?' We told him" (personal letter).

Another incident, which occurred while G.H.R. was at work in the factory, tells of a visitor's dangerously careless behavior. However, since no real harm occurred, the story is told in an ultimately humorous way:

> A call from central office one day required me to produce the basics for an unusual revolver. I learnt that one of the girls in assembly had a boyfriend in the RAF. [He] had the gun as he was an RAF policeman but no holster. The job was done and next leave he appeared at the factory where girlfriend showed him off. He produced the gun and someone took it—pointed it—and it went off. The fool had left it loaded. I found it almost beyond belief. I don't believe anyone was hurt but rumour had it that it killed the manager—he looked alright to me. [personal letter]

A very similar irony is found in wartime material, as in the following story from the diary of William Bernard Regan, who, if his diary had been found by a journalist, would doubtless have been called a cheerful Cockney. Regan's comments are about the first V1 attacks in June 1944: "Nothing on the news about the raid; at 10:00 A.M. Forces news gave out, that rocket planes were used over the south of England. Periodically, throughout today, they have been coming over, but Mr. Morrison says there is nothing to worry about, as he has the situation in hand, or will have as time goes by. Still, we shouldn't worry, he is O.K."

In sum, humor did exist in wartime Britain; it was a technique for survival against the horrors of war and a skill much loved and prized in British culture. As such, it was seized by government propagandists and blown cheerfully out of proportion. Since it existed both in national mythology and in wartime experience, it remains an important part of the stories told by those who remember the war. Such retrospective humor is also a way of letting out one's breath once more, of realizing that one is still alive though others have died, and of not taking this chance survival too seriously.

Love Stories

> Faces came and went. There was a diffused gallantry in the atmosphere, an unmarriedness: it came to be rumoured about the country, among the self-banished, the uneasy, the put-upon and the safe, that everybody in London was in love—which was true, if not in the sense the country meant.
> —Elizabeth Bowen, *The Heat of the Day*

It would be hard to imagine an atmosphere more conducive to sexual excitement than one that combined danger, purpose, constant change, haphazard sleeping arrangements, an influx of foreigners, and the knowledge that one might not live through the night. Illegitimacy and sexually transmitted diseases increased during the war (as did marriage and, especially after the war, divorce), yet many wartime love stories have an atmosphere of innocence rather than prurience. Although wartime circumstances may have swept away the final traces of Victorian morality, from the vantage point of the 1990s, wartime love stories seem charmingly old-fashioned. They are stories in which romance, rather than sexuality, is the central character, yet they seem not prudish but filled with a graceful reticence. My interviewees made it clear that relationships between the sexes had changed a good deal during their lives. G.H.R. describes his weekends with his fiancée, whose place of work had been evacuated to Bournemouth, as "tame by modern standards" (personal letter). Ettie Gontarsky tells of entertaining her boyfriend in the front room of the family flat while her parents were in the shelter but remarks that such sessions were "very innocent, very innocent in those days" (personal interview, 4 April 1993).

Love, like humor, was both an unrationed pleasure and a gesture of mild defiance—it was a way of refusing to give up the normal aspects of life even in very abnormal circumstances. And just as the chanciness and absurdity of wartime life provided many opportunities for laughter, so did the uncertainty and excitement of war lend their aid to sexual love. "It was sheer Hollywood," said Ettie Gontarsky of her American boyfriend: "Here were we, English girls, fed on Hollywood, brought up on Hollywood—Greta Garbo, Joan Crawford, Betty Grable, Clark Gable, you name it—we lived that kind of romanticized—we had these romanticized ideas. Suddenly you've got a boyfriend who is from there, who speaks with the same accent and very nicely too, who rings you up and says, 'Darling, they're playing our tune.' Well, you just melt" (personal interview, 4 April 1993).

Ettie was not the only one who mentioned the films as a model for romantic behavior. G.H.R. writes:

> From World War I, we had the cinema to which most of us went regularly, and it is a question of whether we copied the actors or they us. It did seem at the time that we learnt from the films how to dress, how to fix our hair and also how we treated one another. Coming as I did from working class stock and prejudiced in the working class tradition, the films presented a life of people wealthier than we were but on the whole acceptable. It does seem to me in retrospect that our relationships were very similar, and at a personal level we treated our girls like the men on the films did. As a result I believe girls were respected and treated in a special way. . . . Girls did not expect undue familiarity (?) and relations were warm but strictly chaste. Babies out of wedlock were very rare and society had little sympathy for the couple but especially the girl. . . . During the war all our normal patterns of behaviour were changed. Men got called up and so did women. Women went into industry and the services. Girls and men who were completely unused to it left home and family and very often were put into groups living far from home with no

familiar surroundings. Boredom and loneliness, together with the uncertainty, created problems. Since the future was so uncertain, young
people did things they would never have contemplated. At the same
time, there was an attitude of irresponsibility, far from home and away
tomorrow or soon. Promises were made, especially by men, which on
reflection were forgotten. Probably most young people coped but there
was a substantial number that found problems. [personal letter]

Anne Lubin likewise notes how the strangeness and uncertainty of wartime fostered both romance and danger: "The place was absolutely teeming with uniforms
from all over the world, and it seemed to be terribly romantic as well as exciting.
I'm lucky I never fell. I really am" (personal interview, 13 March 1993).

And yet, as G.H.R. notes, it was "tame by modern standards." Wartime films
are almost unbearably chaste, with marriage portrayed as a pillar of society and
sexual romance sublimated to the romance of doing one's duty in wartime. Retrospective stories of wartime romance are not so improbably pure, but they do have
a certain cinematic quality, a climate of magic and coincidence and the chance
wonder that attends much wartime happiness. G.H.R.'s story of the night he
became engaged is an especially delightful example. The date is 1 September 1939,
the day that Germany invaded Poland, making war inevitable. G.H.R. arrived
home after work and a meeting of a local youth organization:

After the hasty meal, I thought about my ever-loved and what she would
do—I guessed she'd come to find me. We lived $1^1/_2$ miles apart and so
with some trepidation I set out on foot—buses were in a bit of a muddle
and she might walk. Since some minds think alike we met half way—
this was no mean thing since the routes between the two houses were
varied and if we had not met—remember—complete blackness everywhere.

We went to my house—being empty and our future, being uncertain
and possibly short, we decided to spend it together. A couple of hours
later I walked her home, and promising to go to her house the following
evening I walked home myself. [personal letter]

If uncertainty heightened romance, then romance itself was a kind of certainty.
Eileen Scales met her husband on her sixteenth birthday, when she and her grandmother and aunt were helping to clear the debris caused by a bomb in their neighborhood. Soldiers billeted nearby were also helping, among them her future husband:

We started to talk, and I knew him for one week and he was sent to—
that was just after D-Day—and he was sent out to Holland I think
when it began. And I didn't see him for about another year, just used to
correspond, until he came home on leave. Came home about a year later

for a fortnight's leave. And we became engaged and I was seventeen by then. And then he went out again, I think, for about another year. So I didn't see him for another year. . . . And then after he'd been home the second time, they then sent him to Palestine. So I didn't see him for quite a while again. And then when he came home we got married. That was '47. [personal interview, 5 March 1993]

The interrupted courtship, the early engagement, and the eventual marriage between relative strangers of rather different backgrounds (she was a Londoner, he a country boy) were all part of the vicissitudes of war. As things changed, one looked for something that did not. Eileen says:

I suppose I was very young at sixteen to have—or seventeen—to, you know, come to a decision that here is the man I was going to marry. Maybe I wasn't taking it that seriously at the time. I don't know. I mean when you're seventeen I suppose you don't. We were engaged; he bought an engagement ring. And I suppose when things are so dangerous and so unsettled, maybe something like that is something to hold on to. You know for him perhaps the thought, well, there was a girl back home, waiting. Whether we were both really taking it that seriously I don't know. [personal interview, 5 March 1993]

Despite the fragmentary courtship, Eileen's marriage was a happy one. Others were not so lucky. One woman I interviewed found herself at loose ends after the war had put a stop to her education. She made a hasty marriage, and by the time she realized what a serious mistake it was, she had several children and remained in this disastrous marriage for the better part of twenty years. Another woman found her husband so changed and traumatized from his wartime experience that she was in actual danger; she left the marriage very shortly after his return. Many women, of course, waited for husbands or boyfriends who simply never came home. Conversely, many men returned to find that their places had been taken or their wives were busy with babies of uncertain paternity—there were harsh invectives against the sly Canadians, Poles, Free French, and of course Americans, universally acknowledged as "over-paid, over-sexed, and over here." Even Jan Struther, whose "Mrs. Miniver" sketches spoke of an idealized domesticity, found that her previously happy marriage could not survive the five years of separation when her husband was a prisoner of war. Like most wartime experiences, wartime love affairs were shot through with contradictions: the excitement and danger of war, which made romance inevitable, also threatened its very existence. Wartime romance was a game of chance. G.H.R., whose marriage survived a three-year absence while he was in the army and remained happy more than fifty years later, looked back on the way war had changed his life and said, "The gods smile on some of us—not always deservedly" (personal letter).

Horror Stories

> Deep with the first dead lies London's daughter,
> Robed in the long friends,
> The grains beyond age, the dark veins of her mother,
> Secret by the unmourning water
> Of the riding Thames.
> After the first death, there is no other.

> —Dylan Thomas
> "A Refusal to Mourn the Death, by Fire, of a Child in London"

The necessary partners to tales of love among the ruins and defiant laughing in the face of danger are, of course, the ruins and the danger. Horror stories emerge slowly in interviews about wartime life. They are less enjoyable to tell and to remember, and they defy the standard image of steadfast togetherness and jolly camaraderie. Horror stories of this kind barely exist in wartime material, which is not to suggest that wartime sources are free of horrible incidents. But in wartime narratives, the horror exists always to be transcended, to be a stepping-stone to something else, the necessary stage upon which the drama of courage and defiance may take place. In postwar narratives, such morale building is no longer necessary, nor is it legally mandated. In postwar horror stories, the horror itself exists as the central focus, grotesque, purposeless, and bleak. It is not ennobled by fine phrases or subsumed into the story of something else. It simply exists, a grim reminder of the price of war.

That a city besieged by enemy bombing should be a place of terror need surprise no one, but horror stories must fight against the shining official image of wartime London. "There's nothing romantic, nothing exciting about a war," says Kitty Brinks, in defiance of so much that has been said about it. Kitty remembers differently. In the following interchange, one can see that it is I, the interviewer, who is trying to make the story have a happy ending. Such an ending is not permitted:

KB: I remember one sight that I saw that made me feel bad. A man
  sitting on a wall while they were excavating, trying to dig out his
  family. He sat there for three days waiting for his wife and children
  to be dug out.
JF: Did they make it?
KB: I doubt it. Not after three days. They were digging and digging.
  He just sat there as though he just wasn't there; he was there in
  body. His body was there. It was a horrible sight that I can still see
  today. . . . There's nothing romantic, nothing exciting about a war.
  Nothing at all. Because it's not only other people that get killed, it's
  us. And I still see that man sitting on the wall waiting for his family

to be dug out. When someone says to me, "Must have been exciting," oh! Never! It was never exciting. [personal interview, 25 January 1993]

"It's not only other people that get killed," says Kitty, but of course, for those who remember World War II, it *was* only others who got killed. Looking back from the safety of five decades later, one may well be nostalgic for a time that promised at least fifty more years of life, as the present cannot. "Although we were very conscious of being close to death all the time during the war," says R.B., "we're always close to death. But you don't really consider it. I mean, especially when you're young, you think you're going to live forever. Only other people die" (personal interview, 21 April 1993). Being close to death is, as R.B. reminds us, a natural part of everyone's life. But there are horrors that war brings that are not natural, not a path that all of us must take. "There's worse things than death and that's living and being maimed," says R.B. Her story about such an event takes place on the traditional day of the macabre:

I . . . remember an occasion when a young friend of mine had just started work that week . . . in a factory of some kind. And she was working on the top floor and an incendiary bomb came through the roof there, and in the panic of the girls to get away from it, she was knocked onto it. And she had so many operations because her face was badly disfigured and I never—I mean, I didn't see her at that time, I saw her a long time afterwards. But that's always stayed with me and that was on a Friday the 13th. [personal interview, 21 April 1993]

Many people saw the war not as unrelieved horror or unrelieved hope but as a constant interweaving and crosscutting of the two. G.H.R. told many stories of wartime comedy and near-magical coincidences, but he had plenty of stories on the dark side as well. In discussing his experiences as an air-raid warden, he described several funny incidents and then wrote: "Another night heavy bombing including a land mine had fallen about two miles north of us. A lorry collected a contingent to go to aid the locals and help. When we arrived an area about a quarter mile across was level. We were to search in the rubble for survivors—particularly checking shelters. It was all very organised with pairs covering every inch. I was given a young policeman as a partner. As we walked carefully he remarked that some-one had lost a toy doll and he picked it up—then he fainted—it wasn't a toy" (personal letter).

The death of children is one of the most horrifying consequences of war. Eileen Scales, like G.H.R., became engaged during the war and emerged generally unscathed, but she has many stories about others who were not so lucky. The following story is filled with the contradictions inherent in wartime experience, humor and terror, survival and death, chance and irony:

I remember the night too that we had this awful bomb drop. We were all in the shelter and we were in there with these neighbours and this little baby. And my mother, when this bomb hit, almost fainted. She was, you know, came over very faint. This neighbour hadn't got water to throw over her so she threw the contents of a bottle of orange squash over her! The next morning my mother, when we got out of the shelter (of course we had to stay—I suppose it was about three in the morning that it happened), couldn't understand why her eyes were all sticking together! It was horrible. It was a very bad night that, you know. . . . Four or five people were killed outright—it was so sad because the little girl was five and clutching her teddy bear when they dug her out. And the parents of the child had come from somewhere else because the grandmother had said, "It's too dangerous where you're living, come stay with us." And they'd only come the week before and were killed. [personal interview, 5 March 1993]

It is difficult to subsume such tales into one of final success; to the individual teller, it is the dead child who is the focus of the story, not the ultimate British victory. Yet it is possible to subsume such stories into a larger one, for despite many such enemy attacks, Britain ultimately won the war. One hopes that these smaller stories, painful reminders of the tortuous path that wartime took, retain their jagged integrity within the larger picture. What makes these stories ultimately subsumable is the fact that the horror in them is caused by *enemy* bombs and shells. No one is surprised when enemies behave like enemies. What is more difficult to accept—and what rips more deeply at the myth of wartime unity—are the stories in which danger is caused not by enemies but by supposed friends. My interviewees told of many incidents that defied the conventional image of wartime camaraderie, tales of pettiness, greed, profiteering, anti-Semitism, and racism. But I heard stories of actual cruelty mainly from evacuated children.

Evacuation was difficult under the best of circumstances. Even those who were not ill treated might receive relatively little affection; those whose foster families were warm and loving lived in constant fear for their families back in London. Shirley Ann remembers playing with dead kittens as an evacuee because she had no toys. Many evacuees were so homesick that they came back to London within a few months, their families having decided that the physical danger in London was less than the psychological danger of being left in the country. G.D. stayed with a family that she remembers as being stern but kind, but her younger brother was not so lucky. He and three others were mistreated by their foster family until concerned villagers took over and moved the evacuees to other families. Some were so shaken by evacuation that they will not discuss it.

Sometimes mothers accompanied their evacuated children. These children had an obvious psychological advantage, though often the billets did not last, with two adults vying for control of the home. Marian was four years old at the start of the war and was evacuated with her mother and younger brother. They stayed in the billet only nine months, but it was long enough to garner one of the most horrific wartime narratives that I know:

> The lady that we lived with . . . had a couple, at least two evacuees staying with her. And I was telling _____ that there was a little girl about my age or maybe a year older kept complaining that she had pains in her legs. . . . She would walk through the lane and she would stop and have to hold onto the side of the wall. And she was always complaining bitterly about being tired and her legs hurting her. And the lady of this house we lived in said, "It's nothing, nothing," and she got fed up with her in the end. She got her mother to come and take her home and apparently the girl died of rheumatic fever. She had had no medical attention while she was away. [personal interview, 2 February 1993]

This wanton neglect, this mindless cruelty to a child separated from her family so that her life might be spared, is not easily integrated into a narrative that stresses unity, camaraderie, and caring. Perhaps the farther one gets from the center of London, the looser the tale of camaraderie becomes. Many villages in Britain never felt a bomb, and Londoners (like Glaswegians and other evacuated city children) were considered an alien species by many country folk. So the difficulty, as well as the occasional tragedy, of evacuation is played down, when it is mentioned at all. It fits uneasily with standard wartime narratives.

It can, however, be banalized into an evening's light entertainment. *The Mouse-trap*, the longest running play on the postwar British stage, is based on an Agatha Christie novel in which a mistreated evacuee sets about killing those responsible for the evacuation in which he was tormented and his brother killed. He is successful in his revenge and then is led away—to prison or perhaps to a mental hospital, courtesy of the welfare state. The British murder mystery is paradoxically the coziest of genres, and it makes this most horrible crime tame and tidy. In the novel, the fact of evacuation is clearly spelled out, while the play is more ambiguous about the reasons the children were placed in a foster family. Nonetheless, the play is filled with references to the war—rationing is still in effect—and the audiences who first saw it in 1952 would easily guess the reason the children were separated from their family. So the tale of a mistreated evacuee need not even mention the fact of evacuation; such stories need not impinge on wartime memory at all, but only make one think of a successful postwar tourist trap.

Near-Miss Stories

In a seminal article, William Labov and Joshua Waletzky (1967) analyze personal narratives evoked by the question "Were you ever in a situation where you were in serious danger of being killed?" Without realizing it—and without using those words—I was essentially asking the same thing. Again and again, when I asked people to tell me about wartime, about the blitz or shelters or simply what they were doing during the war, I got stories of near misses. These stories were so prevalent, among so many diverse and dissimilar people, that I was forced to examine the significance of this theme. I began to see these narratives as a prime concern of those who remembered and spoke about wartime London, a key metaphor of wartime itself.

Often these narratives were laced with humor, as is the following story told by Ettie Gontarsky, who during the war was a young fashion designer living with her family in central London:

> I remember we were all in the garage, in the Lex Garage Shelter, and an incendiary fell on a house next to ours. . . . When I think about it now, I think, you know, either I was mental or I was so distraught that I didn't know what I was talking about. . . . But I saw my brother, as we heard that there was a firebomb next door . . . which meant that our house was also in danger of setting alight. And I got hold of my brother and if you can imagine, I said, "Philip, please, go indoors and up in my bedroom, there's a box of make-up. Please go and rescue it for me. Please go and rescue my box of make-up." And he gave me the most withering look; he said, "You'll be lucky." [personal interview, 4 April 1993]

Though Ettie self-deprecatingly describes herself as "distraught," she certainly is not panicking or demonstrating any sign of hysteria. Showing no concern for herself or for the fact that she might soon be homeless, she is worried about the items that will enable her to continue her normal life as a fashionable young London woman. Though the irony of the story is highlighted in its retrospective telling, the focus on humor is in line with the wartime emphasis on the Londoner's ability to laugh even when the skies rained bombs. As wartime propagandists were keenly aware, this ability requires courage, discipline, and repression, qualities essential for the fighters of the home front.

My interviewees rarely spoke directly of personal acts of extraordinary courage; blowing one's own trumpet is considered poor form in Britain. Instead, they described bravery in ways that actually downplayed it, making it seem humorous or commonplace. The ordinary was valorized in wartime, and there was a certain quality of grit and defiance exemplified in the refusal to give up one's routine and one's claim to a normal life. The following near-miss narrative, told by Eileen Scales, shows her family's ability to "take it" and "carry on." Eileen was a teenager working in a London office during the war. She lived with her family in a suburban neighborhood in south London and sheltered in an Anderson shelter in the back garden. The following narrative shows the concerns of Eileen's mother:

I think my mother's biggest problem was the meals and whatever were we going to have for our pudding that day! I remember one occasion that was when we were having daytime air raids so it was a case of having to take our dinner or our lunch into the air-raid shelter. And I remember that she'd been saving up her coupons in this book to get dried fruit because dried fruit was so short, there was such a shortage and it was all on ration. And she made this pudding with plums in it, with sultanas and things in it. And when the air raid had . . . sort of ceased up for a little bit she said, "Well, I'll run in now and I'll fetch this pudding." As she came back a bomb dropped and she fell into the air-raid shelter with the pudding! The pudding basin was in thousands of pieces and nobody could eat the pudding. There were pieces of china sticking into the pudding. My mother nearly cried I think that day to think of all that fruit that had gone, all the dried fruit. And we just sat and laughed. [personal interview, 5 March 1993]

In severely rationed wartime Britain, dried fruit and sweets of any sort (including sugar) were in short supply; fresh fruit, particularly bananas and citrus fruits, usually unobtainable. A pudding such as the one made by Eileen's mother would have required weeks of careful planning on the complicated "points" system. Wartime recipes are full of suggestions for using grated carrot or mashed potatoes as substitutes for fruit (see Minns 1980); perhaps Eileen's mother used these substitutes without her family's knowledge, but Eileen remembers the uneaten pudding as on a par with prewar standards. Despite the loss of this delicacy, it is laughter that wins out. Eileen's mother's quiet courage is shown by her very lack of concern for her own safety (she was thrust into the shelter by bomb blast and narrowly escaped injury or death); she wept only for a culinary masterpiece that she could not serve to her family. In this near–miss narrative, the near miss itself is played down; in so doing, the story highlights the family's matter-of-fact courage, humor, and will to continue a normal life.

Yet near-miss narratives did not always contain examples of humor or stoical "carrying on." Often, they simply showed the element of luck that is the survivor's lot. Irene Wagner, a German Jewish refugee, tells the following story of a daylight V1 raid in 1944. She and her husband George, a German political refugee, were on their lunch break; they were working for the British government in a capacity so secret that they still cannot discuss it. Her story is as follows: "Now what happened, during a fateful day, when we went out to lunch, and because my watch had stopped, we went out earlier than expected. We got home and during our lunch, there was a mighty crash. Absolutely fantastic. And on our way back, we noticed that we would have stood in that entrance to our office as the bomb came down, and we would have had it" (personal interview, 1 February 1993). As a demonstration of the arbitrariness of fate, this story could scarcely be bettered. The Wagners' lives were saved not by special insight or bravery but by the failure of a mechanical timepiece, which disrupted their routine. Had they gone to lunch at their normal time, they would not have returned. There is no suggestion of bravely carrying on in adversity or of turning disaster into a joke, simply the recognition that survival often is due simply to luck. The arbitrariness of fate is both disquieting and comforting: it is comforting because it shows that victims cannot be blamed, for they do not choose their fate—a lesson that may have been especially important for the Wagners who, had they remained in their homeland, would have been among its victims. But if one does not choose to be a victim, then contrariwise one cannot prevent it. As many people told me, wartime induced a kind of fatalism; "if the bomb has my number on it" became a popular catchphrase. In other words, if you got hit, then you got hit; there was little that one could do.

In an attempt to ward off or combat the arbitrariness of fate, some people developed special powers. Marjorie Newton, a London schoolgirl at the time, wrote the following:

> As the winter of 1940/1941 went on my mother developed a strange ability to sense whether or not a raid would continue all night. Sometimes there would be a raid and then a lull for hours after which the bombers would return. It was a very cold winter and people in the shelter became restive and wanted to return to their beds. My mother would go into the yard outside the shelter, lift her head, close her eyes and sniff the air, then she would come down and tell us whether or not it was safe to go home. I don't know how she did it but it certainly worked, in fact local police and wardens would consult her during a lull. . . . On 19th March there was a very heavy raid followed by a lull of some hours. My uncle finished his duty period and came down to say he was going home and would bring us a flask of tea. It was bitterly cold that night and the others asked my mother to "have a sniff." She started to go upstairs and I followed her, suddenly she screamed at me to get down. I heard a sound like a great sailing ship and then an enormous crash. We both fell down the stairs and the lights went out. . . . Some of us had torches and a lantern was lit, we were all covered in dust but were not seriously hurt and decided to stay where we were for the time being. Later a warden came down and told my mother that our house had been completely destroyed by a parachute mine and that the gas main outside our house was burning. Some time later two men from the First Aid Post came down the stairs dragging a body, they said he was either dead or dying and they would return later to take him to the mortuary. I saw his face and knew it was my uncle. His face was grey, his hair and eyebrows were burned, he was bleeding from his nose, mouth, ears and one leg. Suddenly he made a rattling sound in his throat and my mother realised

that his false teeth were lodged at the back of his throat and choking him. She forced his mouth open and pulled out his dentures so that he could breathe. Later he was taken to the hospital and released the next week. [personal letter, 4 January 1993]

This story actually tells of several near misses and attempts to cheat fate. First, there is Marjorie's mother, with her uncanny ability to sense the length of a raid by smell.[4] While performing this olfactory divination, Marjorie and her mother narrowly escape being hit by a bomb; they are covered in dust but unharmed. However, their house is destroyed; thus the shelter, and their prescience and sense in using it, has quite possibly saved their lives: another near miss. Marjorie's uncle, who has returned to the house for the homely and very British task of making tea, is caught in the blast and injured; in fact, rescue workers believe he is dead. Again, it is Marjorie's mother who possesses lifesaving power: she recognizes the supposed death rattle as the sound of false teeth caught in the throat; she removes them, and the man is able to return home after only a week in the hospital. In Marjorie Newton's story, the near misses are a combination of luck and prescience, uncanny insight and ordinary common sense. There is also a touch of humor in her uncle's being brought back from the dead by the removal of his dentures.

The preceding stories are what folklorists call "personal narratives," i.e., narratives in which the teller of the tale is also the protagonist. Anecdotes about others were less popular among my interviewees, but some had missed most of the war themselves and had to rely on the experiences of others. G.D., a small child evacuated to the country for most of the war, tells the following tale about a near miss her grandmother experienced. Humor is mixed with heroism in this story, which clearly had become a family legend, but the heroism is performed by the family dog: "My grandmother had a sweet shop . . . very tiny little shop . . . in Hackney, and it was open right through the war. And she had a dog, collie dog it was, Rex. And Rex, the siren went and on this occasion for the first and only time Rex grabbed my grandmother and dragged her under the table. And in fact, there was blast and the room fell about her. But she was safe because she was under the table, and Rex saved her life" (personal interview, 19 January 1993). In this narrative, man's best friend behaves the way Rin Tin Tin did in the silent films of the preceding decades; even dogs are allowed a role in London's famous solidarity and courage. As in many other stories, there is great reluctance to blow one's own horn (or one's grandmother's horn); boasting is considered excessively vulgar in Britain.

In fact, as G.D. and I went through her father's papers, we found a letter commending him for single-handedly rescuing fifteen people trapped in the debris caused by an air raid. G.D.'s father had been an air-raid warden and a founder of one of the largest shelters in London's East End. Like every wartime Londoner, he told many stories about his experiences. But this act of genuine heroism is one he had never told. People were far more likely to praise the heroism of others, both individually (as in this letter about G.D.'s father) and collectively (as in Churchill's ringing speeches in praise of Londoners or general statements about the grit of the cheerful Cockneys). In personal narratives and anecdotes, one's own (and one's family's) courage and sense are shown as nothing out of the ordinary (a way of showing the innate quality of the British people, perhaps); and people's lives are saved by luck, fate, and circumstance as well as by the heroism of ordinary Londoners and loyal family pets.

I originally became interested in near-miss narratives because of their abundance in postwar interviews, but they were widely told during the war as well. Vere Hodgson told the following tale about her friend Mrs. Fisher on 16 November 1940:

> It seems that by a miracle she was in her little lobby doing some ironing at 8 P.M., when the land mine struck. Everything went black. She found herself being choked by cement and debris, and hit by falling masonry. She could smell the escaping gas and hear it hiss. . . . She heard voices calling, and crawled towards what she thought was the door. It was part of a fallen wall!
>
> The road was full of screaming people. Twenty wardens were rounding the people up and taking them out of the twenty houses, because none were habitable. The rain was pouring down. They were walked along to St. Charles' Hospital, where the windows of the Casualty Ward had gone. So they had to sit in the dark . . . in the cold . . . all suffering from shock. Someone finally nailed down the Black-out. Mrs. Fisher's head was bleeding, but it was not much. . . .
>
> Mrs. Fisher is so plucky over it.

Why are near-miss narratives so prevalent? Possibly because this is what my interviewees thought I wanted; I said that I was interested in "wartime," and they gave me the stories most directly connected with the war. Also, near-miss narratives simply make good stories, as Labov and Waletzky discovered with their famous query. There is nothing quite so exhilarating as a near miss; since intensity is most noticeable at points of contrast, nothing makes us feel our aliveness so much as a brush with death. We are then in a sense reborn, while petty worries and jealousies are swept away; the precipice is revealed to us, and simultaneously we are saved from it. A secret Ministry of Information report on morale, dated 17 August 1940, describes the following phenomenon: "Intensified raids have not affected morale; rather the reverse: confidence is increased, opinion is stiffer and there is a feeling of growing exhilaration. The spirit of the people in raided areas is excellent" (INF 1/264, 97/15 H.I.).

Discussion of a near miss was also a way that fear could be rationalized and transferred to others. During the war, any sort of defeatist talk, any talk that could cause "alarm and despondency," was illegal. To express fear for oneself was at best bad form, at worst treason. To speak pityingly and sorrowfully of the death of others was an acceptable way to express and sublimate fear; both the danger and the suffering referred to someone else. Jan Struther, in her Mrs. Miniver sketches, wrote: "To shrink from direct pain was bad enough, but to shrink from vicarious pain was the ultimate cowardice. And whereas to conceal direct pain was a virtue, to conceal vicarious pain was a sin" (1940, 173). To speak of the death of others was one way to express and simultaneously to ameliorate one's own fear.

This may explain why near-miss narratives were so prevalent during the war itself; and they may have lasted because they have been told so many times and because they best express the feel of wartime London. Yet in a sense, any story of wartime is a near-miss narrative: only those who have experienced danger and survived can tell stories about it. Funny stories are funny because one escaped the bomb; horror stories are horrible because others did not. Indeed, the overarching narrative of wartime London, of a courageous people defying bombs and laughing at danger even while they defeated it, is the story of a near miss. It is a story of people who were close to death and defeat, but who ultimately survived and triumphed.

"We were lucky," people told me again and again, a sentiment often expressed by those who seemed to have most right to complain. Irene Wagner had come to London before the war and was followed by her parents and grandmother. After being arrested in Germany, being kicked out of her university, watching her fellow Jews disappear and her country fall apart, she had accepted exile as the price of survival. Yet she told me several times how lucky she had been. And indeed she had been; she knew just how lucky in 1945, when her job for the British government required seeing the first photographs out of Belsen. "There," she said, a secular internationalist who knows a good proverb when she sees one, "but for the grace of God."

Thus it is with all survivors of wartime; they know how lucky they have been. This awareness may explain the nostalgic tinge in many personal stories of wartime, for the danger has past and the teller has survived. History is a story without end, but memory knows the ending. In Britain, tellers of wartime tales know that the war is over and Britain has won, the bombs have stopped falling and can do no more harm. This is one reason why oral sources are insufficient unto themselves: they take account chiefly of history's survivors. History as a whole must also take account of the destroyed and the dead, the true losers of war. In the past, it was commonplace to say that history is written by the winners; with the advent of the social history movement, this statement is no longer quite true. What is true, however, and almost too obvious to mention, is the fact that history is written by those who survive. Dead men and women tell no tales.

Yet the stories of survivors tell us much about the meaning of war and the interpretations, both political and personal, that people carry with them through their lives. Near-miss narratives are, I believe, a metaphor for talking about the war as a whole. Simultaneously tales of hope and tales of disaster, these stories emphasize both destruction and survival, life as brushed with death. In my interviewees' words, the pain and sorrow of wartime is mixed with the joy, the wonder, and perhaps the guilt of having survived. However much they may have suffered, they have little to complain about when compared to the dead. These near-miss narratives show an awareness of how close the tellers were to joining that silent majority—and how lucky they feel to have been spared. Whether by the grace of God or the arbitrary nature of warfare, those who write history or give information to historians are automatically on the side of the blessed.

Historical Narratives

Historical narratives are stories that my interviewees and other wartime Londoners deemed to be of historical significance, though the incidents they describe may not be well known. The two historical narratives that I have chosen to discuss are stories of direct hits on air-raid shelters. Of all the unnecessary tragedies of war, these tales have an especially ironic twist: people were bombed because they went to a place in order to be safe from bombing. As such, they emphasize the individual's helplessness in wartime—precisely the opposite message of British propaganda, which emphasized the important contributions of everyone. This fact may be one reason why these narratives were downplayed and obscured in wartime, and why they figure more prominently in oral memory than in written documentation. While mention is made of these incidents in the historical record, the attention drawn to them is small; in popular memory, they loom rather larger, reminding my interviewees once again that there, but for the grace of God, went they.

At the height of the blitz, in October 1940, more than 150 people were killed when a bomb hit a shelter in the suburban London neighborhood of Stoke Newington. Despite the fact that it was one of the worst shelter disasters of the war, it is virtually unknown. Only a few of my interviewees knew of this incident—one because she had been in it. Vera was a teenager working as a typist during the war. She lived with her family in Stoke Newington and sheltered in the local Coronation Avenue shelter, which consisted of three rooms. They were in the third room on 14 October 1940:

> On this particular night we were settled in our room, my father was laying in his bunk bed, and I was standing by him. And my mother was seated on the bench with my younger brother. My older brother decided

Ludgate Circus, in east central London, at dawn after a night of air raids, 11 May 1941. St. Paul's can be seen in the background. (Courtesy of the Imperial War Museuem)

People sleeping (or trying to) on the platform of Elephant and Castle Underground Station. (Courtesy of the Imperial War Museuem)

Above: Men playing draughts (checkers) in Liverpool Street Station. *Below:* Londoners playing cards in an air-raid shelter in an attempt to stave off boredom. (Courtesy of the Imperial War Museuem)

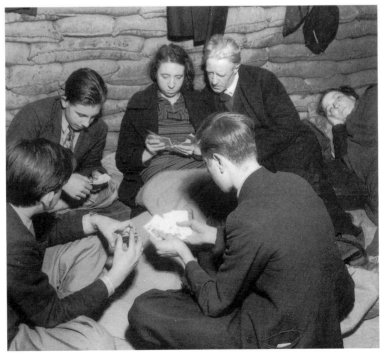

Above: A young couple settles down for the night in an air-raid shelter. *Below:* Orthodox Jews studying in an air-raid shelter. (Courtesy of the Imperial War Museuem)

A nurse comforts two injured children in a hospital after a raid in which their mother, father, and brother were killed, 21 March 1941. (Courtesy of the Imperial War Museuem)

Rescue workers carry a woman on a stretcher after a daylight air raid. (Courtesy of the Imperial War Museuem)

Be like Dad—keep Mum! was one of the many wartime posters reminding British citizens that careless talk costs lives. (Courtesy of the Public Record Office)

Hitler lurks in the background while two men chat in this marvelous wartime poster by Fougasse. (Courtesy of the Imperial War Museuem)

While the *Women of Britain—Come into the Factories* wartime poster *(left)* depicts women's importance to the war effort, *Keep mum—she's not so dumb! (above)* presents women as being dangerous to the cause. (Courtesy of the Public Record Office)

Above, left: Harold Melville Lowry, 1993.

Above, right: Anne Lubin, 1993.

Right: Ettie Gontarsky, 1993.

Below: George and Irene Wagner, 1993.

that he wanted to go for a walk so he and a friend went out; they went for a walk along the road. The air raid was quite thick at that time, there was a lot of gun fire and noise. Suddenly, all the lights went out! And there was the sound of falling masonry and the door that led into our . . . room was blocked. And it was complete darkness. And after the initial shock, somebody called out, "Don't panic! Remember you're British!" I'll never forget that. And nobody did panic but we just, he said, "Just walk towards the emergency exit." Now the emergency exit was on the far side of the room; we were on the extreme right of the room and the exit was on the left. So we had to walk along, my dad got off his bunk and held my hand. We went over and found my mother—it was only a step or two to get hold of my brother's hand and my mum. And we walked along to the exit. We were the last family. And by the time we reached the exit, the water was up to my armpits. The water pipes had broken and we were, we came out soaking. And we climbed up the ladder which led us to the opening which was the emergency exit. And we went out into the night. . . . The first two rooms were completely destroyed, and we had been in the third room. [personal interview, 20 July 1993]

One hundred sixty-four people died in this disaster; of these, over fifty drowned because the bomb struck a water main and the shelter filled with water. Yet the Stoke Newington bombing was and is obscure. Wartime censorship hushed it up at the time, most historians do not mention it, and few of my interviewees had heard of it. Lester Haines, a London filmmaker who has interviewed and filmed survivors of the disaster, was appalled by the incident's obscurity:

There is a definite feeling from the official records that because it was a working-class area away from the centre of London it wasn't so important.
    Even more disturbing is the evidence that because many of the victims were Jews who had fled from Europe to escape Hitler, in some way their deaths didn't matter so much.[5] [quoted in Cooper 1992, 20]

Haines suggests that "the reason it was then forgotten was partly the censorship, partly because the victims were working class and Jewish and partly because it was so early in the war" (20).
    Far better known is the shelter disaster at Bethnal Green, which occurred on 3 March 1943. In 1943 the RAF had begun the bombing of Berlin; the Luftwaffe had promised reprisals, and these were expected by the residents of East London, who had suffered from the intense and concentrated bombing of the 1940–41 blitz. Bethnal Green is situated in the Cockney heart of the East End, and many local residents used an unfinished underground station (Bethnal Green Underground) as a shelter. On the evening of 3 March 1943, as people were entering the shelter,

a salvo of rockets from a nearby gun battery went off. The noise confused people, who misinterpreted the sound and believed it to be the beginning of an air raid. As people hurried down the stairs, someone tripped (some say it was a woman carrying a child), which in turn tripped people rushing in behind. In the space of ninety seconds, 173 people died of suffocation (Kendall 1992, 27–28).

Anti-Semitism, which had obscured the Stoke Newington disaster, set out to explain the Bethnal Green one, and within hours rumors of a "Jewish stampede" swept Britain. Although the coroner of the Bethnal Green disaster said, "There is nothing to suggest any stampede, and panic, or anything of that kind" (Kendall 1992, 29), it is difficult to imagine what else would have caused people to hurry so quickly and thoughtlessly that 173 people could suffocate to death in a minute and a half. Such "un-British" behavior had to be explained. After all, British propaganda had just spent years talking about the lack of panic demonstrated by Britain's besieged population. Vera remembers that when the Stoke Newington shelter was hit, someone called out: "Don't panic! Remember you're British!" The same admonition was flashed on cinema screens during air raids. Since British people do not panic—particularly not the "cheerful Cockneys," who are used to the hardships of life and greet them with a smile—such behavior must have come from a "foreign element."

The Bethnal Green disaster was not so well concealed as the one at Stoke Newington, as Vere Hodgson's diary entry from 6 March 1943 shows: "It was at Bethnal Green, and though they say there was no panic, everyone thinks there must have been. It is a Jewish quarter and Jews have the reputation everywhere of scrambling out of danger as fast as they can, and rather tending to look after themselves." This "reputation" certainly made its way everywhere. The British government was afraid of anti-Semitism and tried to squelch it in the working classes, because anti-Semitism was a sign of divisiveness and hence a threat to morale. (The government was less vigilant in rooting out anti-Semitism in more rarefied circles.) On 9 September 1940 the Ministry of Information had issued the following secret report: "Owing to the behaviour of the Jews, particularly in the East End where they are said to show too great a keenness to save their own skins and too little consideration for other people, there are signs of anti-semitic trouble. It is believed locally that this situation may at any moment become extremely serious" (INF 1/ 264, 97/15 H.I.).

Ironically enough, it was the residents of Bethnal Green themselves who knew that rumors of a "Jewish stampede" were untrue. Jews did live in Bethnal Green, but not in large numbers (in contrast to Vere Hodgson's characterization of the area as a "Jewish quarter"); Jews were far more concentrated in other East End neighborhoods such as Whitechapel. Jews who lived in Bethnal Green often did not shelter at the Bethnal Green Underground, a known haunt of the British Union of Fascists, and instead preferred the Liverpool Street shelter despite the fact that it was farther away. Vere Hodgson seems to realize her mistake; in an attempt to be fair she wrote the following entry two weeks later: "There were only five Jews in the Shelter disaster. The rumour has certainly gone round that the Jews stampeded. But it does not seem to be so at all. The people died of suffocation in a few seconds apparently." A similar impulse to fairness had occurred in the Ministry of Information several years earlier, when it released the following secret report on 11 September 1940: "A certain amount of anti-semitism in the East End still persists, but that is not so much on account of a marked difference in conduct between Jews and Cockneys, but because the latter, seeking a scapegoat as an outlet for emotional disturbances, pick on the traditional and nearest one. Though many Jewish people regularly congregate and sleep in the public shelters, so also do many of the Gentiles, nor is there any evidence to show that one or other predominates among those who have evacuated themselves voluntarily through fear or hysteria" (INF 1/264, 97/15 H.I.).[6]

Harold Melville Lowry describes British anti-Semitism, in contradistinction to Continental anti-Semitism, as "a rather nasty sort of unthinking prejudice. It's not the pseudo-scientific attitude of the Nazis about some races being inferior and that sort of thing" (personal interview, 21 January 1993). Tony Kushner, in his study of British anti-Semitism during World War II, writes, "The two clearest features of modern British antisemitism are that Jews are perceived firstly as a foreign group and secondly as a malevolent power in society" (1989, 9). British anti-Semitism appears to be largely xenophobia, the distrust of an island people for those who have come (or whose recent ancestors have come) from beyond the sea. This insularity can also be seen on the plaque that the bishop of Stepney and the mayor of Tower Hamlets placed on Bethnal Green Underground on the fiftieth anniversary of the Bethnal Green disaster. The plaque reads in part, "Site of the Worst Civilian Disaster of the Second World War," a grotesque inaccuracy unless one realizes that the word "British" is to be understood. (There is a memorial to the Stoke Newington disaster, too: an overgrown monument in Stoke Newington's Abney Park Cemetery.)

Why is Bethnal Green so well known and Stoke Newington virtually forgotten? Anti-Semitism, as Haines suggests, is certainly one factor; it highlighted Bethnal Green by laying blame on the traditional European scapegoat, while allowing Stoke Newington to sink into obscurity as somehow less important. But I believe other forces are at work as well. Stoke Newington was, in a sense, a larger version of what was going on all over the city—civilians being killed by enemy bombs. Because this bomb hit a public shelter, the casualties were high, though when compared with East End shelters, the Stoke Newington shelter was not especially large; it was used by several hundred people as opposed to the thousands who used the Tilbury Shelter on Commercial Road or, indeed, the Bethnal Green Underground. Tragic and horrible as the Stoke Newington disaster was, it differed largely in scope rather than in kind from the many small tragedies that happened each night in private homes and back gardens.

Bethnal Green was something else again. No enemy bombs killed the victims there; instead, death was caused by something that everyone said could not happen: Londoners, in particular the "cheerful Cockneys," panicked and stampeded for shelter. While the Stoke Newington disaster allowed one to hate the perpetrators with a clear conscience, Bethnal Green struck at the mythic heart of wartime London. It is remembered, perhaps, as a nightmarish example of what happened when Londoners did *not* pull together, a horrible cautionary tale in which panic and selfishness were suicidal, and British citizens caused British deaths. Bethnal Green allows none of the righteous anger that could accompany blitz tragedies such as Stoke Newington; indeed, Bethnal Green is a monument to failure. Bethnal Green could not, as Stoke Newington could, be subsumed into generalized tales of British courage and suffering at the hands of the Germans. Bethnal Green did not allow one to turn one's anger "Fresh and whole, against the stranger," in the words of Rostrevor Hamilton's wartime poem "Bias" (quoted in Murdoch 1990, 163). Many tried to blame the "stranger within" and, shamefacedly and grudgingly but with a belief in British fairness, realized that this blame was unfounded. There were no strangers at Bethnal Green. The failure of allies is far more disquieting than the villainy of enemies.

Epochal Narratives

Over against every remembered narrative that I encountered is a great supernarrative of wartime Britain, with London as its central character. In crude and simplified form, the narrative runs something like this: The weak Chamberlain government had pandered to Hitler's megalomania and was finally and reluctantly forced into war because of a promise to defend Poland. During the first year of war, the "phony war" period, Hitler continued his conquest of Europe while relatively little happened in Britain. In 1940 Winston Churchill became prime minister, the Battle of Britain was fought in the skies, and the blitz began. Inspired by Churchill's leadership and outraged by the Germans' wanton attacks on civilians, the British people united as they had never done before. Great and small, rich and poor fought together and defeated the threat of Nazism. In this narrative, London and its people play the role of the hero, a communal protagonist such as one finds in Gerhart Hauptmann's *Die Weber* or Lope de Vega's *Fuente Ovejuna*. London was cast as a place where danger confronted matter-of-fact courage, resilience, and kindness; above all, London was seen as a place of unity.

The communal protagonist of this dark comedy—the unified London populace—has proved to be one of the most durable, overarching, and, in recent years, highly contested images of World War II. Clive Ponting (1991) has pointed out that without American capital, a unified Britain would have been forced to surrender. A.J.P. Taylor (1963) demonstrates that Chamberlain's policy of conciliation was perfectly consistent with European diplomacy at the time, particularly within the Conservative Party of which Chamberlain was leader. Angus Calder (1969; 1991) and Tom Harrisson (1990) have documented myriad occasions during which the London populace was neither unified, calm, nor courageous. Yet this image prevails and remains an indelible part of British political discourse.

This supernarrative, so easily told in retrospect, was in fact created during the war; the ending was told before it had actually happened. Consider, for example, a radio broadcast of J.B. Priestley on 5 June 1940, immediately after Dunkirk. In commenting on this event, Priestley described the successful outcome of the war at a time when it was hardly assured: "And our great-grandchildren, when they learn how we began this war by snatching glory out of defeat and then swept on to victory, may also learn how the little holiday steamers made an excursion to hell and came back glorious" (NSA ref. nos. 2562 and LP2560b5). Winston Churchill's speech on the same subject, broadcast on 18 June 1940, was less sanguine. It is a long speech, full of discussion of military tactics, yet devoid of any genuine military information that might be communicated to the enemy. In the first line, he calls Dunkirk a "colossal military disaster" (unlike Priestley's description of the event as "glorious"), but Churchill assures the listeners that after consulting military advisers, "there are good and reasonable hopes of final victory" (Eade 1951, 204). Victory is not assured; it is certainly possible, but it is up to the British people to bring about victory. Churchill makes this point clear in the final and best-remembered part of the speech: "Let us therefore brace ourselves to our duties, and so bear ourselves that, if the British Empire and its Commonwealth last for a thousand years, men will still say, 'This was their finest hour'" (207). The narrative of ultimate victory was clearly spelled out; it was up to the British people to will the narrative to life.

This remarkable political strategy of treating the war as a pre-scripted drama in which everyone had important parts was a fundamental part of wartime rhetoric, as Churchill was keenly aware. In this same speech, he spoke briefly about the military errors that presaged Dunkirk, then proposed to leave such discussions of the past "on the shelf, from which the historians, when they have time, will select their documents to tell their stories. We have to think of the future and not of the past. . . . Of this I am quite sure, that if we open a quarrel between the past and the present, we shall find that we have lost the future" (Eade 1951, 198–99). The future could be controlled only if past controversies were subsumed into a narrative that would bring about the desired consequences. Hayden White's exegesis of Kant's theory of history is instructive here: "Kant's position was something like this: The way I conceive the historical process, apprehended as a process of transition from past to present, the form which I impose upon my perceptions of it, these provide the orientation by which I move into a future with greater hope or despair, in the face of the prospects which that movement is conceived to have as a *movement toward* a desirable (or *away from* an undesirable) goal" (1973, 57; emphasis in original). Churchill, Priestley, and all the other rhetoricians and ordinary folk who proclaimed victory long before it happened were in accord with Kant's insight; unless one conceives of an event as ending well, one lacks the hope necessary to bring such an outcome about. A comic or happy ending can only occur if one is able to envision it in advance.

If this vision of the war was ultimately comic and in some sense cheerful, it was optimistic only in a very cautious way. The small-scale retrospective narratives can provide a clue for interpreting the epochal narratives. We have seen how the story of the near miss permeates narratives of wartime London and how it can be seen as a metaphor for the war in general. In the same way that each individual life was threatened, so was the life of Britain as a whole. If individuals narrowly escaped disaster, then so in retrospect did Britain itself. This epochal near-miss narrative was, as noted, already being shaped during the first year of the war. The danger was too real and too near for an easy victory to be expected, yet an ultimate victory was always assumed, accompanied though it might be with "blood, sweat, toil, and tears." During the year in which Britain "stood alone" (despite military aid from the Dominions and a massive influx of American capital), the British people were in great danger, yet by dint of unity and courage they survived and triumphed.

A wartime book by Hamilton Fyfe, whose title *But for Britain . . .* sets the tone perfectly, describes the year of the blitz in terms of a near-miss narrative: "But for Britain, the workers of all Europe and millions outside Europe would have been subjected to . . . slavery. There is no doubt as to what the Nazis would have done if no check had been offered to their victorious onrush. That is their idea of a new order, with this addition: destruction of all forms of religion excepting worship of the State, the State being the person or persons who control the machinery of government" (14). Fyfe's story has a communal protagonist as its hero, and this hero is "the British People. Not the Government apart from the people. Not any one class or order. The people as a whole" (7). Although Fyfe praises the entirety of the British people, he gives special mention to Londoners: "By the united testimony of all who were among them during their ordeal Londoners behaved with unwavering resolution to 'take it'" (86).

This placing of London in a privileged position, of using London to represent both the best of British character and the worst of British home front experience, is common in much propaganda, popular representation, and memory. On 14 July 1941 Winston Churchill gave a speech at a London County Council luncheon, in which he praised the entirety of Britain, stating that "London was upheld by the sympathy and the admiration of the other great cities of our island" (with a quick additional reference to Northern Ireland). Churchill honored the provincial cities for their "constancy in a comradeship of suffering, of enduring, and of triumph," a comradeship that has "united us all." But it is London that is the chief object of his praise: "But there was one thing about which there was never any doubt: The courage, the unfaltering, unconquerable grit and stamina of the Londoners showed itself from the very outset. Without that, all would have failed. But upon that rock, all stood unconquerable" (NSA ref. nos. 3843-5 and T3843b1).

London is the indispensable actor in this near-miss narrative, the paterfamilias of the family that is Britain, the head of the nation that is head of the empire. Ministry of Information films such as "London Can Take It" (INF 6/328) and "Ordinary People" (INF 6/330) focus on the destruction of London and the courage of Londoners; the latter film begins with an address "To the future historian: This film was played by ordinary people of London." Though other films and speeches provide montages of pan-British images (miners in Wales, dancers at Blackpool), no other city emerges with as much dominance, as much sheer time devoted to it as London. Yet at times the Ministry of Information listed morale as being higher in the provinces than in London (INF 1/264, 97/15 H.I., 27 May 1940). In fact, a Ministry of Information document from 7 September 1940 mentions complaints from provincial towns about the excessive publicity that London received (INF 1/264, 97/15 H.I.). Even now, there is little general knowledge about the Plymouth or Cardiff or Clydebank blitzes (only Coventry, by the sheer magnitude of the destruction it endured, still has its bitter fame); few speak of Glaswegian evacuees or of the defiance of Liverpudlians. If Britain was united, it was assumed that London was at the helm.

At first glance, it may not be surprising that a nation's capital should represent the entirety of the nation; and indeed, as the governmental, financial, commercial, and artistic center of the United Kingdom, London had no rivals as the seat of power. On the other hand, romantic representations of essential national character usually fasten on rural, rather than urban, images. Indeed, cities have always been problematic for romantic nationalists, containing too many foreigners, too many ethnic minorities, too many people who want to change the essence of the nation rather than preserve it. *Das Volk* is a concept that requires ethnic or racial homogeneity, and cities give the lie to this concept. This is not to say that romantic representations of rural England did not exist; they existed in abundance, from both right-wing and left-wing sources, and Patrick Wright (1985) shows that they lost none of their resonance during the war years. But to these pastoral, timeless images of England's green and pleasant land was added the image of the noble city, the suggestion that the essence of Britain could exist in the narrow streets of Poplar and the crooked back alleyways of Bethnal Green. Beside the feudal squire and the village schoolmaster could stand the Cockney streetmonger and the City banker, and perhaps even the Jew, the Indian, and the Chinese immigrant.

One can see how this narrative and this cast of characters are simultaneously progressive and reactionary. To praise all classes of British society equally was a new and remarkable thing; it gave hope of increased power and influence to the working and middle classes, yet it offered no suggestion that the basic class structure be changed. (In the film version of "Mrs. Miniver," it is the middle-class professionals, not the decadent aristocrats, who emerge as leaders; yet the middle classes remain in the middle.) It is a story in which Britain—not any political philosophy or moral principle—is cast as the greatest threat to Nazism. As such, it is a story that subsumes antifascism and imperialism, internationalism and xenophobia, a well-nigh perfect example of Gramscian hegemony. But what is truly remarkable about this narrative is the way that it was scripted and told before it had happened.

As always, it was Churchill who said it best. In his first speech after becoming prime minister, he declared in a world broadcast that Britain's goal was "to wage war until victory is won, and never to surrender ourselves to servitude and shame, whatever the cost and the agony may be" (Eade 1951, 184). On 18 June 1940, directly after the fall of France, Churchill gave another famous speech, in which ultimate victory is still assumed, though it is tempered with the acknowledgement of danger:

> What General Weygand called the Battle of France is over. I expect that the battle of Britain is about to begin. Upon this battle depends the survival of Christian civilization. Upon it depends our own British life, and the long continuity of our institutions and our Empire. The whole fury and might of the enemy must very soon be turned on us. Hitler knows that he will have to break us in this island or lose the war. If we can stand up to him, all Europe may be free and the life of the world may move forward into broad, sunlit uplands. But if we fail, then the whole world, including the United States, including all that we have known and cared for, will sink into the abyss of a new dark age made more sinister, and perhaps more protracted, by the lights of perverted science. Let us therefore brace ourselves to our duties, and so bear ourselves that, if the British Empire and its Commonwealth last for a thousand years, men will still say, "This was their finest hour." [206–207]

This is, in fine, the story of World War II from the officially sanctioned British perspective—a great danger, a period of suffering stoically borne, British courage and unity in the service of a common goal, ultimate victory, the restoration of freedom to the peoples of the world. That these events had not actually happened when the speech was made seems a mere detail; the structure of the story was in place, and the British people all had their parts to play.

We know now that the story did come true: the remarkable political strategy of creating a narrative and then setting policy that will allow people to enact it was apparently successful. A Home Intelligence report on morale, prepared on 13 June 1940, shows that Churchill was very much in accord with the mood of the people. Though they differed in their levels of optimism, people expected the same ending to the story:

> Depression and pessimism are at a high level but reaction is "flat" and without high emotion. People are waiting for the fall of Paris which is regarded as inevitable although the feeling is widespread that this will not mean the end of the war either for France or for ourselves.
>
> At the same time belief in ultimate victory is still general although this belief is now qualified by such comments as: "We might as well commit suicide if we didn't go on believing in victory," "I suppose in the end we shall win," "The cost of winning does not bear thinking about." [INF 1/264, 97/15 H.I.]

Of course, government researchers could only gauge people's thoughts from what they said, and since defeatist talk was illegal, people may have been less than willing to express such opinions to government officials. Yet wartime diaries show a similar point of view.

Josephine Oakman, an artist who lived in Chelsea, kept a detailed diary of the blitz, in which she described the appearance of battle-scarred London, the sounds of guns and sirens, and her sense of wartime spirit, alternately praising Londoners' morale and grumbling when people did not pull together. On 24 February 1941 she described a film that rang true to her own narrative of the blitz. The film is *The Great Dictator*, made by the former East Ender Charlie Chaplin: "I saw the Chaplin film today and would like the text of the last speech of Chaplin's against 'dictators.' I thought it magnificent. To think our England and Greece are fighting against all this—just together—for liberty, justice and humanity; it is good to be of England." Chaplin's allegorical rendering of World War II clarified the issues for Josephine Oakman; it expressed both the risk to humanity that Nazism posed and the justness of England's cause. On 24 August 1941 she presented her own narrative:

> We had now had a year since our blitz started in earnest last autumn— it had been a strange year and in many ways a terrible one. I have learnt

many things—things of what are really worthwhile in life. Material things seem to vanish like smoke in importance—it is better to have one's friends around than all the gold on the earth. The greatest thing is service—and being kind to others—to first help and serve and to look for no gain. I have lost friends, a home and possessions and yet I am still here. *I have several times missed death by inches and I still remain.* I want to see this war to the end—it is my one wish—and see all the terrors of cruelty of these air raids as things of the past—and see the beginnings of a lasting peace—which—God willing will endure! [emphasis added]

Her narrative is a near miss for herself and her country, but—as she painfully acknowledges—not a near miss for all. The outcome of the war is never in doubt; the only things in doubt are the date at which victory will come and whether or not the peace will endure.

Of course, no historical source is without its problems; the most private writing becomes an act of public self-presentation by the mere fact of placing it in an archive and allowing people to read it. People give us access to the sources that they want us to see, and they may not allow us to view them in an unflattering or shameful light. As G.D. and I went through her father's papers, she would not permit me to quote from those that she felt gave "the wrong impression," nor did she give those papers to archives. Memory, as Maurice Halbwachs reminds us, is a social phenomenon, and people may not allow us access to memories that are currently judged to be incorrect. The same phenomenon can be seen in the oral history interview. During one interview, I asked questions of a woman while her friends listened and occasionally commented. When I asked, "Did you ever think Britain would lose?" she stopped and thought for a moment. Before she could speak, her friends chimed in with, "No!"; after a few seconds, she too said, "No." As Halbwachs remarks, "It is in society that people normally acquire their memories. It is also in society that they recall, recognize, and localize their memories. . . . It is in this sense that there exists a collective memory and social frameworks for memory; it is to the degree that our individual thought places itself in these frameworks and participates in this memory that it is capable of the act of recollection" (1992, 38).

Herein lies the central problem in current debates about wartime London: are people remembering properly? Is the story being properly told? We know that the end of the story came true; we are less sure of what this story leaves out. Part of the problem lies with what Hayden White terms "emplotment," the way in which the form of the story demonstrates the historian's judgment of past events. Following Northrop Frye, White singles out comedy, tragedy, romance, and satire as four of the most common modes of historical representation (1973, 7–11). Much wartime material and many postwar reconstructions tell the story as a romance, in which heroic actors bring about the triumph of good over evil. This view glosses over instances of selfishness, greed, apathy, and lack of agreement among the "good" characters. Interestingly, it does not gloss over the danger and wickedness of the enemy, for such threat is necessary for the romantic hero to have something to overcome.

No one is more hostile to this point of view than Paul Fussell. He tells the story of World War II as a satire, "the precise opposite of this Romantic drama of redemption" (White 1973, 9). To Fussell, the popular wartime narrative leaves out virtually everything: it is a tissue of lies, half-truths, and sentimental nonsense: "For the past fifty years the Allied war has been sanitized and romanticized almost beyond recognition by the sentimental, the loony patriotic, the ignorant, and the bloodthirsty. I have tried to balance the scales" (1989, ix). Fussell, an American, criticizes both American and British wartime propaganda so thoroughly that one is left with the conclusion that the entire war was simply a gargantuan waste. But the satire is a parasitic genre, depending as it does on a preexisting narrative, and Fussell concentrates more on deconstructing the old narrative than on building a new one. As such, his story is so fragmented (possibly to show the incoherence of wartime thought) that there is essentially no story left, only chaos and rage. For Fussell, the old narrative is in ruins, but he supplies no new one to replace it.

Few scholars go as far as Fussell. The dominance of the old narrative is so strong that one may fight it but not defeat it; Fussell's story shatters on it, but the old narrative does not break. Many historians have essentially accepted its basic plot structure while at the same time pointing out its simplifications and omissions. This kind of emplotment might be judged a dark comedy or tragicomedy, grimly expressed by A.J.P. Taylor: "The British stand in September 1939 was no doubt heroic; but it was heroism mainly at the expense of others" (1963, 26). Tom Harrisson is one author who uses this sort of emplotment. Faced with the discrepancies between the records of Mass-Observation in the 1930s and 1940s and the memories of people in the 1970s (sometimes the same people remembering the same incidents), Harrisson opted unequivocally for information "recorded at the time on the spot" (1990, 327). His conclusion is to dismiss memory from consideration (even, to be fair, his own) and to trust only the written record: "The record . . . can seem improbable today because it reads so differently from the contemporary, established concept of what 'really happened' in that war. There has, in particular, been a massive, largely unconscious cover-up of the more disagreeable facts of 1940–41. . . . It amounts to a form of intellectual pollution: but pollution by perfume" (15). Harrisson's wartime data suggested that the notion of a unified, cheerful British populace was, at best, simplistic; he describes many incidents of depression, dissatisfaction, selfishness, and outright panic. At the same time, Harrisson cannot entirely reject this vaguely defined "established concept of what 'really happened'": "Under all the varied circumstances, the final achievement of so many Britons was enormous enough. Maybe monumental is not putting it too high. They did not let their soldiers or leaders down. Not infrequently, indeed, they propped their leaders up, in a situation where leadership at the local level was lacking" (278).

On a different subject but in a similar vein is Clive Ponting's *1940: Myth and Reality*. Ponting begins the book with his own version of the "current widely accepted view of what happened in 1940" (1990, 1). After setting up this straw man, he declares that "when we examine the historical record, however, not one of these statements turns out to be true" (2). Ponting's "widely accepted view," unlike Harrisson's, deals with governmental and financial matters; and he rightly chronicles the facts that may irritate a complacent view of 1940: incidents of governmental misjudgment, for example, and the fact that "standing alone" against Hitler meant being propped up with massive amounts of foreign, particularly American, aid. However, though he struggles against the popular images, he does not entirely escape them, nor does he wish to:

> The purpose of this book is to strip away the myth and examine the events of 1940 from a different perspective. The result is a radically different, less comfortable view of Britain's "Finest Hour." This book goes behind the scenes to examine many of the facts and episodes that were kept carefully concealed at the time. The fact that the emphasis is on high government policy and not on the details of military campaigns, nor on feats of individual courage and heroism, nor on the human suffering of war, is not to deny or denigrate them in any way. The choice was made deliberately to deal with those aspects of 1940 so often neglected or played down by other books. *We must never forget those who died or suffered in the Second World War in order to defeat a vile and evil system.* [2–3; emphasis added]

On the other hand, Angus Calder does not think that Ponting's view is terribly radical. Calder writes, "Ponting writes as if exposing scandalous untruths and cover-ups: in fact there is virtually nothing in his book which was not known by scholars, and all interested members of the public, in the sixties" (1991, xiii). If Taylor writes about diplomacy, Fussell about propaganda, Harrisson about behavior, and Ponting about political policy, Calder writes about everything. In his earlier book, *The People's War*, he discusses everything from military strategy to the wartime use of cosmetics; he also sets out his own lucid, compassionate, wryly skeptical story of the war:

> The war was fought with the willing brains and hearts of the most vigorous elements in the community, the educated, the skilled, the bold, the

active, the young, who worked more and more consciously towards a transformed post-war world.

Thanks to their energy, the forces of wealth, bureaucracy and privilege survived with little inconvenience, recovered from their shock, and began to proceed with their old business of manoeuvre, concession and studied betrayal. Indeed, this war, which had set off a ferment of participatory democracy, was strengthening meanwhile the forces of tyranny, pressing Britain forwards towards *1984*. [1969, 18]

In his later book, *The Myth of the Blitz*, Calder looks less closely at the "facts" and more closely at the "myth." Writing from the vantage point of 1991, he believes that the myth has lost its "old dominance," despite its persistence in "a vast number of texts still current . . . and a great deal of 'common-sense' thinking" (xiv). The book is as much about how people discuss and remember the war as it is about the war itself. But Calder recognizes the important connections, the fact that people remembered and talked about the war while it was still going on, and that a narrative scripted in advance enabled a desired end to come about:

> Myth may distort what has happened. But it affects what happens. The 'story' of the Blitz and individuals' own personal 'Blitz stories' were mythologised within 'everyday life' in terms of existing mythologies. . . . Believing that they were 'making history' in harmony with the Absolute Spirit of 'England' (or 'Britain'), people tried to believe as that spirit seemed to dictate. Heroic mythology fused with everyday life to produce heroism. People 'made sense' of the frightening and chaotic actualities of wartime life in terms of heroic mythology, 'selecting out' phenomena which were incompatible with that mythology. But, acting in accordance with this mythology, many people—not all, of course—helped make it 'more true.' [14]

Calder's use of the term "myth" is fair-minded and not pejorative; he insists that myth "should not be taken to be equivalent to 'untruth,' still less to 'lies'" (xiii). Yet the use of the word myth is always a method of distancing; the term may not be insulting, but it always refers to the beliefs of somebody else. Myth simplifies and selects and flattens out experience; it reduces the confused lives of millions to a single, neat story line. But can any epochal narrative, even the most meticulously researched history book, do anything else?

Calder's analysis is brilliant, his books probably the finest explications of the British home front. But they are not definitive, and they are not even in accord with all of his fellow historians, far less with the millions of others who remember and speak about the war. As Arthur Marwick points out, what one sees depends upon where one stands:

I believe that there is some truth in the myths, and that, above all, for good or ill, the Second World War did profoundly change British society. In part, of course, judgment depends upon what your standards are, what sort of change you believe to be possible in human society. It is no reflection on Angus Calder's impeccable scholarship to point out that he is a committed socialist. Without any doubt at all, the Second World War did not produce a socialist society. But I would prefer to take as my standard of measurement the state of British society in the 1930s, rather than some hypothetical ideal state. [1976, 11]

Yet one disturbing assumption remains throughout this debate: the notion that these "myths" were swallowed wholesale by the people for whom they were fashioned, that "the people" (whoever they might be) accepted the simplistic narrative as true with none of the critical skepticism shown by Calder, Harrisson, Fussell, and others. There has, in fact, been little attempt to discover if so-called "popular beliefs" were held by actual people. Popular beliefs about wartime London are curiously disembodied; they float in air and rest like fog on London, apparently with as much power to blind. Yet the comments of my interviewees are filled with the same contradictions that one finds in scholarly works. Anne Lubin suggested I read *The People's War* in order to find "the parts not covered in cheery official records" (personal letter, 12 January 1993). When I asked her about the popular image of the unified London populace, she replied:

People remember what it suits them to remember. If I tell you that the first thing that greeted me when I went for my interview, having volunteered to work in the factory, was a woman who sat there saying, "You wait till you get inside and see all those bloody Jews in there, all swanning around, getting out of the army." Words to that effect. And I thought, "My God, what are we fighting for?" But also there was a feeling—if somebody, if your water was cut off, there was no difficulty about getting a kettle of water . . . or anything; doors were open, and people did try and help one another. [personal interview, 13 March 1993]

"People remember what it suits them to remember." Memories and the events they recall are, as Anne shows, highly contradictory. During the war, viciousness coexisted with kindness, solidarity with selfishness. Indeed, how could it be otherwise for an event that lasted six years and affected millions of people? Is it logical to expect that solidarity existed every minute of the war, for every person in London? At the same time, should we consider all reports of London unity a propagandistic sham when we discover evidence to the contrary?

My interviewees' comments on the epochal narratives are instructive here; they know these narratives well and believe them to be both true and false. London was simultaneously unified and fragmented, exciting and horrible. Ettie Gontarsky's comments on the war show her knowledge of the epochal narratives and her own interpretation of them: "It was a time that I hope will never happen again. But—and one can romanticize, which is dangerous to romanticize about war—but I think one has to say that some good things happened during the war which might not have happened. Like people forming friendships, relationships, cementing relationships, creating new ties with people you might never have done under different circumstances" (personal interview, 4 April 1993). Her comments show her understanding of the war as a necessary crisis, a time of unavoidable pain and unavoidable purpose, which one tried to face with as much spirit as possible: "I'm sure that for a lot of people, they lived in a way which they hadn't lived up to the war, in the sense they had a sense of purpose. Which many people didn't have. There was a sense of purpose. We had to win the war. That was no questions about that. Whatever our political views, if any. Whatever our religion, if any. We had to win the war. So there was a strong sense of purpose, a strong sense of service. . . . There was a sense of danger, a sense of excitement, a sense above all of purpose" (personal interview, 19 April 1993). This is no sentimentalization of catastrophe, but a statement of political allegiance: to Ettie, the war had both purpose and meaning, achieved at great price. The war was an amalgam of humor and pain, personal courage and mass destruction, none of which can or should be forgotten.

Eileen Scales's comments on the war are similar to Ettie's; they highlight both the suffering that war brings and the unique camaraderie that shared suffering engenders. Again, what you see depends upon where you stand; Eileen's politics inform her interpretation: "This was our country and it was a common cause that we were all fighting for. And it's sort of all for one and one for all sort of thing. . . . I think it made you very, very patriotic and as I say it made people, I think personally, much nicer to each other" (personal interview, 5 March 1993). Yet increased kindliness was matched by increased danger. Eileen was a schoolgirl of twelve at the start of the war; by its end, she was engaged to a soldier in the infantry. Her perspective changed with her growing maturity and awareness of danger: "I suppose at twelve it was quite an exciting time. But when you grew older, I think you realized how awful, you know. And when you got to know young men that were in the forces and then they'd perhaps be killed. I got to know quite a lot of young men and quite a lot of them were killed, and you then realized, you know, what a dreadful, dreadful thing it all was" (personal interview, 5 March 1993).

For George and Irene Wagner, the war meant a complete disruption, the trading in of their old lives for new ones. Because of this fact, the war had a special urgency, an unquestioned necessity. Irene told me, "The work which we were doing during the war was, I think, to say, 'Thank you' to people who rescued us, in a way" (personal interview, 4 March 1993). More than those who had watched the rise of Hitler from the relative safety of England, the Wagners knew the strength of the enemy they were fighting. Most British people whom I interviewed (with the exception of soldiers) told me that they never feared or even thought that Britain might lose the war. Those who had some experience with Germany saw things differently. When I asked Irene if she ever thought that Britain would lose, she replied: "I was very, very afraid, I think, in the first year. You know, when France fell, and—but I was too busy to think about that. I don't think for one moment I thought we would lose after the first shock of France falling. And then, after the Battle of Britain, I knew: 'Britons never, never, never, ever shall be slaves.' With the determination, you know, not to let this happen" (personal interview, 23 April 1993). In her ironical quoting of "Rule, Britannia," Irene shows her growing acceptance of the British perspective on the war: there was danger and hardship but also the determination to emerge victorious.

Narratives that include incidents of disunity, fear, and selfishness are far more subtle than romantic tales that gloss over such things as though they did not exist. Yet if these narratives are framed as dark comedies, then their ultimate judgment is that the war ended well, if not happily. Indeed, romance is often considered a subgenre of comedy, differing largely in atmosphere, presentation of characters, and simplicity of ideas rather than actual emplotment. Those who point out the contradictions and omissions of the standard wartime narrative—incidents of lack of unity, dependence on American finance, the terror of war itself—have made the narrative more subtle and complex and have in a way improved it. As scholars and rememberers fight against this standard narrative, they are highlighting the parts of the narrative that they believe require most attention; they are not discarding it wholesale or replacing it with alternate narratives.

Doubtless there exist those who believe that the defeat of Hitler was a bad thing or that the British people did nothing while their leaders did everything or that any war is indefensible, but by and large, they express their views with silence.[7] During the war, such views were treason, and the traitorous Lord Haw-Haw was the best-known exemplar of such a view. Even pacifists find their place within this wartime narrative: conscientious objectors contributed to the war effort through organizations such as the Friends Ambulance Unit. Some prewar pacifists, such as the writer A.A. Milne or my interviewee Harold Melville Lowry, gave up their pacifism during the war, believing that Nazism was so great an evil that it threw the evil of war into shadow. Even those who, for religious or personal reasons, remained absolute pacifists throughout the war, offer no counternarratives or alternative explanations; pacifism is mute when confronted with fascism.

A.J.P. Taylor wrote: "I am glad Germany was defeated and Hitler destroyed. I also appreciate that others paid the price for this, and I recognize the honesty of those who thought the price too high" (1963, 26). The question of the price of victory is at the heart of debates on World War II, a question for which each person may have a different answer. Britain was never defeated, but it was weakened and scarred; both individually and collectively, the British people had suffered, and this suffering did not end completely when the peace treaty was signed. Britain emerged from the war with massive debts, with shortages and rationing that lasted until the mid-1950s, with its cities in ruins, its empire disappearing, and its military strength eclipsed by the United States and the Soviet Union. At the same time, the postwar era ushered in the National Health Service, free university education, and other bulwarks of the welfare state. And the fear of sudden death or national defeat—so real and yet so obliquely expressed—was over. The near-miss narratives show how prevalent this fear was and at what price victory was bought. People now ask, as they never could during the war, "Was the price worth it? Was victory so much the sweeter for being preceded by suffering? Did the lessons learned by war build the New Jerusalem on England's green and pleasant land?"

The other question that looms large in the debates about "what really happened" in World War II is not about the time period itself but the way it is remembered. As Patrick Wright says, the war has been "redeclared," and the enemies may look a little different now, the wartime goals different from the ones declared in 1939. In a country where the memory of World War II holds so much sway, each creates the wartime victory in his or her own image. And many ask, as did my interviewee Fred Mitchell, "What the hell was it all for?" (personal interview, 18 May 1993).

Paul Fussell's vitriolic rage at cheery memories of wartime focuses on an important omission: what British and American memories often leave out is the death and dismemberment of soldiers; such memories concentrate instead on the joy of survival. Fussell's target is not really the war itself or the soldiers who fought it, but those who represent and remember it improperly. Yet, while we cannot accept romanticized views of a happy war, neither can we accept Fussell's notion that only horrific memories are valid. If we take seriously the memories of those who lived through wartime, then neither point of view is more real than the other. War leaves in its wake misery and destruction; it may also leave behind the unique camaraderie of shared suffering and an awareness of life more intense and perhaps more valued for its constant brushes with death. To complicate matters, World War II destroyed a system of government more cruel and violent even than war itself. It is up to each person to take account of the price that has been paid and, in so doing, to decide which memories are most important and most worth keeping.

The past, as Halbwachs tells us, is always *reconstructed*, and it is reconstructed for a reason. Perhaps people cannot remember thinking that the war might be lost because they never said it, never saw it in print, and know now that they won. Yet the war was won at a great price; it was not an easy victory, but a near miss. If the war was won by the ordinary people of Britain (as wartime propaganda said again and again), then ordinary people deserved something in return. In this way, the war can be used to criticize the present, just as in wartime it was used to predict the future.

5

London Pride
Music and Wartime London

> *Tommy Handley:* Well, I suppose I better face the music. How are you, bandmaster?
> *Bandmaster:* I'm absolutely allegro, your Worship.
> *Tommy Handley:* Oh, that's fine. Last time I saw you, you were slightly pizzicato. You'd been out on the baton.
> *Bandmaster:* Impossible. I may have been suffering from an attack of cadenza.
> *Tommy Handley:* Yes, you probably had a fugue in the throat.
> "ITMA," January 1942

Few art forms cover so broad a base as the one called music.[1] Some arts, such as theater, are essentially communal, while others, such as literature, are in large measure solitary. Some are basically the province of amateurs, such as storytelling, while others are largely the domain of professionals, such as sculpture. Yet music encompasses all these realms: it ranges from the communal forms of symphony and choir to the solo vocalist or concert artist to the solitary music student practicing in a small room. Music ranges from the highly virtuosic, in symphonies and chamber orchestras and opera companies, to the completely nonprofessional: the exhausted parent singing a lullaby to an infant or the worker who chooses to lighten work with a song, whether it be the communal chantey of the sailor or the solitary singing of the housewife. Music is essential to ritual: it is part of public ceremonies such as weddings and funerals; it also exists in the solitary prayers of individuals. It is the sine qua non of the art form dance; it is a fundamental, if often overlooked, part of cinema. With the wide availability of secondarily oral forms of music, such as radio and recorded sound, it is likely that many people spend some part of each day listening to or producing music.

Yet music has no obvious referential or material function. It cannot feed the hungry or house the homeless. Only rarely does it impart information or foster understanding. In moments of emergency, music is usually absent. Troops may march into battle to the sound of pipe and drum, but once the fighting has begun, soldiers listen to the orders of officers and the sounds of guns and bombs. Firefighters must talk in order to coordinate action and rescue survivors, but they need not sing; indeed, singing might well be considered distracting or frivolous. Like other art forms, music is considered the product of leisure time, a pleasure rather than a necessity.

Yet music, like other art forms, rarely remains in this marginal position; it crops up in the most unlikely places. In extended periods of crisis, rather than sharp moments of emergency, music almost always appears. During World War II, people sang in the POW camps of Singapore and Sumatra, in the death camps of Auschwitz and Birkenau, and in partisan brigades behind enemy lines. In Eichstätt, Germany, Allied prisoners of war even put on a music festival. In Great Britain, people sang in the armed forces, in the factories, in the air-raid shelters, and at home. Throughout the war, people composed, performed, and listened to music on numerous occasions, formal and informal, amateur and professional. It seems that music, while not essential to human survival, is nonetheless an essential part of human life.

But what is music? This question has long puzzled musicians, ethnomusicologists, sociologists, and philosophers. The English word "music" has no exact translation in many languages and no exact equivalent in many cultures. Most definitions of music that strive for universality are dissatisfying and tautological; essentially, they boil down to "Music is whatever people say music is." John Blacking writes: "Music is a product of the behavior of human groups, whether formal or informal: it is humanly organized sound. And, although different societies tend to have different ideas about what they regard as music, all definitions are based on some consensus of opinion about the principles on which the sounds of music should be organized. No such consensus can exist until there is some common ground of experience, and unless different people are able to hear and recognize patterns in the sounds that reach their ears" (1973, 10). The vagueness in Blacking's definition is inevitable; music's intangibility and cultural variance make a general, universal definition of music well-nigh impossible. The most specific part of Blacking's definition, "humanly organized sound," covers far more than music. Language is humanly organized sound, as are doorbells and air-raid sirens and banging on the ceiling with a broom when the neighbors are too loud. What makes music different is the fact that it is considered a special form of communication. Music, whether well or poorly done, is considered an art form, and its purpose tends to be affective rather than referential. One can, for example, speak and sing the same words, but the difference between these two performances is more than one of timbre. To sing words is to make some sort of comment that the words themselves do not.

In wartime Britain, music existed in many forms and was used for many purposes. Both the use of music and the image of people making and listening to music contributed to wartime hegemony. Song lyrics proclaimed loyalty to Britain and to the war effort and assumed an ultimate victory. Popular music cheered people and enabled them to continue their duties with hope and optimism. Art music was seen as a sign of civilization, one of the things for which the war was being fought. In this chapter, I examine the use of music and the image of music in wartime London, and look at the ways that this art form contributed to wartime hegemony and wartime life.

The Use and Image of Music

As stated earlier, music is often considered an inessential, leisure-time activity, despite its prevalence in many people's lives. Paradoxically, the nonemergency nature of music was one of the things that made it beloved in wartime London. The idea was that people who create or listen to music are those who are living normal lives, with time for relaxation and art. They are not people who are afraid or without hope, but people who know how to enjoy life and can create beauty and meaning for others. Thus the image of the person enjoying music is precisely the image that the government wished to create of the wartime Londoner. Frank E. Huggett, in his book on wartime music, remembers a perfect manifestation of this image in a newspaper headline: "On 30 September 1940, the *Daily Mirror* had a headline: 'LET THE PEOPLE SING? YOU CAN'T STOP 'EM!' The picture below showed Cockneys dancing and singing in the devastated streets of the East End to the sounds of a harmonium perched precariously on the debris of their former homes" (1979, 109; emphasis in original). Thus the cheerful Cockney becomes the singing Cockney, whose matter-of-fact courage and love of a good time remains unabated; Cockneys do not allow bombs and ruined homes to spoil their fun. There is, of course, no way to determine if people are Cockneys from a newspaper photograph, but Huggett knows how to properly interpret the *Daily Mirror*'s intent. He continues the image with his own commentary: "In one East End pub, the customers went on singing, even though their voices could scarcely be heard through the continual concussions of high explosives, while the landlord went round with a collecting box for the Spitfire Fund. When an underground shelter in a factory in south-west London was hit and the water main was shattered, the girls in one section sang *Roll Out the Barrel* to their trapped workmates" (109).

Singing is a good way to communicate with people trapped by debris, for the voice carries more effectively in song than in speech. For the person trapped, singing was a declaration of survival; it also told the rescuers where to look. Although the fact of singing may be purely functional, the choice of song is ideological and shows the singer's point of view. Basil Woon, in his wartime eulogy to his fellow Londoners, reports the story of a woman trapped under five tons of masonry that had to be moved by hand. When a hole was made to pass oxygen to her, she could be heard singing "Land of Hope and Glory" (Woon 1941, 34–35). Both the woman's singing of a patriotic song and Woon's reporting of this story contributed to the wartime image of a brave and united population that would never give up, that proclaimed love of their country and loyalty to their side even when the enemy threatened to crush them.

More than fifty years later, Eileen Scales remembers an incident uncannily similar to the one mentioned by Woon. Whereas Woon's wartime story never hinted at the possibility of death, Eileen's postwar story shows that even the bravest and most patriotic can be defeated in war: "The person that had an upstairs flat there, an elderly lady, I suppose she was about sixty-five, was actually alive when she was dug out. And we could hear her singing while they were digging her out 'There'll always be an England.' You could hear her singing and I think she lived for about a month and had broken legs and was terribly injured. But we could hear her. . . . We could actually hear her singing 'There'll always be an England' while they were digging for her" (personal interview, 5 March 1993). Though Eileen's story tells of a sad wartime reality that would have been downplayed during the anxious, morale-building days of the war itself, both stories emphasize the ways in which ordinary citizens used songs to show their patriotism and courage. This is precisely the state of affairs that the government wished to bring about.

Music became a linchpin of home front morale. On 22 May 1940 the Ministry of Information made the following suggestions in a secret report: "Action to improve morale in air-raid shelters. Tell actors that they are counted upon to keep people cheerful, lead singing, etc. Have words of songs ready to hand round. Tell people to bring gramophones, games and toys" (INF 1, 250). The ministry had other suggestions for making the blitz fun, and sponsoring open-air rallies was one of them. On 23 July 1940 Sir Wyndham Deedes wrote to Sir Kenneth Clark, commenting favorably on a rally that had just taken place: "The success of the Hendon rally shows that this is the moment to encourage communal singing and open air dancing, if possible. People are rather tired at present and have a feeling of suspense. . . . They should be able to have community fun and dancing and singing would be extremely popular. For heaven's sake let us get rid of this feeling that the MOI is out to depress and spy on people! Let us provide an antidote by giving the people music and some active form of communal life that they can join in and thoroughly enjoy!" (INF 1, 250).

The choice of songs was as important as the fact of singing; the British government had no wish to encourage rousing choruses of "Deutschland, erwache!" or the Horst Wessel song.[2] The songs of the Hendon "Rout-the-Rumour Rally," held on 21 July 1940, were chosen to be as patriotic, hopeful, and inclusive as possible. They were selected to represent an almost careless assurance of victory at a time when things looked their worst. The song-sheet program contains a few hymns, such as "Fight the Good Fight" and "O God, Our Help in Ages Past," to assure people that they were fighting with God on their side. It has a few World War I classics, such as "Pack Up Your Troubles in Your Old Kit Bag," to remind people that Britain had beaten Germany fairly recently and could do so again.[3] One of the World War I songs, "It's a Long Way To Tipperary," also served to embrace the Irish contingent. "Men of Harlech," a song of Welsh victory over the Saxons, made a similar call to Wales. "Loch Lomond" was the Scottish offering, despite its sad tone and the fact that it is not a war song at all. "John Peel," a traditional song about fox hunting, represented the English heritage. Well-known patriotic songs, such as "Land of Hope and Glory" and "Rule, Britannia," emphasized the national and imperial power of Britain. "It's a Lovely Day Tomorrow" and "The Long, Long Trail" stressed the principle of hope. Though few of the songs were overtly political, all were chosen for their political effectiveness.

Not only songs but other forms of music were chosen as proper conduits for public feeling. It was believed that certain kinds of music could canalize emotion in ways helpful to the war effort. On 10 July 1940 a Ministry of Information morale report stated: "Many people feel a need for martial music, processions and bands, and other stimulants of righteous aggressiveness. The sight of Dominion troops in London has been heartening, but there have been many suggestions that opportunities should be found for parades and marches" (INF 1/264, 97/15 H.I.). Eileen Scales, whose fiancé was in the infantry during the war, remembers her own reactions to martial music:

> If you heard military music then it all sort of made you feel rather patriotic and a bit proud of your country, you know. Military music still does that to me anyway. I think, you know, all the battles that different regiments have fought, and they've always been very proud of their battle honours and things like that. So military music always does tend to make me feel a bit emotional, but it also did then. . . . Yes, the song, "There's Something about a Soldier." There used to be something about a soldier, you know, something that made you feel a bit proud and patriotic. [personal interview, 3 May 1993]

Other kinds of music could stimulate a feeling of togetherness by emphasizing the "Britishness" of the music played. According to Ian McLaine, a Ministry of Information planning committee "suggested that the BBC make the greatest possible use of folk tunes and national music and the press be persuaded to emphasise the theme of what Britain means to its citizens" (1979, 72). The BBC's listings of wartime radio programs show a wide variety of British music and musicians, including music hall songs, Gaelic work songs, several BBC orchestras, and the Band of the Scots Guards playing the "Internationale." Another point of view on the power of music is presented by Major A.H.B.R., who wrote in a letter to his wife on 2 November 1940: "I did hear a delightful concert a short time ago when Schumann's Concerto in A minor was played in part by Miss Myra Hess (I think it was she) along with a few other delightful pieces including her adaptation of a Bach Chorale—I agree with you entirely and . . . Myra Hess said the same— now more than ever is music necessary as a sort of mild sedation" (Imperial War Museum Department of Documents 88/21/1).

Finally, the need for some sort of relaxation and entertainment was recognized. Music was an excellent choice because it was cheaply and readily available; it could be produced by anyone who could croak out a tune. Grand opera was no longer mounted at Covent Garden, but music appreciation classes increased. Music could exist anywhere, at any time; one could even sing in the cold and dark of an air-raid shelter. George Orwell wrote in January 1942: "A people at war . . . cannot get on without rest and amusement. Probably these things are more necessary in wartime than at ordinary times. And yet when you are fighting you cannot afford to waste precious materials on luxury goods, because this is primarily a war of machines, and every scrap of metal used up in making gramophones, or every pound of silk used up in making stockings, means less metal for guns and aeroplanes, or less silk for parachutes and barrage balloons" (West 1985, 71). Thus a people at war should shun amusements that require expensive consumer goods, clothes, or labor and should encourage more democratic forms that can be home-made. Orwell writes: "The amusements which can be encouraged . . . are games, sports, music, the radio, dancing, literature and the arts generally. Most of these are things in which you create your amusement for yourself, rather than paying other people to create it for you" (72).

An astonishing number and variety of activities arose from this policy of music promotion. Many of these activities, as noted, encouraged people to make their own music. Songbooks designed for amateur use were published, such as Lawrence Wright's *War-Time Songs*, subtitled "Nearly 200 Popular Choruses from 'Rose of Tralee' to 'Boomps-A-Daisy'; Specially Chosen for Camp Concerts, Community Singing, Parties, Clubs, Etc." Like the song sheet from the Hendon rally, Wright's songbook is broad-based and inclusive, though it leans more to lighter fare. It has a large selection of popular songs, including "Ain't Misbehavin'" and "Yes! We Have No Bananas"; English folk songs, including "The Bailiff's Daughter" and "Widdicombe Fair"; Welsh songs, including "All through the Night" and "The Ash Grove"; Scottish songs, such as "Annie Laurie" and "Auld Lang Syne"; and Irish songs, such as "Cockles and Mussels" and "The Minstrel Boy," the last being one of the few that has anything to do with war. It also includes a generous selection of American songs, such as "Clementine," "Carolina Moon," and "John Brown's Body"; the World War I classic "Mademoiselle from Armentières"; a few songs written for the occasion, such as "Adolf" and "They Can't Black-Out the Moon"; and a version of "Vive La Compagnie," which proclaims, "Let ev'ry good fellow now fill up his glass / And drink to the health of our glorious class."

Reactions to this bombardment of musical propaganda were mixed. John Hargrave Wells Gardner was angered by what he considered emotional manipulation focused on an improper outcome. In 1940, fully aware of the propaganda value of music and the government's exploitation of it, he wrote:

> Another example, by which the mood of the people was gradually prepared for war, is to be found in the revival of songs that were popular during the Boer War and the war of 1914–18. From the time of the Armistice to 1935–36 (when Rearmament began in earnest) no one played "*It's a long way to Tipperary,*" nor "*Pack up your troubles in your old kit-bag.*" . . . And then, when it was necessary to say to the people at large, "War is pretty well inevitable, so you'd better begin to feel a bit more warlike—you'd better begin to feel the spell of armies on the march—the mass spell of ordered action," the spellbinding was begun, not in words alone, but in the old-associations-link-up of the old tunes. . . . There is nothing inspiring in any of this song-propaganda, but all of it together has a hold upon the imagination. It casts a spell. Whether it is the kind of spell from which a New Britain, a New Europe, a New World can emerge—a world free from social-economic insanity—is extremely doubtful. I should say it was the same old spell, an evil spell. [1940, 125, 127]

Moira, a small child during the war, also remembers a conservative, imperialist use to which music was put, though on a much smaller scale. She describes musical activities in the village school where she was evacuated during the war:

> Some of the ones I can remember from school are those awful patriotic songs like "Land of Hope and Glory, Mother of the Free," and we used to have to—this again ties in with the war—we had to wear red shorts (which our mothers had to make), white blouses, and the big girls . . . had to wear these blue paper-covered things on their heads and do marching! To things like "Land of Hope and Glory." It was all patriotic, you see. But it was very Tory patriotic because they had to—Miss _____ was encouraging them to go into service with the gentry and that's the last thing they wanted to do. You know, be servants. [personal interview, 16 January 1993]

Others remember wartime music as a way that people passed the time to make it more bearable. Anne Lubin, recalling wartime community singing, remarked, "I think there's something happens, a chemical reaction happens when you start either talking or singing that cheers you up" (personal interview, 13 March 1993).

Singing was something that anyone could do, a way that ordinary people could create their own entertainment and simultaneously show their optimism and mettle. On 28 February 1943 Vere Hodgson remarked approvingly on a line from a popular song, "If you're up to your neck in hot water, be like the kettle and sing." Even while bombs were whistling in the dark, people could sing.

Singing London: Music in the Shelters

The image of people singing in air-raid shelters is one of the most powerful and carefully maintained of all wartime London motifs.[4] Several people told me that they did not personally experience shelter singsongs, but they thought that such events were more common in the large shelters of the East End. The documents of one such shelter, the Tilbury, show plans for the formation of shelter choirs and note that "assistance in getting these going can be obtained through the C.E.M.A., the Evening Institute, the local churches, and musical societies" (private papers). Indeed, such activities received wide encouragement and publicity. On 5 October 1940, BBC announcer Robin Duff broadcast from an air-raid shelter in the Kennington section of east London (NSA ref. nos. 2951 and LP2943f7). He reported, "If there was any noise from outside, they started singing." He then played examples of the shelter's musical activities, which included a group singing new lyrics about the shelter to the tune of an old song.

Such activities were found not only in the working-class districts of central London and the East End. A Ministry of Information report from 28 August 1940 describes the suburban neighborhood of Greenwich: "Greenwich contact reports: Women in shelters singing to drown noise of H.E. bombs" (INF 1/264, 97/15 H.I.). These activities did not meet with universal approval. On 31 August 1940, the Ministry of Information morale report was less encouraging than the one of three days earlier. The commentary is ironic and, like much material from wartime Britain, laced with Shakespeare: "On some Estates, shelter marshals run public shelters and organise community singing and games of darts in public spirited manner successfully murdering sleep" (INF 1/264, 97/15 H.I.).

Memories of wartime shelter singing abound. Many of them are so similar to BBC presentations and Ministry of Information pep talks that one wonders (and will never know for certain) how much is remembered experience and how much is remembered propaganda. Ivy Regan, in a moving and detailed written account, describes the terrifying ordeal of the first large air raid of the blitz. On 7 September 1940 this raid battered the Isle of Dogs, the East End district where she and her family lived. As a tonic to the terror and uncertainty of the raid, singing and Cockney humor behaved in precisely the ways that the government wished them to. As she and her neighbors sheltered in a school near their homes:

Sticks of bombs whistled down and the air was literally torn apart in a loud rushing noise as they sped earthward. Everyone instinctively crouched. Holding my breath in an agony of suspense I waited for the blast, fully expecting to be blown to pieces. The bombs exploded, rocking the great building to its foundation; but by some miracle the school escaped unscathed and nobody was hurt. But the awful expectancy had been too much and I sensed a rising panic as the overwrought women burst into tears, and the little ones sensing their fear began to scream. Something had to be done and done quickly; so with parched throats a few of us tried to sing. Then my old Dad, possessor of a fine rich tenor voice, began to sing something they all knew, "Just A Song At Twilight." It was touch-and-go at first as he tried to adjust his dry throat. There was a sudden hush as they listened to him sing; then here and there a few voices around us joined in—then more—and soon it became a swell as they sang the lovely old refrain with him. What a tonic that was! To hear those tired folk lift up their voices in song—then more songs—and the wits among us with their spontaneous Cockney humour had us all laughing in no time. [Violet Ivy Regan Papers]

An on-the-spot account of the same night, recorded by Mass-Observers in the East End neighborhood of Stepney, describes a very different reaction to singing. As bombs fell outside, an Air Raid Precautions (ARP) helper in a street shelter tried to lift people's spirits by singing "Roll Out the Barrel." A middle-aged man shouted at her, "Shut your bleedin' row! We got enough noise without you" (Harrisson 1990, 62). The ARP helper tried again with another song, but could get no one to sing with her and finally gave up. Mass-Observers do record more successful attempts at shelter singsongs during the Battle of Britain and during the long period when the blitz had become routinized as daily life. Several of my interviewees have vague memories of singing as a time-filling activity in dark, cold Anderson shelters; they remember singing popular songs such as "Run, Rabbit, Run" and children's songs such as "Ten Green Bottles." Joan Gray remembers an unsuccessful attempt to behave the way cheerful Cockneys were supposed to: "When the war first started and the bombing started, we sort of tried to sing to hide the bombing, but it didn't really work" (personal interview, 15 April 1993). Anne Lubin, on the other hand, remembers being cheered by shelter music, community singing, and organized concerts. She also remembers a time when music helped after the raid was over:

I can remember a conductor on a bus. There'd been a bad raid that night—this was in London—been a bad raid, and a lot of people might well have been involved, I don't know, but I know the bus was quite quiet, which was unusual, 'cause people very often would talk to one another, especially after a bad raid, and someone would say, "Oh, what was it like round your way?" and that kind of thing. But the bus was very subdued, and the conductor suddenly burst out with one of these songs—I've forgotten which one it was—and you know, immediately, the whole atmosphere lifted. And everybody started talking to one another again. [personal interview, 13 March 1993]

Singing, like humor, became an index of patriotism. It was a way to show optimism and courage, to banish sorrow, to bring normal pleasures into abnormal circumstances. But singing was not the only form of music known to wartime Londoners. Instrumental music was also used to combat more ominous sounds. On 22 October 1940 Vere Hodgson wrote in her diary: "Our musical box is lovely. Its sweet melody is in contrast with the odious noises of the Merry-go-round in the sky." And even the odious noises in the sky could be contemplated with some equanimity if they were considered a strange variety of music.

London Music: The Symphony of War

The discordant and threatening sounds of war were often humanized and diminished by referring to them in terms of music. On 19 March 1944 Vere Hodgson began a description of an air raid with the words "The band began to play." On 3 April 1945 she described a train journey: "It was lovely, too, not to depart to an orchestra of Flying Bombs, as I seem to have done so often—or to the menacing rumble of a Rocket." Quentin Reynolds, speaking over an air raid in the opening commentary of the film *London Can Take It,* says: "These are not Hollywood sound effects; this is the music they play every night in London—the symphony of war" (INF 6/328). In *Listen to Britain,* a Crown Film Unit production about music in wartime, the Canadian Leonard Brockington says in the foreword: "Blended together in one great symphony is the music of Britain at war. The evening hymn of the lark, the roar of Spitfires, the dancers in the great ballroom at Blackpool, the clank of machinery and shunting trains, soldiers of Canada holding in memory their 'home on the range,' the B.B.C. sending truth on its journey round the world, the trumpet call of freedom, the war-song of a great people, the first sure notes of the march of victory, as you and I, Listen to Britain" (INF 6/339).

Listen to Britain was made in 1941 and 1942, and it focused on the music and sounds of wartime Britain, combining high art and folk art, popular songs and military bands. It shows Myra Hess playing a Mozart piano concerto in the National Gallery while the audience (including the queen) listens spellbound. It shows an unnamed woman in an ambulance depot singing a bel canto rendition of "The Ash Grove" to her slightly bored coworkers. It shows the bells of Big Ben playing their signature tune, women in a Middlesex factory singing "Yes, My Darling Daughter" as they work, and the variety artists Flanagan and Allen singing "Round the Back of the Arches" to an appreciative audience in a factory canteen. The film ends with a choral rendition of "Rule, Britannia." The descriptive material provided by the Crown Film Unit shows that "listening to Britain" meant paying attention to natural and mechanical sound as well as to music; all were part of the "symphony of war."

Listening to Britain also meant paying attention to the sounds and voices of different classes: farmers in their fields, workers on the night shift, soldiers marching through a city street:

> While larks sing in the peace of the country at evening, their notes are drowned by the roar of Spitfires and the clatter of tractors. As the blackout curtains of a small house are being drawn another familiar sound is heard—Joseph McLeod reading the six o'clock news. . . . In the Tower Ballroom at Blackpool those on leave or off duty, are dancing to "Roll Out the Barrel," the strains of which are interrupted by the clanging of a cage at a pit-head as miners go on the night shift. We hear the familiar clink-aclank-clink of shunting trains. Inside a stationary passenger train, some Canadian soldiers sing "Home on the Range." Meanwhile the aeroplane factories are working non-stop and the hard metallic symphony of war production is drowned by a bomber taking off outside. [INF 6/339]

Ministry of Information films met with varying success; some were far more popular than others.[5] *Listen to Britain* touched a chord in a young airman serving in Southern Rhodesia: "'Listen to Britain' . . . was a great source of joy to me . . . showing that even in War time music is playing a bigger part in the lives of those at home than it did in peace time" (INF 6/339).

Other Ministry of Information films concentrated on specific musical topics. Films were made about the pianist Myra Hess and the song "Lili Marlene." Another ministry film described CEMA, the Council for the Encouragement of Music and the Arts (INF 6/471). The precursor of the Arts Council of Great Britain, CEMA was founded in January 1940 with the intention of bringing first-rate music, theater, and art to people who did not ordinarily have access to such things. CEMA sponsored concerts of art music in provincial towns, factory canteens, historic buildings, and rest centers for the homeless and also provided funds for the formation of music clubs (as noted, the Tilbury Shelter planned to ask CEMA for help in forming shelter choirs). The introduction to the CEMA film declared: "This Council was started in the first winter of the war, to bring pleasure in the highest forms of inspiration to those millions who were, as it were, blacked out in the general black-out all over Britain at that time. This Council took music and the arts . . . to factories, mining towns, sea ports, which may have suffered in the war, or may be cut off from their normal source of entertainment" (INF 6/471).

CEMA, like many wartime innovations, kept one foot in the left wing and one in the right, borrowing from the socialist desire to make the good things in life available to workers and the policy of noblesse oblige that brings culture to the benighted ("blacked-out") masses. In the CEMA film, which lists Dylan Thomas among its authors, art and culture are presented as hallmarks of civilization, while the freedom to choose one's preferred cultural products is in sharp contrast to Nazi censorship:

> *Man*: What's the point of all this 'ere art? Pretty pictures don't win anything. Not now anyway.
> *Newton*: We all know what we're fighting against, but don't you think we sometimes forget what we're fighting for?
> *Man*: Not pretty pictures.
> *Newton*: Yes, but they're part of it. We've got to fight because if we didn't we wouldn't be free. Free to work, to play, to listen, to look at what we want to. [INF 6/471]

Far better known than CEMA was ENSA, the Entertainments National Service Association. ENSA's primary mission was to bring entertainment to the troops, though it did sponsor concerts in shelters, factories, and rest centers as well. Whereas CEMA tended to concentrate on high art, ENSA painted with a much broader brush, sponsoring programs that featured variety artists and comedians as well. In fact, ENSA was often considered a refuge for second-rate actors and comics who would have been out of work during peacetime; a wartime joke claimed that ENSA stood for "Every Night Something Awful." This comment is unfair considering the range of ENSA's activities and talent, but it doubtless represented many people's experience with the organization. Anne Lubin, who left her native London to work in a war factory in Birmingham, remembers ENSA coming to the factory canteen:

> I can remember one or two that they had in the canteen when I was in Birmingham. They were abominable. I mean, a couple of oranges up your jumper, and that was supposed—a man, you see—supposed to be absolutely hilarious. Very poor comedy. I cannot remember a good ENSA show. Not at all. There must have been some. . . . I think all the best people were in the forces and entertaining the forces, and we got the leftovers. . . . They were not witty; they were just dirty. I mean, I don't mind a dirty joke if it's really witty—I could tell you a few myself—but these were not; they were just plain dirty. (personal interview, 13 March 1993]

Mass-Observation found similar sentiments during the war. In one factory, the workers' committee "actually complained about the low quality of the humour in many E.N.S.A. concerts, and requested more music and straight stuff. Two C.E.M.A. concerts (classical, instrumental and vocal music) have been very successful, and attempts have been made for more" (quoted in A. Calder 1969, 372). This preference delighted ENSA's director, Basil Dean, a theatrical producer whose own taste led to more high-brow fare. ENSA did provide a large number of high art concerts during the war years. For example, in 1943 and 1944, ENSA provided concerts for war workers that featured major British symphony orchestras. Walter Legge, in a report about ENSA's activities from September 1943 to July 1944, writes: "Throughout the season the programmes were built on the highest artistic levels, without any concession to what is usually regarded as 'popular taste.' This policy has proved to be much to the liking of war-working audiences" (1946, 309).

In the same years, ENSA sponsored concerts of symphonic music to forces personnel. A book on wartime art and entertainment shows amazement at the good taste of the masses: "Although many of the men were hearing this type of music for the first time, they listened with concentrated attention and expressed their appreciation in the most enthusiastic manner. Naturally not all the music provided by E.N.S.A. was up to this standard, but the experiment showed that the most unlikely audiences will appreciate good music if given the chance of hearing it" (Myers 1948, 108). Dean had long wanted to bring classical music and theater to the troops but had been checked by authorities who felt that such fare would not be appreciated. Richard Fawkes suggests several reasons for their eventual change of heart: "The criticism of all but the best variety shows, the lack of talented singers and dancers and the growing need, discovered in the adversity of the Blitz, for entertainment of more lasting value. That a symphony orchestra should prove as popular as a dance band came as a surprise" (1978, 72). Similarly, an Old Vic tour of Wales, sponsored by CEMA, was a rousing success. The audience particularly liked a production of *Macbeth* in which the man with "vaulting ambition" was portrayed as Hitler (Fawkes 1978, 71).

Despite ENSA's many concerts to war workers, its primary focus was on entertaining the troops. *Worker's Playtime,* on the other hand, concentrated on providing lunchtime entertainment at factory canteens. "We're not in any way in competition with the E.N.S.A. concerts that go round to a number of these factories," said John Watt, director of *Worker's Playtime.* "We're just trying to help" (NSA ref. nos. 4125 and LP4125b1, 26 October 1941). *Worker's Playtime* leaned toward popular music and light, music hall fare and was broadcast at 12:30 P.M. over the BBC. On one broadcast, Ernest Bevin, the rough-voiced, trade unionist minister of labour, introduced *Worker's Playtime* by stressing the importance of its audiences: "Victory can only be secured through work" (NSA ref. nos. 3411 and LP3404f7, 25 and 28 October 1941). The Ministry of Labour helped finance the program, perhaps to ward off the dangers of all work and no play. Though a child during the war, Shirley Ann listened to *Worker's Playtime* broadcasts and remembers their own brand of humor: "They would always have a quiz. And there was one quiz; Wilfred Pickles used to get somebody from the audience to come up to give a little bit of quizzing. And I can always remember one coming up and he said, 'What does a woman wear that a man never sees?' And you had to try and guess that. What does a woman wear that a man never sees? And this is going back years now, and I still remember it. Don't give up! [laughs] Perfume" (personal interview, 18 February 1993). Fred Mitchell remembers *Worker's Playtime* productions coming to the factory where he worked, but he had a better way to spend the lunch hour. With many women in the factory, lunchtime was "courting time," and canteen entertainment took a definite back seat (personal interview, 18 May 1993).

Whereas *Worker's Playtime* allowed workers a time for play, *Music While You Work* allowed them to listen to music while still working. *Music While You Work* played light instrumental music for brief periods during the workday, and many factories played these broadcasts for the benefit of their workers. Anne Lubin remembers looking forward to the broadcasts:

> It broke the morning up. It was very monotonous working in a factory, at least what I did was, and so you knew that when *Music While You Work* came on in the morning, you knew that you were halfway through the morning; it wouldn't be long till dinnertime. And the same thing again in the afternoon, round about three or half past three, you had it once again, *Music While You Work*. They discovered that if you played it all the time, it had no effect on people, but if you had a half an hour at a time, people could look forward to it, and it had an effect on production, so they said. And people would sing along. They didn't have any vocals on that; they only had tunes. But people sang along with them, whatever they were playing. [personal interview, 13 March 1993]

Music While You Work began on 23 June 1940 with its midmorning and midafternoon sessions; a 10:30 P.M. broadcast was added in 1942 for the benefit of the night shift. Because it was broadcast over the radio, it was heard by millions, both in and out of the factory. Nonetheless, its target remained the industrial worker. A Ministry of Information report from 12 July 1940 discusses a factory in south London: "Woolwich factory reports wireless and gramophone music have greatly increased workers' cheerfulness: 'staff working busily and happily in spite of long hours and do not seem unduly tired. This is proved by freedom from serious accidents'" (INF 1/264, 97/15 H.I.). The purpose of *Music While You Work* was not sheer humanitarianism. As Anne Lubin mentioned, a cheery, energetic, uninjured worker is a productive one. Frank E. Huggett quotes a wartime factory report that claimed: "The music exhilarates the workers without acting as a harmful distraction. When the set was shut down for a week, there was a 20 per cent drop in output" (1979, 65). If the Ministry of Food was responsible for bread, then *Music While You Work* provided circuses.

In music, as in many other things, the primary disseminator was the British Broadcasting Corporation (BBC). The sole broadcasting network in Britain during the war, it was divided into two stations: the Home Service and the Forces Programme. The Forces Programme, which began in February 1940, specialized in light music and other entertainment suitable for listening in noisy forces canteens. The Home Service was much more varied, and a typical week might include radio drama, the leftish inspirational broadcasts of J.B. Priestley, the middlebrow-intellectual *Brains Trust*, the news in several dozen languages, and music of all kinds. Prior to the war, the BBC had paid little attention to listener preference and had offered the public what it felt was good for them, the radio equivalent of cod liver oil. John Reith, director general until 1938, had banned dance music and variety programs from broadcasting on Sundays. Such musical autocracy was unbecoming in a people's war. It was also embarrassing to discover that people were turning to foreign broadcasting stations in order to hear the light music denounced by the BBC. The BBC relented by degrees, though not without a fight. It continued to argue for the composition and broadcasting of rousing patriotic songs, despite the fact that most such songs left listeners cold. Sentimental ballads were the popular songs of the day, and this music was requested most often by those in the forces and on the home front. This music was also the kind targeted for eradication by the BBC's stern "Anti-Slush Committee." Spike Hughes wrote in 1945 of the struggles still going on between the BBC and the public: "Today, thousands of servicemen overseas ask to hear Miss Vera Lynn singing 'Miss You.' They are not allowed to hear it, because the B.B.C. considers it would be harmful to morale and remind the sailor too much of home" (1945, 80).

Although the BBC lamented the taste of the majority, it could be cheered by the preferences of a substantial minority. The BBC's Listener Research Department discovered a sizable audience for art music, noting that those who preferred symphony concerts, grand opera, and chamber music were a minority of the population but a very large number of people. The public's appreciation for art music grew substantially during the war, and the BBC attempted to increase this trend still more. Finally aware of the value of audience input, the postwar BBC invited members of the general public to join its Music Panel: "The only condition of membership is a real interest in serious music and a willingness to co-operate" (Silvey 1946, 174).

Despite its disdain for popular taste, the BBC did increase its presentations of popular music, and such fare became available on Sundays as well. B.E. Nicolls stated in the BBC Year Book for 1943 that "it was essential that our troops should not feel that the BBC was letting them down by leaving it to other stations to provide the light entertainment that they chiefly wanted" (quoted in Huggett 1979, 52–53). Huggett suggests, somewhat patronizingly, the reason for the popularity of the sentimental ballads: "For the unsophisticated these simple songs of hope could express all their most intimate yearnings more readily than they could ever have done themselves; but it was not sentimentality alone that made them so popular. People were conscious then, as they are even more now, of the contrast between these songs' optimistic sentiments and the grim reality of their wartime lives: the irony helped to distance them from events and to make them more bearable" (42).

The popularity of such music made it incumbent on the BBC to provide it for listeners. In November 1941 *Sincerely Yours—Vera Lynn* began broadcasting (Lynn 1975, 97). Billed as a "sentimental presentation by Howard Thomas," this half-hour program consisted of Vera Lynn's renditions of songs requested by overseas servicemen.[6] Vera Lynn also decided to visit servicemen's wives who were in the hospital having babies, so a chosen few heard personal congratulations beamed from back home by Lynn herself. She speaks, with becoming humility, of her role: "I was simply acting as a message carrier between separated people, and through the words of a song I told one what the other wanted to say. They may have quarrelled, they might have been shy—like most people; there was always a song which would convey what they couldn't say for themselves" (98).

The BBC also found a song for every occasion. In order to create musical hegemony, the BBC granted concessions to the public in the form of popular and sentimental music; at the same time, it continued to provide messages suitable for wartime and for inspiring a loyal and warlike spirit. These messages were sometimes far from subtle, such as the antiphonal trumpet fanfare "Come If You Dare" from Purcell's "King Arthur" (played 19 September 1941) or a male voice choir rendition of the children's song "London's Burning" (played on 4 July 1942). Music hall songs were designed to cheer people up (and were a concession to popular taste); more serious feelings might be stirred by the haunting sound of Highland pipes, played by Scottish regiments in Britain and on the Continent. Vere Hodgson, an assiduous radio devotée, remarked with pleasure on a broadcast of this type: "To hear the Highland pipers over the radio in St. Valery was cracking" (8 September 1944).

More elaborate musical presentations were also broadcast. One remarkable example is called "Marching to Victory," which aired on 11 August 1940 (NSA ref. nos. 2577-9 and MT2577). The program begins with the sound of soldiers marching, an order to "Halt!," then the words: "We halt for a moment the marching feet of hundreds of thousands of men of the British empire to talk about the music they've brought to the shores and country lanes of Britain. Music you've never heard before, perhaps, but music that's putting new life into the mother country." "Marching to Victory" concentrated not on British music but on music from the Dominions and the empire—one of the few acknowledgments that "standing alone" meant getting substantial aid from an empire that numbered 500 million people. The title came from a song of the New Zealand Expeditionary Force:

We are the boys from way down under,
Marching to victory,
We're not afraid of Hitler's plunder,
We'll put him where he should be.

Making a careful distinction between Nazis and everybody else in Nazi-controlled and Nazi-occupied lands, the song optimistically proclaimed, "The Poles, the Czechs, and Germany as well / Will fight to put the Nazis on the shelf."

The title song was not the only selection from the antipodes; a sizable number of songs from "down under" were represented on "Marching to Victory." Several Maori songs were played in the Maori language; a song composed by a Maori corporal (in English) was featured as well. "Waltzing Matilda" needed no introduction, but the lovely Australian folk song "The Road to Gundagai" did. The introduction to a Maori haka (a dance accompanied by chanting) proclaimed admiration for all these rough-and-ready ex-colonials, from sun-drenched Australians to hearty Canadians: "They've brought an electric something with them, a courage, a confidence, a swagger, new blood, new hope and in the songs they've written, homely or heroic, swinging or sentimental as the case may be, they speak to us of the lands they've left behind them, of the deeds they hope to do, and of what they think of the enemy, which is plenty. Listen."

Music from the Dominion of Canada was prominently featured in "Marching to Victory." The Royal Canadian Air Force sang, "Wait till we get them in the air, boys" with the same innocent swagger beloved by British pilots in the summer of 1940. This song, which discusses the activities of the conquering hero, contains a line that caught the censor napping: "In every house, there'll be a maiden laden." An instrumental piece, a version of "Road to the Isles" played by a brass band, linked Canada with its British roots. The announcer proclaimed, "The Canadian Highland Regiments haven't forgotten the 'Road to the Isles,' the songs of their ancestors. Once again, they've brought back Scottish music to lead Canadians into battle." Few songs could be less suited to marching than "Road to the Isles,' with its irregular rhythms and lilting dance tempo, though the brass band does its best to iron out such irregularities.[7] The adaptation of traditional Scots music by a Canadian regiment was part of a mythic linking of the soldiers with "their ancestors"; it is doubtful that all members of Canadian Highland Regiments were descendants of Highland Scots, any more than all the members of British Highland Regiments were actual Highland Scots.

An Indian announcer made a further connection between exotic foreigners and exotic highlanders as he moved the program away from Western music and toward the rest of the empire:

So far, you have mainly heard the martial music of the West, the music of brass and drums and marching boots, the music which catches the ear and the heart of 140 million people in the empire. But there are 500 million people in the British empire. What about the 360 million, the majority of the British empire, Indians? They too have a fighting tradition. But it's not the tradition of heavy boots marching and brassy trumpets blowing. It is the ancient tradition of the spear and the sword, the swift foot and the cunning hand, the lone warrior and the mountain passes of the Himalayas. There beneath the snows on the northwest frontier live a proud and ancient people, the Patans, whose music has perhaps something in common with that of the hill people of the Scottish Highlands.

The loyalty of Indians toward their colonial rulers was not assumed during the war. Indeed, a large amount of propaganda was aimed at getting Indians to fight for, rather than against, the British; George Orwell, to take a renowned member of this enterprise, served as talks producer of the BBC's Indian section from 1941 to 1943. A letter to Sir Malcolm Darling, head of the Indian section, from the Indian novelist Mulk Raj Anand indicates the tensions that many Indian intellectuals had to face. Anand, torn between his antifascist sympathies and his dislike of British colonialism, turned down his old friend's request for help:

> Since the breakdown of negotiations between the Viceroy and Gandhiji, the position of Indians in this war has become very invidious. . . . Even those who have the most distant affiliations with the Congress, are bound to feel a certain sense of national humiliation if, with full awareness of the internment of hundreds of their compatriots and the savage sentence on Pandit Nehru, they do anything to help the war effort. . . . And the one question that has been taxing my mind all these months is how to reconcile that affiliation with my belief that fascism would destroy all I stand for. I am afraid the British Government has done nothing which may help to solve the dilemma which faces some of us. . . . This enforces on us a kind of vague neutrality. [West 1985, 15]

Although this tension was largely ignored in home front propaganda, "Marching to Victory" was one of a few friendly nods in the direction of the subcontinent that contained the "majority of the empire," though Malays and Chinese Singaporeans (among others) might resent this division of the empire into Westerners and Indians. The Indian announcer of "Marching to Victory," with his educated voice and upper-class English speech, sounds as though he might be more at home at an Oxford college (or with George Orwell and Sir Malcolm Darling at the BBC) than on the mountain passes of the Himalayas or in the remote villages of the Scottish Highlands. His description of a "proud and ancient people" to whom warfare is an art, rather than the bloody business of machines and insensate slaughter, presents the Patans as "noble savages" who prize warfare as a cultural tradition.

At the same time, the announcer represents the "majority of the empire" as a people skilled in war, a people proud of their culture, a people who outnumber their masters, a people to be reckoned with.

A different invocation of tradition came from Newfoundland, at the time a British-run Dominion. An updated, anti-Hitler version of the sea chantey "Row, Bullies, Row" turned a bawdy work song into a lighthearted song of war. The new song, with its easy assurance of ultimate victory, proclaimed: "Row, row, bullies, row / The Newfoundland boys have Hitler in tow." The Newfoundland boys will not be enthralled by "Liverpool judies," as in the original song. This time, it is they who wield the power and speak of Hitler as an easy prey.

People's reactions to the BBC's musical barrage varied. On 6 December 1942 Vere Hodgson wrote: "Such a lot of lovely singing [on the wireless]." Yet on 24 January 1943 she wrote: "There are very few good songs on the wireless now." Many of my interviewees spoke with affection of Glenn Miller and other American-style dance bands. Certain songs were remembered as being ubiquitous: "The White Cliffs of Dover," "Run, Rabbit, Run," and "We're Going to Hang Out the Washing on the Siegfried Line" among them. Creina Musson compared wartime popular music with present-day offerings: "Oh, yes, had some good songs in those days. A bit of tune to them unlike the awful noise they have nowadays" (personal interview, 28 July 1993). Anne Lubin remembers that "popular music was very melodious. Mostly, of course, it was 'Darling, I love you, I long to see you again' type of thing, you know, 'When the moon is blue, and so am I too and I'm longing to see you again' type of thing. And Vera Lynn, of course . . . it wasn't bang-bang; I mean, you could sing the songs, so everybody did" (personal interview, 13 March 1993).

At the same time that the BBC was increasing its broadcasts of popular and light music, a substantial proportion of the population was discovering an interest in art music. The popularity of CEMA and ENSA symphony concerts has already been noted. BBC listener research showed a decline in hostility to art music between 1941 and 1942 and a small but significant increase in enthusiasm for symphony concerts, chamber music, and plays (Silvey 1944, 164). Music appreciation classes at the Workers' Educational Association (WEA) increased a hundredfold between 1938 and 1944 in almost all parts of the country (Workers' Educational Association 1946, 240).[8] The WEA speculated on a number of reasons for this increased interest:

> I do not think there can be much doubt that broadcasting has had a stimulating effect on public taste in music. . . . In a less spectacular way, C.E.M.A. had undoubtedly contributed, especially as W.E.A. Branches have taken a prominent part in the organisation of C.E.M.A. concerts, and . . . have often followed them up by using them as propaganda for the organisation of classes.

> Apart from this . . . many people actually engaged in the war effort have taken up Musical Appreciation as a relaxation. It is a real and justifiable escapism, and a tonic which has strengthened their morale. Finally, the number of tutors who possess the necessary technique for teaching adults to appreciate music has increased. [Workers' Educational Association 1946, 241–42]

The oblique reference to the increasing number of trained music teachers masks the sinister circumstances of its happening. George Wagner discussed one reason for this explosion of music:

> Now, there was one factor which improved the scene a bit. Among the German and particularly Austrian Jewish refugees who had come to Britain, there were quite a considerable number of very good orchestral players from German and Austrian local symphony orchestras. And they filled up, insofar as they were not interned first[9], they filled up the orchestras and made for quite a decent standard and gave sort of first impetus to the fantastic development of music in Britain after the war. And a lot of musical tastes were raised or kindled for the first time. People no longer said, "Oh, classical music, bloody awful." [personal interview, 23 April 1993]

The BBC, understandably enough, took the credit for bringing classical music to those who had not heard it before and for fostering a new interest in art music throughout the nation. R.J.E. Silvey, the BBC's listener research director, quoted the testimony of a north-countrywoman who kept house for her father: "Before I had radio I had no interest or understanding of music and first came to love good music through listening to the Promenade Concerts. To the B.B.C. broadcasts of all that is best in music I owe the only real pleasure I have ever had—and acknowledge a debt of gratitude that can never be repaid" (Silvey 1946, 172). One does not know whether to rejoice for a technology that can bring happiness to unfortunates or to weep for someone whose life was so straitened that her only pleasure consisted of hearing concerts beamed from far away.

Unlike the "Merrie England" folk revival of the early part of the century, the wartime music boom laid little emphasis on working-class folk and rural music, outside of a few obligatory radio broadcasts. The class-stratified nature of English music was treated as another opportunity for democratization, yet in this case the opening of opportunity to the working classes meant a simultaneous and concomitant denigration of working-class music itself. Books on wartime music tend to concentrate on art music, with occasional nods to music created *for* the working classes, such as American-style jazz and sentimental popular ballads. Music actually created *by* the working classes, such as music hall and folk song, gets extremely short shrift. The image of the benighted worker slowly awakening to the golden dawn of "good" music is captured by Gladys Crook in a rosy article entitled "New Audiences." It is worth quoting at some length:

> A well-known pianist who has toured in factories for C.E.M.A. since the earliest days of its inception says: "When we first started these concerts, the workers appeared indifferent and almost resentful when they found the sort of programme we intended giving. On a second visit they were definitely interested, but rather afraid of showing it, lest their neighbours should think them a bit queer. Now, they all give us a marvellous welcome and show keen interest and enjoyment all the way through."
>
> These remarks would undoubtedly be endorsed by all the very many fine musicians who have done this work. It is a stimulating experience to see hundreds of tough-looking workmen, mostly in caps and dirty blue dungarees, listening spellbound to Bach and Purcell played on the oboe, an instrument many of them had never even seen before. Clustering around the player afterwards they asked about the instrument, showing the keenest interest in it as well as in the music performed. It is unlikely that any of those men would previously have visited the local concert hall if that same distinguished player had been appearing, and equally probable that many of them will do so for his next visit. [1946, 78–79]

One can practically hear her crying, "They simply need to be taught, the poor things!" It should be pointed out, however, that the poor things might not have had much money to spend on concertgoing after feeding a family on £2 per week; and it is doubtful that a workman, should he venture into the concert hall to hear his favorite oboist, would be welcomed in his cap and dirty blue dungarees. Musical sound has no inherent class connotations, but the accoutrements of musical performance are filled with them. One of the remarkable accomplishments of the wartime concerts was to adapt the presentation of classical music to a working-class milieu: concerts were cheap or free, were performed at lunchtime, and in many cases, were taken to people's places of work. Since first-class musicians such as Myra Hess and Yehudi Menuhin performed at these concerts, it was not a case of selling the castoffs at bargain price. At times, custom may be stronger than law, and breaking the class-bound customs of art music presentation was no easy thing.

Spike Hughes, scoffing at cockeyed optimists like Gladys Crook, writes about concerts in army camps and factories: "Much as I hate to doubt that these musically illiterate thousands do enjoy Good Music, I am churlish enough to think that they listen to Good Music because they are fed-up, far from home, have the music brought to them and have little freedom to escape to do the things they want to" (1945, 97). However, in the next sentence, he declares that soldiers who served in Italy developed a genuine love for opera because they were able to see it "in its native surroundings of gilt, plush, garlic and encores" (98). Hughes's cranky skepticism about any newfound love of art music among the working classes is balanced by his desire for a kind of musical mix-and-match bar, where all classes can get all kinds of music off the peg:

> It isn't just a question of "selling" music by informal presentation; it is a question of setting a good example. Music (i.e. "good" music) has a thoroughly bad reputation among the masses, towards whom the so-called "music-lover" behaves as an unnecessarily and unbearably superior person.
>
> We are supposed to be living in a democratic age. Well, democracy isn't all a matter of raising the lower ones up; the higher ones have got to come down and see what's going on in the four-ale bar, and then everybody can graduate to the saloon-bar and a good time can be had by all. [91]

Though much wartime music was a form of needed escapism, equally important were the many musical compositions that took the war itself as subject matter. Many popular songs were written to comment on wartime themes: "Coming in on a Wing and a Prayer," "The White Cliffs of Dover," "In Der Führer's Face," "Oh, What a Surprise for the Duce," "We're Going to Hang Out the Washing on the Siegfried Line," and "Don't Let's Be Beastly to the Germans" among them. Art musicians also composed pieces that reflected wartime concerns. Some plied their musical trade in the service of government agencies, such as William Walton, who wrote film scores for the War Office and the Ministry of Information. (One of his compositions was the incidental music of Olivier's *Henry V.*) Others composed pieces about specific wartime events, such as Ralph Vaughan Williams's 1945 "Thanksgiving for Victory," first performed on VE Day, and Michael Tippett's 1941 "A Child of Our Time," which incorporates African-American spirituals (some of which compare the plight of African-American slaves with that of Hebrew slaves in Egypt) in its musical representation of the rise of fascism.

Constant Lambert's "Aubade Héroïque" was inspired by his being in the Netherlands with the Sadler's Wells Ballet Company at the time of the Nazi invasion; the idea came to him on the quay in Rotterdam as he waited for the boat to take him home. A well-nigh forgotten solidarity with the Soviet Union is revealed in titles such as Elizabeth Maconchy's "Stalingrad" and Sir Arnold Bax's "Ode to Russia." Even a work such as "Peter Grimes," which has nothing to do with the war and was composed by the conscientious objector Benjamin Britten, could be venerated because it was composed by a British composer during the war—an example of the greatness of the British spirit under adversity. Since British composers had long suffered an inferiority complex with regard to their German and Italian counterparts, artists of Britten's stature (with his felicitous surname) were especially to be cherished. Rollo H. Myers writes: "In spite of the material dangers and difficulties to which this country was exposed during six long years, spiritual and artistic values were never lost sight of or allowed to be submerged in the heat and dust of the struggle. Musically, Britain has won her spurs and can now face the future with confidence. Gone are the days when it was possible for foreign nations to refer to her as 'the land without music.' It was never true, and never less so than today" (1948, 139).

For many people, it is music that brings back the feel of the war years more surely than anything else. Frank E. Huggett writes:

> For every generation, the popular songs of its youth have a perennial appeal, recalling those sunny days when the feelings were still warm and unclouded by suspicion or disillusion; but for millions of people who lived through the Second World War, the songs of 1939 to 1945 have a special meaning that they will never lose. . . . Some of them, such as "We'll Meet Again," "A Nightingale Sang in Berkeley Square," "Lili Marlene," "The White Cliffs of Dover," "The Anniversary Waltz" and many more are engraved so indelibly by the pressure of personal association upon the memory that even now some people find the recollections they evoke too poignant to bear with equanimity. [1979, 8]

Alfred Schutz has written about the peculiarly time-based dimension of music, the fact that music must be grasped step-by-step (polythetically) and thus is grasped at the same time by all beholders. We cannot skim music as we do books or glance at it quickly as we might visual art; music forces us to conform to its time dimension. At a concert, we cannot hurry ahead or linger behind our fellow listeners; the nature of music requires us to listen together. Schutz points out that "it will 'take as much time' to reconstitute the work in recollection as to experience it for the first time" (1971, 173). Recorded sound even makes it possible for us to listen to exactly the same sounds that we heard years before and in so doing, to reexperience an event of the past. Sound may linger in memory, but it also has the ability to bring the past into the present.

In public presentations of wartime Britain, music is used to maintain and revive an image of the past—an image of unity, courage, and cheerful patriotism. A recent television film of *Dad's Army* used a Flanagan and Allen tune as its theme song, a song that asked, "Who do you think you are kidding, Mr. Hitler?" In the film, members of the local Home Guard sing "All Things Bright and Beautiful" as they capture a German spy in the village church. On Valentine's Day 1993, BBC Radio Two presented "Forces Sweethearts," a program of music and readings predominantly from the First and Second World Wars. At the taping of the show, the audience waved paper Union Jacks and sang along as Dame Vera Lynn led wartime standards such as "The White Cliffs of Dover," "Roll Out the Barrel," and "Bless 'Em All." At the Imperial War Museum's World War II exhibit, "Run, Rabbit,

Run" and other popular songs play continuously; at the Winston Churchill Britain at War Theme Museum, which opened in 1992, "Rule, Britannia" plays in the gift shop.

Private memory can provide an astringent counterpoint to such complacent musical reconstruction, for memory can show that public presentation did not always match private reception. Anne Lubin remembers: "'There'll Always Be an England,' that was terribly popular. Actually, I always hated that song, I'm afraid, because I detest this so-called patriotism which makes my country right all the time and there's never any criticism of it, because that's the real meaning of chauvinism. And I don't like it at all; I think it breeds very nasty sentiments in people. It means that anything that's not of your country is awful. . . . So that was never one of my favourites. But it was a very popular song" (personal interview, 13 March 1993). Her comments show the delicate umbrella that hegemony builds. Anne was a Jew and an antifascist; as such, she was strongly in favor of intervention and volunteered for work in a war factory even before she was called up. Yet her reasons for supporting the war did not involve the mindless patriotism that she felt was invoked by songs like "There'll Always Be an England." This song, written in 1939, optimistically declared that "England shall be free" and ignored any mention of the future status of Scotland, Wales, or Northern Ireland. Its patronizing claim "The Empire too / We can depend on you" supports a vision of imperial might and rigorous maintenance of the status quo. This was not the England— not the Britain—that Anne Lubin fought to defend.

S.H. also remembers being uninspired by the kind of rousing music that the government thought necessary: "Songs of defiance were purely propaganda. They weren't sung by and large except on the wireless. . . . People might join in. Nowadays they will sing them as a reminiscence but I don't think that people went round singing songs because . . . some interfering clever neighbour would say, 'I don't know what you've got to sing about when so and so was killed last night,' you know. You wouldn't go around singing like that except when they gathered in sort of pep-up groups maybe" (personal interview, 22 March 1993). Shirley, a child during the war, finds that war songs and memories have an appeal in retrospect that they did not have at the time. She found the war traumatic, but nonetheless feels nostalgia for it now. When I asked why, she replied: "I guess it's part of your childhood, I suppose. Well, for me. I'm quite a romantic anyway. So tunes and Vera Lynn and, you know, the songs like 'White Cliffs of Dover'—everything is going to be all right when the war is over. I don't know, it's sort of an ambivalent feeling of fear and yet looking back and thinking, 'Oh, yes, I remember that'" (personal interview, 22 January 1993).

Others remember wartime songs associated with specific personal events. The songs seem to act as a fixative to memory, anchoring it in time and commenting on it simultaneously. The songs were war songs because of the time period in which they were sung and composed, yet the lyrics often focused on happier topics such as lovers meeting. This built-in irony between the violence of war and the soothing sweetness of wartime songs may have added an extra poignancy. Ettie Gontarsky explains: "The songs went very deeply with me. And of course they were about us. And what was happening. And if they were romantic and if we were having a romance at the time—and I did have two or three during the war, or three or four, which were rather nice—the songs involved a memory, like this particular one with this American; I don't even know if he's still alive. 'Darling,' he rings up, 'Darling, they're playing our tune.' It was sheer Hollywood. It was romantic. But it was lovely of its kind" (personal interview, 4 April 1993).

"It was sheer Hollywood." Hollywood provided many images of wartime Britain, of which *Mrs. Miniver* was probably the most famous. The Hollywood films naturally featured American music, which proved very popular in wartime Britain. Dance music was especially beloved; when Glenn Miller died on his way to entertain the troops in France, many people were devastated. G.H.R. writes, "The British music was either funny-satirical or patriotic but the American import was sheer escapism" (personal letter, 8 May 1993). Many people remembered learning songs from films or seeing films in which music was presented as an index of civilization, living on in spite of the Nazis. *Dangerous Moonlight*, a 1941 film, featured Anton Walbrook as a Polish pianist playing his Warsaw Concerto while bombs rained outside—a spirited defense of beauty and civilization against the forces of destruction. A London housewife remembers her response to this film: "I can still remember seeing that film as if it was yesterday. I was feeling very depressed as my husband was in the desert and I had not heard from him for weeks. My daughter suggested that we should go to the cinema as she knew that I liked Anton Walbrook. I loved the film and although I came out of the cinema in tears, the music made me think that everything was worthwhile" (quoted in Huggett 1979, 82).

Some personal memories of music have a similarly cinematic quality. In linking songs to specific memories, people provide a musical backdrop for their own lives. Vera's story is one such memory:

> There's one song, it was called "I'll be Around." You wouldn't know it. When I worked at this club . . . I met somebody. A very, very nice young man and we were walking together along Piccadilly and there was a dog fight. You know, the aeroplanes; it was during an air raid. And we were walking along, and this young man had been a singer in a band and he was, as we were walking and watching, he was walking along singing this song in a beautiful voice. And you can picture the scene, we were walking along and he was singing and there they were killing each other or

fighting for their lives up there. And the ack-ack guns, the anti-aircraft guns were shooting. But he was singing and we were walking along. It was, we were oblivious to everything else, I just heard him singing this song. I've always remembered. [personal interview, 20 July 1993]

In sum, music was used for manifold purposes in wartime Britain. It was used to entertain, to inspire, and to cajole; it was used to make people forget their troubles and to concentrate on the serious business of winning the war. London, as the center of broadcasting, recording, and the major symphonies, exerted an enormous influence over the music of the nation. Musical hegemony was achieved largely through *urban* music; whether art or popular, it was music created in cities and disseminated to the rest of the country. Folk and rural music might be played on the radio to emphasize mythical links of Britishness, but even these songs were chosen by an urban government or an urban-based broadcasting station. Several songs were written especially for the capital, such as Noël Coward's stirring "London Pride" or the haunting Maschwitz and Sherwin ballad "A Nightingale Sang in Berkeley Square."[10] London's symbolic capital remained unabated, its image as seat of power and defender of civilization only strengthened by its position as the center of the British music world. It was in cities such as London that one could sing while bombs rained outside. It is time now to turn to the musicians themselves. I will concentrate on two professional, London-based musicians who adapted their art to the circumstances of war and, in so doing, were looked upon as heroines.

The Musicians

In print, memory, and archival documents, one can find mention made of a wide variety of professional musicians: the American bandleader Glenn Miller, his English counterpart Geraldo, the Cockney entertainers Flanagan and Allen, the music hall performer Gracie Fields, and the concert violinist Yehudi Menuhin. Female vocalists crooning sentimental love songs were the rage; as George Wagner acerbically puts it, "Some females with cast-iron vocal chords made great reputations and a hell of a lot of money" (personal interview, 23 April 1993). In this musical barrage two people stand out, in part for their popularity as musicians and in part because they came to symbolize a spirit of musical defiance to Nazism. In their hands, music was a spiritual achievement and an ordinary human pleasure, the sort of thing that British people were fighting to preserve. Though both musicians toured during wartime, their home base remained London and their identities that of Londoners; they were the musical quintessence of wartime London. Vera Lynn's popular ballads were so much in demand by service personnel that she was dubbed the "Sweetheart of the Forces." The concert pianist Myra Hess organized and played in inexpensive lunchtime concerts at the National Gallery, in the center of blitz devastation. Though it is tempting to see Vera Lynn as representing working-class popular music and Myra Hess as representing middle-class art music, their positions were actually more complicated. Both came from the margins of British society, and both ended up symbolizing its center.

Vera Lynn

Vera Lynn was born in the working-class neighborhood of East Ham, in the East End of London. She was a child performer, and though only a teenager when the war began, she was already a seasoned professional. When war broke out, she had performed as a band singer, recording artist, and radio artist; she had even sung on the fledgling medium of television, which ceased broadcasting during the war. Her specialty was the sentimental ballad; among her signature tunes were "We'll Meet Again," "Yours," and "The White Cliffs of Dover." Lynn wrote in her autobiography: "For the most part I sang sentimental, wistful songs. They may have been the ones I was best at, but they were also the ones the troops asked for" (1975, 98). Spike Hughes analyzes Lynn's style as representing the essence of Cockneyism, a style that struck a chord not only with the troops but with the home front as well:

> During the war I have been living over a small factory in London; the girls in the workshop sing above the noise of the machines, and everything they sing (ranging from the "Volga Boat Song" to "We'll Meet Again") they sing as it might be sung by Miss Lynn. The effect is pure Cockney, for there is a Cockney way of singing which is as characteristic of our musical life as *bel canto* is characteristic of Italy.
> The most easily recognisable features of what we might call "Bow Bell Canto"[11] are frequent breaks in the voice and a whining intonation which is accentuated by the convention that turns all sentimental songs into songs of a broken heart, regardless of the subject-matter of the lyric.
> Miss Vera Lynn herself is a Cockney, born and bred. As a performer she has developed the natural characteristics of her native style of singing to a highly successful and commercial degree. Even when she sings a song like Jerome Kern's "Long Ago and Far Away," which is a song dealing with a new-found love, Miss Lynn convinces the listener that she has lost everything. The Cockney tradition dies hard, but while the tradition lasts, Miss Vera Lynn will remain an almost perfect example of the Local Girl Who Made Good. [1945, 79–80]

Hughes's rendition of the Cockney is not one of constant cheerfulness, but one that emphasizes sentimentality. Though gender may account for some of the differences between Hughes's analysis of Lynn's Cockneyism and more common presentations of cheerful, wisecracking Cockney men, the consistent thread is that of turning hardship into pleasure. Vera Lynn may not be cracking jokes while her heart breaks, but she is singing; misery may not be funny in her hands, but it is entertaining, even optimistic. "We'll Meet Again," one of her most famous songs, is actually a song of parting, but the lyrics emphasize the imagined pleasure of future reuniting. Lynn writes: "Ordinary English people don't, on the whole, find it easy to expose their feelings even to those closest to them. In November, 1939, and for a long while after, the unpretentious off-the-peg sentiments of 'We'll Meet Again' would go at least a little way towards doing it for them" (1975, 81). The combination of Lynn's optimistic lyrics and sentimental style is like the pleasure of a good cry. It is also the pleasure and happiness of wartime London, pleasure sharpened by its closeness to pain, happiness and normality turned noble because they exist in defiance to crisis.

Part of Vera Lynn's appeal lay in her own personality. Spike Hughes writes: "Miss Lynn's appeal to the male public has . . . a great deal [to do] with being a sister-substitute. The cultivation of sex-appeal is not part of her stock-in-trade; to a million servicemen stationed away from their families Vera Lynn is a kind of kid sister who reminds them of home. She has the same kind of voice, the same lack of sophistication, the same need for protection. She is a thoroughly Nice Girl and she sings the songs they like" (1945, 80). Women enjoyed Lynn's singing as well; as Angus Calder says, "She was the 'Forces' Sweetheart,' but their sweethearts liked her too" (1969, 363). Of course, there were many women in the forces, to whom Vera Lynn seemed like a trusted friend rather than a sweetheart. It was fortunate that the Forces' Sweetheart was someone whom men would like to kiss (chastely, as a good-night kiss) and women would like to pal around with.

Lynn was also cherished for her devotion to the simple, ordinary pleasures of life and her sincere belief in songs scorned by the elite but loved by the masses. In her autobiography, she quotes a "middle-aged listener," a veteran of World War I, who wrote to *Radio Times* in 1941 about the charms of the Forces' Sweetheart:

> The words of her songs may have been so much sentimental twaddle. But she treated them with as much tenderness as though they were precious old folk songs, as though they meant something, something that she believed in and assumed that her audience believed in too. . . . It may not have been great art. Who cares? I can only confess that if twenty-five years ago that young soldier of an earlier generation could have heard Vera Lynn singing to him—as if to him alone—simply and sincerely, all the silly, insincere songs about home and the little steeple pointing to a star and the brighter world over the hill, that old war would have been made so much less unhappy for him. [1975, 94]

Lynn praises this anonymous author's ability to pinpoint the essence of her singing. She presents herself as talented but trained only by experience, a musician who stands with the masses rather than apart from them, a singer who gives her audience the musical equivalent of sugar candy because she loves it too. She is the polar opposite of the austere art musician who provides culture to those who understand it; instead, Lynn is a kind of musical Girl Guide: "So, what did I have? A voice which gave the impression of being higher than it actually was. . . . arising from that a need to have most songs transposed down into unusual keys—which automatically gave them a 'different' sound; a very accurate sense of pitch, which apparently I'd been born with; clear diction, which might have been my way of compensating for what I knew to be a rather cockney speaking voice; and a genuine respect for simple, sentimental lyrics, which I could sing as if I believed in them because I *did* believe in them" (1975, 95–96).

Her warm, unpretentious style was matched by a desire for service; in wartime, entertaining the troops meant helping those who were helping her. Though Hughes sees her as needing protection, Lynn's decision to entertain troops abroad showed a very real courage; she chose to go to Burma, where entertainment was most needed, because it was a place that most entertainers (not to mention soldiers) preferred not to go. It was her own idea to visit servicemen's wives who were in the hospital having babies and then to broadcast these visits on her program "Sincerely Yours—Vera Lynn." The desired effect of this simple, homely touch can best be described by Lynn herself: "To be able to say to some poor boy serving out in Burma or North Africa, or somewhere at sea, that I'd actually been to see his wife and that I'd taken her some flowers and talked to her, was like getting hold of their hands and putting them together. . . . I quickly found out that while it was marvellous for the handful of lucky ones, it was also good and reassuring for those who didn't get chosen because they'd know that the contact was there, and that it worked" (1975, 98).

Lynn's autobiography, written in a witty and conversational style, discusses not only her career but also the simple, ordinary pleasures of her life, such as meeting her husband and earning enough money to move to a house with a bathroom. In America, such down-home appeal would probably be attributed to a small-town or country girl. In wartime Britain, however, Vera Lynn exemplified the touted virtues of the Londoner. Like the king, she remained in London except when duty took her abroad; she did not escape to America as she so easily could have. Yet unlike the king, she was portrayed as an ordinary person keeping the home fires burning, an ordinary wartime Londoner, a cheerful Cockney par excellence. Her autobiography eschews politics but brims with patriotism and avows her loyalty to the institution of the monarchy. She was ignorant of the political ramifications of "Sincerely Yours—Vera Lynn" during the war but acknowledges it later as another way that her singing could help her compatriots:

> Although I didn't hear about it at the time, the programme did have some slight warlike intentions, in that the War Office had expressed

concern at the pernicious influence that "Lili Marlene," a German female voice using Lale Andersen's recording of the song "Lili Marlene" as
a signature tune, was having on the British troops, who used to tune in
to her. Apparently she used to imply that the wives of British serving
men were up to all sorts of things in return for black market butter and
meat while their men were away at the front. What was needed was our
own radio antidote to it. [1975, 97]

The solution was to counter the "sexy, seductive voice" of Lale Andersen by "using me in the rôle of a believable girl-next-door, big-sister, universal-fiancée" (97).

Vera Lynn, portrayed as an ordinary Londoner who carried on with cheerfulness and courage, became a symbol of wartime spirit, an icon of patriotism, a wartime Londoner writ large. Her absolute devotion to British society and her
symbolizing of its mainstream is especially interesting in light of her marginalization
by this society. Her songs were scorned and derided by many, popular taste and
popular music treated with condescension at best, contempt at worst. Personally,
Vera Lynn was a young, working-class woman, an East Ender and a popular singer,
married to another East End pop musician who also happened to be a Jew. Yet
nowhere in her writing is there any indication that she *feels* marginalized; to the
contrary, she presents herself as absolutely representative, for that is what ordinary
means. In wartime, the margins became the mainstream: the cheerful Cockneys
symbolized the true repositories of British spirit, the essence of the folk, the salt of
the earth. Far from showing any resentment toward a society in which working
people cannot afford bathrooms, she is proof that *democracy works.* Lynn's rise from
her bathroomless house in East Ham to the heights of international stardom and
finally, decades after the end of the war, being made a Dame Commander of the
British Empire showed that the myth of social mobility had come of age in Britain.
Possibly it was another American import, along with Spam and nylon stockings.

Reactions to Vera Lynn's singing varied. A number of my interviewees said
that they preferred the more robust style of the richer-voiced Anne Shelton. Tastes
were moving in that direction even during the war. A readers' poll from *Melody
Maker* of 16 March 1940 shows a list of favorite women vocalists, with Vera Lynn
as number one and Anne Shelton not mentioned. A similar poll of 13 May 1944
shows Anne Shelton as number one and Vera Lynn not even among the top four
(Huggett 1979, 184). Vere Hodgson wrote on 22 July 1944: "I find Vera Lynn
soon palls. It is more like moaning than singing." Nearly fifty years later, Creina
Musson said, "Then of course, there was Vera Lynn, the Forces' Sweetheart. I never
met any of the forces that liked her. . . . But she became a sort of institution and
she's still alive, she's still singing. The one they all liked was somebody called Anne
Shelton" (personal interview, 28 July 1993). I.E.W. had similar tastes but in retrospect could understand the charms of the Forces' Sweetheart: "I wasn't terribly

keen on Vera Lynn. . . . I liked Anne Shelton, I thought she was much better. But, of course, since the war I have now realized the appeal of Vera Lynn. She had a certain poignancy in the way she put over a song and the songs which she sang. It must have been, for people who were in love and away from each other, it must have been very poignant" (personal interview, 7 May 1993). Jack and Poppy Morris, on the other hand, liked both singers. In response to my question, they discuss the attractions of a singer who, like Jack, came from the East End of London:

JF: Did you like Vera Lynn?
PM: Yes! I did quite.
JM: Genuine sob in her voice.
PM: And her diction was perfect. I mean, she hadn't been trained, not
    a proper trained singer but her diction was—
JM: A Cockney from the East End of London, you know.
PM: You could hear every word she was saying. She had an appeal, this
    woman, you see. [personal interview, 1 July 1993]

Others mentioned Vera Lynn with little evaluative comment, simply as a popular singer of the day, part of the musical landscape. Today, Vera Lynn's style sounds hopelessly dated, for sentimentality is no longer in vogue. Yet she perfectly exemplified the musical fashion of her time. Her voice is pleasant, her musicianship excellent, and her renditions of sentimental songs refreshingly free of affectation (though the same cannot always be said of the instrumental accompaniment to her singing). Unlike working-class singers who sang music hall songs for the entertainment of the working classes, Vera Lynn sang for all British people in defense of a British way of life. As the war was supposed to do, Vera Lynn broke through class barriers; she brought mass culture to people of all walks of life. In so doing, she upheld British society as a model of democracy and declared that people like herself would see to it that there would always be an England.

Myra Hess

> Glad memories come, of old, long-distant days
> When I, with many hundreds, saw and heard,
> And joined with many hundreds in her praise,
> Glad memories, all, with no remembered word,
> But with the sense that she who played perceived
> The world undying, that composers know
> At moments, as reward for years of woe,
> She touched the deathless world and we believed.
> —John Masefield, "Remembering Dame Myra Hess"

No wartime musician is remembered with more respect or reverence than Myra Hess. Even those who never went to a chamber music concert (and would have been utterly bored had they done so) spoke of her with pride. Hess was born in 1890 to a middle-class Jewish household in London. She made her professional debut in 1907 and was a well-known concert pianist by the time World War II began. Unlike Vera Lynn, she never had to defend the music she played. Art music was inherently respectable, though a woman artist performing it was not. In the late-Victorian era into which Hess was born, a woman appearing on stage was unusual and somewhat shocking. Yet there was never anything shocking about Myra Hess. Wartime and postwar material present her as a kind of chaste goddess of music, a Diana of the keyboard. Descriptive material from a film made about her life puts it well:

> Music has been her life-long passion. She was taught to play the piano as a small child, in the same way as other children of her acquaintance were taught, but her parents had no intention of making her a professional musician. Indeed, when the girl told them of her ambition they were astonished and dismayed. It was not unusual for women to become music teachers, instructing pupils privately or as members of the staff of a girls' school; but it was a very different thing for a woman to earn her living as an instrumentalist on the concert platform. . . . But music so filled her whole horizon that Myra Hess was quite determined she would devote her life to nothing else. [INF 6/29]

Vera Lynn's personality was an inherent part of her appeal, but Myra Hess's personality is virtually absent; she is treated as a kind of conduit for the music itself. Whereas Lynn sang of earthly delights that everyone knows, Hess presented spiritual joys that are beyond one's knowing: "Some famous instrumentalists have permitted their own personality and mannerisms to become too obtrusive; but there is nothing flamboyant or self-assertive about the playing of Myra Hess. An utterly truthful rendering of the music is her dominating desire on the platform. In her playing of tranquil legato passages there is a spiritual beauty which remains a memorable experience to all who have had the rich delight of listening to this great woman artist" (INF 6/29). The emotional and unrestrained playing of "some famous instrumentalists" (particularly Jewish instrumentalists) might be better received on the Continent than in Britain. Hess, on the other hand, was a Jewish musician who behaved like an English lady.

If Myra Hess had simply been a dedicated and talented pianist, she probably would not be remembered as a wartime heroine. What changed her status was her decision to hold a series of lunchtime concerts at the National Gallery. Her idea was to provide music (with an emphasis on chamber music) at a time convenient for war workers, in a central location, and for a nominal price. The first concert was held on 10 October 1939, with an entrance fee of one shilling. More than one thousand people attended this concert, and so many people had to be turned away that the concert was repeated later that afternoon. Like the CEMA concerts in factories and shelters, the National Gallery concerts provided music to a new audience in a wholly new way, and a wartime institution was born.

Hess played at the first concert and at many others; even when she was not the featured performer, the National Gallery concerts were her brainchild. The most popular composers proved to be Mozart, Beethoven, and Bach, but British composers were prominently featured as well. The director of the National Gallery said:

> Myra Hess has not allowed the highest standards to be relaxed—never in her own playing, and never, so far as is humanly possible, in the choice of artists who play here. To maintain this sense of quality, this feeling that these are standards which must survive all disasters, is the supreme function of the arts in war-time. Those of us who are connected with the Gallery can never be sufficiently grateful for the fact that, through the art of music, it has been able to fulfil in war essentially the same purpose which it fulfilled in peace—that of maintaining through beauty our faith in the greatness of the human spirit. [quoted in Myers 1948, 116–17]

To these comments, Rollo Myers added his own thoughts: "Without that faith it is difficult to see how the country could have survived" (117). Hess is presented here as one who held aloft the torch of civilization against the forces of barbarism. Her courage and that of her fellow musicians was demonstrated by the fact that even when the National Gallery was bombed, the concert series continued.

No work on wartime music would be complete without a prominent reference to Myra Hess. *Listen to Britain,* the Ministry of Information film about wartime music, had "National Gallery" as one of its working titles; perhaps it planned to concentrate on the National Gallery concerts or to use the concert series as a symbol of wartime music in general. The film shows a clip of Hess and the RAF Orchestra playing Mozart's piano concerto in G. Even in this brief clip, the power of Hess's artistry is apparent, and the audience—from the queen to the workers with their sandwiches—is spellbound. Hess's concentration is so complete that one understands the transcendence attributed to her. She is simply dressed in black, her hair pulled back in a bun, her hands strong and in control, her face suffused with passion. For some forces personnel serving abroad, *Listen to Britain* was a glimpse of home. G. Maurice Turner, serving with the RAF in Southern Rhodesia, wrote a letter of appreciation for *Listen to Britain* in which he said: "Particularly did I enjoy Myra Hess and the R.A.F. orchestra playing (in part) a Mozart Piano Concerto. It was really a first class effort. I am sure such a film is a source of joy to we [*sic*] fellows who have been away for two years" (INF 6/339).

The symbolism of Myra Hess remaining in London and providing spiritual beauty, undeterred by bombs, was an important part of her appeal. Yet an equally important part was the democratizing nature of the National Gallery concerts themselves. In a people's war, she brought to all classes music usually reserved for the elite. Again, to quote descriptive material from the film about her life: "Dame Myra Hess has a deep sense of her responsibility to the public. She believes it to be the paramount task of an artist to maintain and present those 'permanent values without which' as she has said 'a country must suffer spiritual disintegration and decay. This is a vital function at any time,' she declared, 'and war increased rather than diminished its importance.' It is with whole-hearted devotion that she served her country during the war by her timeless work in 'maintaining through beauty our faith in the greatness of the human spirit'" (INF 6/29). This dedication was rewarded in 1941, when she was made Dame Commander of the British Empire.

Folk memory has preserved the fact that Myra Hess was Jewish, but one would be hard-pressed to find this information in any of the promotional material written during or soon after the war. Her Jewishness was considered either unimportant or unfortunate. Instead, she was presented as the repository of "permanent values," an example of "the greatness of the human spirit" that surpasses ethnicity or religion. Thirty years later, such specificity was acceptable; Marian C. McKenna's 1976 biography of Myra Hess mentions her Jewish heritage in the first paragraph. McKenna's descriptions of Hess's family and early life are filled with a romantic exoticism, of which the following passage is fairly representative: "Myra was always proud of her Jewish ancestry. . . . As Sir Neville Cardus once observed, music is not a language the English speak from the heart, as the Slavs and Italians do; and this may have influenced Myra in looking more to her German and Jewish origins as a source of that intellectual and spiritual stimulus which is the nourishment of all art. Some of her Christian friends, only half in jest, expressed the wish that they could also claim some Jewish blood; perhaps then they, too, would be more musical" (1976, 2).

Despite the anti-Semitism endemic in wartime Britain, public reactions to Hess were wholeheartedly approving. Postwar memory also retains this reverent image of her. Jack Morris, though he was "more interested in girls than music at the time," attended one of Hess's concerts at the National Gallery (personal interview, 1 July 1993). In his comments, we can see the popular image and propagandistic intentions of the National Gallery concerts, as well as the way that Hess's name is inextricably linked with them: "This Myra Hess thing started in the Blitz to keep the morale of the people up because they played right throughout all the banging and the bombs. . . . Myra Hess and Harry Cohen were responsible for a wider audience getting interested" (personal interview, 1 July 1993). Before the war, classical music was for "eggheads," certainly not for everyone. But the National Gallery concerts were different. Jack Morris explains: "They were cheap at lunchtime. . . . People came in off the streets. And it was, it was right in the center of London,

Trafalgar Square is virtually the center; well, center of the West End anyhow. And they popularized it, and people could meet friends and chat in comparative safety" (personal interview, 1 July 1993).

J.D. worked in a central London office during the war. Though she was generally more interested in other things, she also went to a few Myra Hess concerts. As a working-class teenager, she was part of the new audience targeted by the National Gallery enterprise. Like Jack Morris, she mentions convenience, location, and price as factors that made this concertgoing possible and attractive:

> I wasn't that crazy about serious music at the time, but you know, it was there so I thought well, I might as well go. . . . They were in the National Gallery. . . . and they used to get Dame Myra Hess to give piano recitals. And they were always packed out with servicemen and everything. I think it was pretty cheap too. . . . And it was lunchtime and, of course, I only had an hour for lunch. And being about seventeen, you know, you don't want to spend your lunch hour listening to classical music. You'd rather eat, but I did go to a couple of those. [personal interview, 26 April 1993]

Even people who never went to the National Gallery concerts spoke of them with pride, as a part of the wartime improvement of many aspects of life. Anne Lubin did not attend any National Gallery concerts but mentioned them as part of "a revival of what you might call the good things of life" (personal interview, 13 March 1993).

Creina Musson, a physical education teacher, knew a friend of Myra Hess. As such, she was the only person I knew who spoke about Hess as a person rather than some disembodied spirit of music: "She was a real comic, Myra Hess, and they used to have great fun. . . . Myra Hess used to lie on top of the piano and play down like that and lie on the floor and play" (personal interview, 28 July 1993). This description is quite a contrast to Hess's austere public image, but McKenna concurs, providing a more bohemian picture than one could glean from the famous photographs of a plump, middle-aged woman seated at a Steinway. McKenna writes: "Her youthful determination to make her own way, her defiance of taboos like smoking in public, and her subsequent zest for Rabelaisian stories and vulgar jokes may be viewed as varied forms of rebellion against hypocrisy and the stultifying atmosphere characteristic of Victorian parlours" (1976, 13). Creina Musson's comments on Hess's public image are quite different. Creina went to several of the National Gallery concerts and remembers them with great affection. She says: "A very great pianist in England who had stayed, she actually had a contract to go to America when war broke out. She was an English Jewess, Myra Hess. . . . She was so popular, Myra Hess. So loved by everybody" (personal interview, 28 July 1993).

Not everyone whom I interviewed spoke about the National Gallery concerts; the audience for art music, as the BBC polls discovered, grew substantially during the war but remained a minority. Myra Hess was responsible for helping to increase this minority and she is remembered as a symbol of civilization at a time when barbarism threatened. At the same time, "Her mission is not only to interpret the work of great composers to those who can appreciate it, but also to enable more and more people to make contact with beauty by learning to love the finest in music" (INF 6/29). Little is remembered about Myra Hess the person beyond the fact of her ethnic marginality; instead, it is Myra Hess the symbol that has endured. Born in a century when Jews and women experienced unprecedented emancipation, she ended up symbolizing the greatness of the British spirit and bearing a title of the British empire. Like Vera Lynn, Hess represented both the progress of democracy and the fact that democracy grew firmly in British soil. The left could celebrate the breakdown of barriers, the right be reassured that society had changed little by letting a few more members into the club. And delicious ironies remain about these two musical heroines of wartime who had mildly transformed the mainstream by becoming part of it. In a patriarchal society at war, these two musical symbols were women: one a working-class teenager crooning despised sentimental ballads, the other a middle-aged Jew who bore the same surname as Hitler's second-in-command and played world-class renditions of Mozart and Beethoven.

The Music

Choosing a few pieces of music out of wartime London's musical array was not an easy task. I have chosen to look at three songs and one piece of art music that were especially common in memories and in wartime material. All of these pieces of music suffered interesting permutations during the war. Two of the songs I have chosen, "The White Cliffs of Dover" and "We're Going to Hang Out the Washing on the Siegfried Line," were English songs designed to inspire and cheer the British population. "Lili Marlene" was a German song that proved so popular with Allied (and Italian) troops that it was subject to constant transformation. And Beethoven's Fifth Symphony, a citizen of the world, provided one of the most interesting musical symbols of the war. Many other songs could be added to my list—the national anthem "God Save the King" or the Cockney classic "Knees Up, Mother Brown," to name a few—but I hope this small but varied sample will provide some indication of the roles of wartime music.

"The White Cliffs of Dover"

Popular songs are among the surest ways to inspire wartime memory. Shirley, one of my interviewees, provided a long list of popular songs that she remembered from the war years and commented, "If you hear them again ever, they remind you of the war" (personal communication, 23 January 1993). Frank E. Huggett, in his book about songs and memories of World War II, writes: "The popular songs of the Second World War are one of the most neglected aspects of its history, yet for millions of ordinary men and women living at the time they were of supreme importance in sustaining morale, in helping to identify and to express feelings, and in providing much-needed relaxation and entertainment. Their impact was so great that even now there is almost nothing else which can recapture so precisely the atmosphere of wartime and all its changing moods" (1979, 7). One of the most famous of these popular songs was "The White Cliffs of Dover," a sentimental ballad par excellence. It was a song of hope and love for Britain, despite the fact that it was actually written by two Americans. It was a Vera Lynn favorite and, like her, a child of its time. Anne Lubin liked "The White Cliffs of Dover" but did not consider it of lasting value: "Oh, it was sickly sentimental, but it was appropriate for its time. . . . And most popular songs are not really lasting, are they? They're just musical ephemera" (personal interview, 13 March 1993).

If "The White Cliffs of Dover" was an ephemeral song, it emphasized the temporary nature of wartime. Unlike other wartime ballads that virtually ignored the subject of war, "The White Cliffs of Dover" focuses on the idea that present hardships will yield to future delights. Though war is not actually mentioned, the song's intent is unmistakable:

> There'll be blue birds over the white cliffs of Dover,
> Tomorrow, just you wait and see,
> There'll be love and laughter and peace ever after,
> Tomorrow, when the world is free. [quoted in Stephens 1987, 91]

It is a song oriented toward the future, toward a "tomorrow, when the world is free," when blue birds will fly peacefully around the white cliffs. Possibly, the blue birds represent happiness, or, as Brian Murdoch suggests, they are "the peace symbol coupled with the national symbol" (1990, 187). In wartime, they signified a Britain that did not actually exist, a Britain that was yet to be. The images of this peaceful, perfect Britain are a revitalization of its rural past:

> The shepherd will tend his sheep,
> The valley will bloom again,
> And Jimmy will go to sleep
> In his own little room again. [quoted in Stephens 1987, 91]

Again, the obliqueness of the references to war does not mask the meaning; such intent would have been particularly clear to wartime audiences. Present listeners might be puzzled, but wartime audiences would have known instantly that Jimmy was not sleeping in his own room because he was in an air-raid shelter. The images invoked are unashamedly pastoral despite the fact that rural Britain suffered relatively little in comparison with the cities, particularly London. In places with shepherds and flowery valleys, Jimmy was probably sleeping in his own room anyway. It was in London and environs that this principle of hope was most needed, and the fantasy of sheep-covered hills and blooming valleys could be part of a fantasy of a peaceful and better world, a tomorrow filled with "love and laughter." Wartime propaganda discussed the future in stirring speeches and detailed outlines of social programs; sentimental ballads could describe the future with dreamy images and soothing melodies.

W. Ray Stephens, author of *Memories and Melodies of World War II*, tells an oddly sentimental near-miss narrative that he links to "The White Cliffs of Dover": "During the Battle of Britain days, while I was stationed in Godstone, south of London, directly under the flight path of the air raids, we had quite a number of bombs fall all around us and even in town. One morning we went to look at the latest hit near a large estate home. The Anderson shelter had received a direct hit and all that remained was a gaping hole. For some unknown reason, the family and two boys had decided to sleep in the house that night—so Jimmy would have his own bed back" (1987, 90). None of my interviewees claimed such a dramatic association with this song, yet when asked about wartime music, virtually everyone mentioned it whether they personally liked it or not. Fred Mitchell, a teenager during the war, invented new words to the song with his friends, but he refused to repeat such scurrilous lyrics fifty years later (personal interview, 18 May 1993). Moira called it "a bit sentimental but, you know, it's the sort of thing that people liked" (personal interview, 16 January 1993). Shirley explains its appeal: "It was all about tomorrow. 'Tomorrow when the world is free' was one of the lines from it. I suppose I felt, presumably, that" (personal interview, 22 January 1993). Irene Wagner was unimpressed with the song's sentimental charms but found it an indelible part of the wartime landscape: "It was so patriotic, it was so soppy— oh, I dislike it intensely. But yes, that is what reminds me of the war" (personal interview, 4 March 1993).

Like day nurseries, Spam, and women working, "The White Cliffs of Dover" was a part of wartime London, a part loved by some and despised by others. The song spoke of a time when Britain would be a better place but linked this improvement to the mythical joys of rural England. It was sweet and unpretentious, hopeful and sad, for it spoke of joy only in an imagined future. Like "It's a Lovely Day Tomorrow" and "We'll Meet Again," it gave comforting and soothing reassurance, promising that everything would be all right if people would only be patient, if they would only "wait and see." How long this waiting might last, the song did not venture to say.

"Lili Marlene"

It was "Lili Marleen" in the original German; in English, it was usually rendered "Lili Marlene." It was that rarest of entities: a popular song that gained critical acclaim. Yet it was more than a song; it was a wartime phenomenon. To discuss it simply as an evocative wartime ballad, a German equivalent to "A Nightingale Sang in Berkeley Square," is to miss an important part of its history. "Lili Marlene" leapt national and linguistic boundaries with ease, gathering new lyrics and new associations as it did so. It belonged to the Germans, the Italians, the English, the Canadians, and to many more besides; an English film made about it even referred to it as a "trophy of war" (INF 6/360). "Lili Marlene" was primarily a soldier's song, fantastically popular with the troops but less so with the home front. Yet many on the home front were familiar with the song, and the BBC played it on the radio in a variety of languages. It is especially interesting for our discussion because of its constant metamorphoses; it contributed to musical hegemony in many different ways and for diametrically opposed causes.

"Lili Marleen" was originally a poem. Hans Leip, a young soldier during World War I, was in love with two women who were merged into one in his poem. His Lili Marleen stands with him by the lantern outside his barracks, where all can see that the two are in love. Yet as a soldier, he is called away from his love and sent to battle. He wonders who will stand with Lili Marleen if he is killed, and in the final stanza he glimpses her through the mists surrounding his grave. Leip wrote the poem in 1915, perhaps feeling a premonition that he would soon die. (He didn't; he died in 1983 at the age of ninety.) The poem was published after the war in a collection called *Die Kleine Hafenorgel* (*The Little Barrel-organ*). There is some debate about the publication date of the collection, and a Ministry of Information film, made in 1943 and 1944, puts the date at 1930. However, in light of "Lili Marleen's" enormous popularity, the film tried to stress the song's links with democracy and antifascism, such as noting that Hamburg, the town where it was written, was "the last German stronghold to fall before Hitler's attack" (INF 6/360). In light of these claims to democracy, it might have been embarrassing to mention that the song was published with Nazi approval, though most sources list the publication date as 1937. Leip wrote a tune to go with it, but his tune never really caught on; the melody that sent it around the world was written by Norbert Schultze. Leip was very likely neither a Nazi nor a Nazi sympathizer, but there is no way to make a good guy out of Schultze, an employee of Goebbels's Propaganda Ministry and the author of such ditties as "Bombs over England." Lale Andersen's recording of the song, made shortly before World War II, used the Schultze melody, and this was the recording that swept Europe and North Africa.

Many legends have sprung up about this famous recording, particularly in battles with the Afrika Korps, where it was played by German-controlled Radio Belgrade each night at 9:57 P.M. Martin Page writes of these legends: "There were stories of the British and the Germans moving into battle against one another, both singing *Lili Marlene*. There was a German rumour that at El Alamein, the 51st

Highland Division launched an attack in the hope of capturing a copy of the record. Later, it was claimed that both sides would sometimes cease firing a little before ten o'clock at night, and resume shortly afterwards, so that they could hear it on the radio" (1973, 86). "Lili Marlene" was indeed a trophy of war, a tool of morale that each side fought to claim. A soldier, writing to Page about an experience in Italy, tells of a time when the song turned its back on its German forebears and acted as an Allied decoy to lure German troops:

> A small party of German soldiers had been drinking in some little café on their side of the line and when they had had enough and decided to go, they linked arms and lurched off along the road in what they believed to be the direction of their billet. . . .
>
> It seemed a terrible long way, but after several rests, they heard the strains of *Lili Marlene* coming from a building by the side of the road. They burst in, convinced that they were among friends at last, only to find that they were in our regimental cookhouse, where our cooks were having a bit of a party. They were duly put in the bag. [86–87]

Whether these stories were true or not, the popularity of "Lili Marlene" cannot be denied, as the many variations on its lyrics attest. An unusually faithful translation occurs in a Canadian version, which played on the BBC on 12 September 1943 (NSA ref. nos. 7624 and T7599b7). The singer is a Canadian soldier in Sicily, his old-fashioned tenor accompanied only by violin and whistling. Other versions preferred not to dwell on the dead soldier and the sweetheart who finds someone else when he is gone. Several versions of "Lili Marlene" stress the theme of the loyal couple waiting patiently for the day when they would be together again. Oswald Edwards, a private in the Second Army, arranged a version for two voices and piano. The English words he used were attributed to an "Unknown 'Tommy'" and begin:

> Outside the barracks by the corner light,
> I'll always wait and wait for you at night,
> We will create a world for two, I'd wait for you the whole night
>   through—
> For you—Lily Marlene, for you—Lily Marlene. [Oswald Edwards
>   Papers]

Brian Murdoch reports that Lale Andersen recorded this English version after the war (1990, 251). These lyrics bear a very strong resemblance to an Italian version of the song; according to Murdoch, the English words were in fact based on the Italian ones (178). The Italian version is far more romantic and hopeful than the stark, ultimately pessimistic words of Leip's poem. In the Italian version, Lili Marlene's face and smile sustain the soldier as he marches through the dirt, and the final stanza is the polar opposite of the dead soldier gazing at his beloved through the mist:

> Present me with a rose to keep against my heart
> Bind it with a thread of your golden hair.
> Perhaps you will cry tomorrow
> But afterwards you will smile
> With me, Lili Marlene, with me, Lili Marlene.

A further contrast can be seen in an Italian presentation of the song, which played on the BBC on 12 September 1943 (NSA ref. nos. 7624 and T7599b8). As opposed to the simplicity in Lale Andersen's German version and the pleasant amateurishness of the Canadian soldier, the Italian version is professional and cheerful. A tenor soloist sings, in bel canto style, to the accompaniment of the municipal orchestra of Ionia, Sicily. The accompaniment is light and playful, with a strong downbeat and a variety of instrumental trills, and one can hardly doubt that Lili will be reunited with her lover.

Allied soldiers wrote many English lyrics to the tune of "Lili Marlene." One version reported by Page expresses an English soldier's fear that his place back home will be taken by an American. A common theme in soldiers' songs, "My Faithless English Rose" is just as pessimistic and far more savage than the original "Lili Marlene":

> I've just returned to England from somewhere overseas,
> Instead of love and kisses, the girls gave me the breeze;
> Said they preferred the Yanks and gum,
> A little jeep, a country run,
> My good-time English sweetheart,
> My faithless English Rose. [quoted in Page 1973, 121]

An Australian version, entitled "The Dive Bombers' Song," declares that Lili Marlene will not be reunited with her lover because as a German soldier, he will not survive the Allied attack:

> Get the right deflection,
> Check reflector sight,
> Give your speed correction,
> And see your range is right.
> Then you can press the tit, old son,
> And blow the Hun to kingdom come,
> Poor Marlene's boy-friend will
> Never see Marlene. [quoted in Page 1973, 87]

The popularity of "Lili Marlene" caused a certain amount of anxiety in Whitehall, both because the song was a German product used to cheer German troops and because it emphasized the themes of parting and being replaced by someone else. An official English version was commissioned, and the popular songwriter Tommie Connor provided a version that stressed faithfulness and re-uniting as surely as did "We'll Meet Again." Murdoch says, "Hans Leip's original is sentimentalized into the common theme of the sweetheart who will still be waiting" (1990, 178). Anne Shelton and Vera Lynn recorded the Connor version in England, as did Marlene Dietrich in the United States.[12] In the final stanza of Leip's poem, Lili's mouth appears to the dead soldier through ghostly mists; in the Connor version, Lili's mouth waits for him and sustains him as he "rests" in his billet. Whereas Leip's soldier haunted his sweetheart, Connor's soldier is haunted only in dreams:

> Resting in a billet just behind the line,
> Even though we're parted, your lips are close to mine,
> You wait where that lantern softly gleams,
> Your sweet face seems to haunt my dreams,
> My Lili of the lamplight,
> My own Lili Marlene. [quoted in Boni 1947, 203]

As noted, Vera Lynn described the War Office justification for her program *Sincerely Yours—Vera Lynn* as an English counteroffensive to "Lili Marlene": "The War Office had expressed concern at the pernicious influence that 'Lili Marlene,' a German female voice using Lale Andersen's recording of the song 'Lili Marlene' as a signature tune, was having on the British troops, who used to tune in to her" (1975, 97). Here, "Lili Marlene" is not merely a song but the personification of the seductive German female.[13] Whereas Vera Lynn may have provided an anti-dote to "Lili Marlene," it was clear that no mere antidote would do; the song was so popular that it had to be captured and rendered a spoil of war. A Ministry of Information film entitled *The True Story of Lilli Marlene* was made in 1943 and 1944. It speaks of "Lili Marlene" as a trophy "captured in the Libyan Desert in the Autumn of 1942" (INF 6/360). It then gives a cinematic history of the song, describing Lale Andersen as "a little Swedish girl."[14] The film supplies yet another set of English lyrics for the song, and the blond woman representing Lale Andersen sings:

> In the dark of evening,
> Where you stand and wait,
> Hangs a lantern gleaming
> By the barrack gate.
> We'll meet again by lantern shine,
> As we did once upon a time,
> We two, Lili Marlene,
> We two, Lili Marlene. [INF 6/360]

In translation, the themes of faithfulness and reuniting are emphasized, though the original Lale Andersen version stressed the opposite.

In the film, the capturing of the song and its rehabilitation from a bit of Nazi propaganda to an English trophy is correlated with Allied victories in North Africa. Rommel's elite Afrika Korps was a fearsome enemy, and "Lili Marleen" was its favorite song. As German victories in North Africa fed German optimism, the invasion of the Soviet Union began, and "Lili Marleen" continued to keep company with German troops. The film discusses a Lale Andersen Winter Relief Fund and shows Emmi Goering (a poor man's Wagnerian soprano) singing "Lili Marleen" at the Berlin State Opera House. Lale Andersen is depicted, wearing a long white gown and holding a swastika flag, singing in English to a nightclub full of German soldiers. The film's German announcer says: "The popularity of Lili Marlene spread with the victories of the glorious wehrmacht [*sic*]. Only last week, the 150th Lala Anderson [*sic*] Cafe Bar was opened in Germany, and a statue of Lili Marlene was erected on the Smolensk Road" (INF 6/360).

Victories in North Africa marked the turning of the tide for the Allies, a point that was obvious when the film was made in 1943 and 1944. Defeat of the Afrika Korps at El Alamein and Algiers were crucial first steps to Allied victory, and "Lili Marlene" became one of the spoils of victory in North Africa. Denis Johnston reports in the film: "So the Eighth Army swept on to El Agheila, capturing on its way 800 miles of desert, 75,000 prisoners, 5,000 tanks, 1,000 guns, and the famous enemy's song of Lili Marlene" (INF 6/360). In the film, Lale Andersen is rehabilitated in Allied eyes by the ancient principle of "The enemy of my enemy is my friend." She is shown as an inmate of a concentration camp, trying to send messages to her native Sweden, and saying, "All I want is to get out of this terrible country."

After the victory at Stalingrad, "Lili Marlene" was turned on its head: "Now it was our chance; now it was the B.B.C.'s turn to send a message from Lala Anderson [*sic*] to the German troops, to send the tune back to Germany—the same tune, but with different words, and a different singer—Lucie Mannheim" (INF 6/360). Lucie Mannheim's voice is less well-suited to cabaret singing than Lale Andersen's, but it has greater depth and passion. The lyrics to Mannheim's version are extraordinary; they are told not from the point of view of the soldier (as in all other versions), but from that of Lili Marlene herself, who is heartbroken when her lover dies. In the final stanza, she suggests another use for the lantern where the two used to meet. Lucie Mannheim is shown singing in a recording studio, and she sings the final lines with such force that a technician in the booth looks up in surprise:

Fuehrer, I thank and greet you,
For you are good and wise,
Widows and orphans meet you
With hollow, silent eyes.

Hitler, the man of blood and fear,
Hang him up from the lantern here,
Hang him up from the lantern
Of your Lili Marlene. [INF 6/360]

The final version in the film is one purportedly written by the Eighth Army. Once again, the commentary presents the song as a trophy of war: "Lili Marlene was born in the docks in Hamburg, and then she went to Berlin, and then through to Belgrade. She was sent to the desert and was captured, and then she was transformed and marched with the armies of liberation into the heart of Europe" (INF 6/360). Lili Marlene appears here as a rehabilitated camp follower, escaping her German creators and taking her place with the victorious Allies. The Eighth Army version proclaims:

Afrika Corps is vanished
From the earth,
Smashed soon will be
The swine that gave it birth
No more to hear that lilting refrain
Each night again, that soft refrain,
With you Lili Marlene,
With you Lili Marlene. [INF 6/360]

In 1944 another set of satirical lyrics to the tune of "Lili Marlene" appeared. This version was in response to a remark attributed to Nancy, Lady Astor, who supposedly referred to the troops fighting in Italy as "D-Day Dodgers." (Lady Astor hotly denied that she said anything of the kind.) This savage reply to her purported comment ends with:

Look around the hillsides, through the mist and rain,
See the scattered crosses, some that bear no name.
Heartbreak and toil and suffering gone,
The lads beneath, they slumber on,
They are the D-Day Dodgers who'll stay in Italy. [quoted in Page
    1973, 162]

Though "Lili Marlene" was certainly part of the musical landscape of wartime London, as the various BBC broadcasts attest, few of my informants spoke of it when asked about musical memories. Perhaps this is because "Lili Marlene" was, first and foremost, a soldier's song, and the people whom I interviewed were in large measure civilians. "Lili Marlene" was also a rarity among World War II songs in that it actually spoke of the hardships of war. Most wartime songs stressed a future time of peace and happiness, while "Lili Marlene" spoke of the uncertain present. Even in its most sentimentalized versions, it was still the song of a soldier parted from his lover by war. It was given a privileged place in the BBC Radio Two broadcast on Valentine's Day 1993, and it is prominently mentioned in every published source on wartime music, yet its importance seems to have been greater on the battlefield than on the home front. It calls forth memories more bitter and stark than those evoked by "In the Mood" or "The White Cliffs of Dover." If home front music was largely escapism, then we can understand the secondary place given to "Lili Marlene"; how much better to think of "We'll Meet Again" than of the soldier dying on the Continent or the woman waiting by herself in the lonely street.

"We're Going to Hang Out the Washing on the Siegfried Line"

"We're Going to Hang Out the Washing on the Siegfried Line" was a popular song, but unlike "Lili Marlene," no one claimed it had artistic merit. A cheerfully bombastic song with a catchy tune, it showed the British love for puns in its comparison of the German fortifications along the French border (the Siegfried Line) with a clothesline. Written in 1939, it showed an optimism that can only be attributed to ignorance of German military strength. W. Ray Stephens writes, "This was another early attempt at patriotic bravado during the first few months of the war, when neither the songwriters nor the military knew what was really going on" (1987, 14). Its suggestion that winning the war will be as easy as washing clothes seems reckless and callous in retrospect:

> Whether the weather may be wet or fine,
> We'll just rub along without a care,
> We're gonna hang out the washing on the Siegfried Line
> If the Siegfried Line's still there. [quoted in Stephens 1987, 15]

Stephens calls it "an unfunny piece" that fell "flat on [its] cadences when it was quickly realized that . . . the German Siegfried Line had closed for the laundry business" (7).

Despite a general agreement that "We're Going to Hang Out the Washing on the Siegfried Line" was not a great song, it is one of the most widely remembered songs of the war. My interviewees mentioned it far more often than more critically acclaimed songs such as "London Pride" or "A Nightingale Sang in Berkeley Square." Their judgment of the song, however, was not generally favorable. Fred Mitchell, when asked about songs of the war, mentioned "The Siegfried Line" and then added, "And all that rubbish" (personal interview, 18 May 1993). S.H. and his wife had a disagreement about the popularity of "The Siegfried Line." When she mentioned the song, he said, "We didn't go around singing that rubbish!" (personal interview, 22 March 1993). She insisted that people did indeed sing the tune and later mentioned dancing to it (personal interview, 22 March 1993).

Harold Melville Lowry, who was a soldier during the last few years of the war, gave a soldier's response to wartime songs, in particular "The Siegfried Line": "There were some very bombastic ones in the very early stages of the war about 'We're Going to Hang Out the Washing on the Siegfried Line,' where, as I'm afraid we tend to do, we very much underestimated our enemy. But these are the sort of attitudes which are commoner amongst civilians than they are amongst soldiers. I think soldiers quickly get a respect for their enemy" (personal interview, 21 January 1993). Soldiers knew that the Siegfried Line would prove to be more trouble than a clothesline. Thus it is not surprising that this song which belittled the difficulty and sacrifice that combat soldiers faced, should be more popular with those at home, who preferred to think of victory as something readily obtainable and easily won. It was only toward the end of the war, when victory was actually in sight, that the complacent silliness of "The Siegfried Line" could be appreciated by soldiers. W. Ray Stephens writes: "In 1945, when the Allies did reach and breach the German Siegfried Line, there were a few feeble choruses sung for that occasion, but only in remembrance. . . . Lyricist Jimmy Kennedy's words came home when . . . as a Captain in charge of a Second Army Convoy, he passed through the Canadian sector of the Siegfried Line and saw another sign saying 'This is the Siegfried Line' and underneath some army socks and a bra, etc. was another big sign to the effect 'And this is the washing!'" (1987, 14).

Whereas the many polyglot, transnational versions of "Lili Marlene" are well known, the fact that "The Siegfried Line" inspired a German parody has been forgotten.[15] I have seen no mention of the parody in any published or archival source, nor did any of my interviewees speak of it. I happened across it by accident in the National Sound Archive in London. It was written in 1941 or 1942, when Germany was winning the war. On 27 September 1944, when the Allies were winning, Godfrey Talbot played the recording on the BBC. Talbot introduced the parody by recalling the original song, already out-of-date five years after it was written: "You remember the popular song at the beginning of this war, the one called 'We're Going to Hang Out the Washing on the Siegfried Line,' a song which, you will also remember, passed out during the dark days when we retreated from France. What I didn't know until recently was that soon after the days of Dunkirk, the Germans took this 'Siegfried Line' tune of ours, and they made a jeering, triumphant parody out of it, laughing at us for imagining that we should ever crack that great line of theirs" (NSA ref. no. LP33654b8).

It seems that both sides underestimated the enemy. The German parody of "The Siegfried Line" is an extraordinary and chilling piece. It begins with a trumpet fanfare, which is soon joined by a brass band. Then a clarinet, with the band accompanying, plays the first two lines of "The Siegfried Line," interspersed with more trumpet fanfares. The last two lines of the tune are played by the full band and lead into the singing (in English) of the first stanza:

We're going to hang out the washing on the Siegfried Line,
Have you any dirty washing, Mother dear?
We're going to hang out the washing on the Siegfried Line,
For the washing day is near.

But the final line of the stanza is not completed—a bomb comes screaming down, and the singing stops. After a few moments, the singers begin the stanza again, but they only get as far as the first line when another bomb crashes down. Many bombs fall now, and we hear desperate voices crying, "Stuka! Stuka! Mother dear!" Still more bombs fall, and then, very slowly, a few singers begin to sing the first line. They are interrupted in the middle of the line by more bombs, and the final "on the Siegfried Line" is sung by only one person, who sobs out these few words before he too is silenced. A horn plays for a brief interval, then the band returns with a loud, triumphant tune; in Talbot's words, "taking over the song in crashing Teuton style." This tune is the prelude to a choral rendition of "The Siegfried Line" in German. The German lyrics use the same tune and pick up the theme of laundry in a mocking taunt. Yet the final irony belongs to Godfrey Talbot, who mocks the notion of German victory by saying, "That's the gramophone record which the Germans made, laughing at us with our own song. I'll bet they don't sell many copies of that record in Germany now. The wheel has turned full circle. The laugh is now on the enemy" (NSA ref. no. LP33654b8).

"We're Going to Hang Out the Washing on the Siegfried Line," like "Lili Marlene," was a cultural artifact that was treated as one of the spoils of war. Yet because the value of this artifact was not rated very highly, few noticed or cared about its capture by the enemy. In the end, when the enemy succumbed, a few feeble attempts to take back the song were made. These attempts are now well-nigh forgotten, but the song itself is not. It is remembered as an example of the mood of arrogant complacency with which the British went into the war, the mood that changed quickly with the tragedy of Dunkirk. Such arrogance, such careless assurance of victory, was part and parcel of the British refusal to give up or to admit that defeat was possible. And the day did come when British washing hung on the tattered remains of the Siegfried Line.

Beethoven's Fifth Symphony

Britain was accustomed to borrowing a certain amount of musical inspiration from the Continent. Though music critics asserted that the twentieth century marked Britain's musical coming of age and insisted that Britain could no longer be called "the land without music," it was as common in wartime to hear music by Beethoven, Bach, and Rossini as by Elgar and Purcell. Two of Britain's finest composers, Ralph Vaughan Williams and Benjamin Britten, were going strong during the war, a fact that helped Britain's musical self-esteem. Nonetheless, it would have been impossible to please art music aficionados without substantial offerings from German and Italian composers. Spike Hughes's comments, while not exactly accurate, represent the wartime mood: "It seems curious that the B.B.C. and the rest did not celebrate our own entry into the war with a riot of home-grown music. Instead, the air was filled with the sound of the march from Wagner's *Tannhäuser*—until Italy came into the war, since when everybody has had a go at the overture to Rossini's *Tancredi*. Fortunately, there are no Japanese composers of note" (1945, 97).[16]

If German and Italian music were inevitable, associations with their fascist homelands were not. British and Allied musicians sought to make Continental music their own. Myra Hess playing Beethoven and Yehudi Menuhin playing Bach in critically acclaimed performances had a built-in irony that required no comment. Just as German popular music was captured as a trophy of war, so was German art music. The Allied use of Beethoven's Fifth Symphony was an especially ingenious example of this reversal of associations. Beethoven, the democrat, the symbol of the German Enlightenment, was seen as the repository of a noble German culture that the Nazis were busy destroying. As such, he was the representative of a transcendent European culture in which the Nazis had no part. The "fate-knocking-at-the-door" theme from his Fifth Symphony was a call to all democrats, all Allies, all who loved freedom; it was also a statement to the Nazis that fate would soon be knocking at their door.

I was first alerted to the musical symbolism of Beethoven's Fifth by one of my interviewees, G.H.R. In a letter of 25 February 1993 he wrote, "Beethoven V was linked with Churchill's famous finger sign so lots of people listened to it for the first time." In response to my request for more information, he wrote: "Beethoven's Fifth . . . begins with a repeated motif of three shorts and a long— • • • —. In Morse code this is V (for Victory) and it formed the famous Churchill two finger sign (copied probably from Agincourt). There was some attempt to encourage anti-German sympathizers on the continent to tap out this rhythm since the Germans were aware of its significance to us—and hence could be tormented. I believe in France, however, that singing 'Auprès de ma Blonde' was more common" (personal letter).[17] After a Danish woman told me, without prompting on my part, that the BBC played Beethoven's Fifth when Denmark was liberated by the Allies, I began to look more closely at this fascinating cultural inversion.

According to Charles J. Rolo, the use of the letter V to represent victory came from the appropriately named Victor de Lavaleye, the BBC's program organizer for Belgium (1942, 173–74). Lavaleye was searching for a visual symbol that would have meaning for both Flemish and Walloon speakers and that could be easily written in the dark. He chose the letter V—standing for *Victory* in English, *Victoire* in French, and *Vrijheid* in Flemish—as a symbol that could easily be chalked up on walls when no one was looking. The BBC encouraged people in France and the Low Countries to write the letter V on walls and other public arenas as an anonymous visual expression of defiance to the Nazis.

In 1941 the V symbol was transmuted into sound. Rolo writes:

> Somebody . . . had struck upon the idea of incorporating the Morse signal for V into British broadcasts. It immediately occurred to all concerned that this Morse signal (• • • —) was the rhythmic theme of numerous pieces of music, in particular of Beethoven's Fifth Symphony, one movement of which, based on this theme, is called "Fate knocking on the door." On his June 27 broadcast, Colonel Britton introduced the V sound to his audience. The next day, the BBC's program for French listeners carried a special feature entirely built around the V sound. Not only were the theme of the Fifth Symphony and the Morse signal abundantly used, but the feature demonstrated in a striking manner how every sound in the daily life of a French village or town could be made into a V: the school mistress calling her children by clapping her hands in V rhythm; trains rattling through the night; dogs barking and cocks crowing at dawn; customers calling for the waiter in the village cafe; the blacksmith hammering on his anvil—all created a V symphony worthy of the best sound effects of a Réné Clair film. [1942, 178]

I have been unable to locate this French broadcast, but an apparently similar piece played on the BBC on 27 February 1942 (NSA ref. nos. 4000 and T3999b2). This remarkable work, entitled "Symphony in V," was arranged by Ludwig Koch. It incorporates natural, mechanical, and human-made sounds that demonstrate the V rhythm and, in some cases, the descending intervals from Beethoven's Fifth.

"Symphony in V" begins with the sound of bombs falling and exploding, then the sound of an airplane engine. The first V sound comes after the airplane: a relatively slow, single-tone rendition of the V rhythm made by a mechanical device such as a car horn. It is followed by a faster and higher-pitched V rhythm, also single-toned and made by a mechanical device. The second V sound is interrupted by bombing, but it soon returns at a quicker tempo. Next we hear the bells of Big Ben and the sounds of city traffic; a car horn honks out the V rhythm as Big Ben strikes the hour. Then a Caribbean-style orchestra plays, with some interesting rhythmic flourishes on the V rhythm and a variety of tonal patterns. Sounds of conversation and the clink of cutlery come next; against this backdrop, someone strikes a utensil against a glass and taps out the V rhythm and notes. Next is a dance orchestra, whose tunes have a rhythmic pattern of three shorts and a long, but no other resemblance to Beethoven's Fifth. The wind blows next, and metallic objects rattle in a V rhythm. A train whistle blows a mournful and sustained V pattern, which increases in tempo as the train begins to move, and we realize that the train is chugging in V rhythm. Bells ring next and various mechanical devices sound alarms in V rhythm. The threatening sounds fade, and we hear birds singing; one bird call, louder than the rest, is in V rhythm. More mechanical sounds, perhaps another train, overlap the bird calls; then one hears actual knocking at the door in V rhythm. Finally, we hear an orchestral rendition of this portion of Beethoven's Fifth Symphony. Applause is appreciative but scattered at first; finally, it too settles into the V pattern.

There was some attempt to reclaim Beethoven's Fifth by the Germans; it was, after all, a piece by a German composer. Goebbels played the Fifth Symphony on German radio and claimed that the V stood for "Viktoria." But the Allies did not listen. Beethoven's Fifth continued to symbolize Allied victory and German defeat. The BBC made full use of these associations when it made Beethoven's Fifth the signature tune for its broadcast *London Calling* (NSA ref. nos. 6586 and T6573b7, 9 February 1944). Private citizens also shared these ideas about Beethoven's Fifth. In 1940 a young soldier stationed in London went to concerts on his nights off but never told his friends for fear of their merciless teasing. His description of the Promenade concerts of August 1940 stresses both the individual pleasure and the communal comfort he drew from music, in particular Beethoven's Fifth: "In the evenings, whenever I could, I made my way to Queen's Hall and joined the patient throng of Promenaders who drew strength and solace from the ageless music. . . . Friday night was Beethoven Night at the Proms. The Fifth Symphony went down particularly well, I thought. With its opening theme in the minor key—you know, the "Fate knocking at the Door" thing—and the eventual glorification of triumph in the major, it seemed somehow to express the mood of wartime London in an uncanny way that I'm sure everybody felt just as much as I did" (Len Waller Papers). In a radio program broadcast on 31 December 1944, the BBC played the V rhythm after descriptions and commentary about D day. Then a working-class male voice said: "That's the V sign. V for victory. Maybe we'll get it this year after all, now the invasion's on" (NSA ref. nos. F44/214 and LP24739–40). And when victory finally came to Europe, another BBC broadcast showed a drum beating out the V rhythm and notes, while the bells of St. Margaret's, Westminster, played accompaniment (NSA ref. no. LP36346b10).

Just as land was captured and men were captured, so were cultural artifacts taken as prizes of war. Sometimes they could be recast by the captors and used against those who had held them first. Such artistic inversions did not seem traitorous, but a transcendence of national boundaries. Beethoven's Fifth, like the many refugee musicians who played it, escaped Germany and fought for the Allies; it played in celebration of Allied victory. Yet it stayed in Germany as well and played in defense of the Reich. Each side claimed it, and each side sought to play it more.

———————— 6

Present Tense
Memories of Wartime London

> In marching, in mobs, in football games, and in war, outlines become
> vague; real things become unreal and a fog creeps over the mind. Tension
> and excitement, weariness, movement—all merge in one great gray dream,
> so that when it is over, it is hard to remember how it was when you killed
> men or ordered them to be killed. Then other people who were not there
> tell you what it was like and you say vaguely, "Yes, I guess that's how it
> was."
>
> —John Steinbeck, *The Moon Is Down*

Any study of the past is in some sense a study about memory. The past is gone
irretrievably, but memories remain, providing us with information and yielding
meaning about past events. Even historical sources apparently created "on the spot"
are the creations of memory; a general's account, a newspaper report, and a descriptive letter are all created after the events that they recount. Memory is thus inherent in any historical study. Though there is certainly a difference between a memory
of five hours and a memory of fifty years, it is not always clear how this difference
is manifest; the more recent memory is not necessarily the more accurate or the
more meaningful. When events are shared and collective memories become as
important as personal memories, society is given a mirror image of itself, and
memories become sites of political discourse. Thus the search for meaning in both
collective and personal memory becomes a quest for political answers. One looks
through the lessons of the past in order to answer the questions of the present.

I began this study with a fairly simple idea of the "finest hour"—Greer Garson
as Mrs. Miniver singing bravely in the bombed-out church, Winston Churchill's
broadcasts inspiring and uniting people in all parts of the country. I wanted to learn
about the human experiences behind this golden image—the real-life Mrs.
Minivers—to turn my two-dimensional portrait into a three-dimensional one. I
learned that the finest hour cannot be taken simplistically, that it does not and cannot
hold true for all people and all moments of the war, but that it does have validity
for some people and at some times, though often with substantial modifications.

I learned that class, gender, and ethnicity could make an important difference in the ways that one experienced and hence the ways one remembers the war. Though class, gender, and ethnicity do not dictate what a person thinks, they often determine one's personal experiences and how one is treated by others. I also learned that discussions and criticisms of the past are often discussions and criticisms of present-day politics. Memories of the past are points of contrast to the present; such memories focus attention on present-day concerns by highlighting their similarities and their differences to past events.

The use of memory for political purposes provides the scholar with a fascinating glimpse into present-day political questions. By analyzing the memories that were shared and emphasized by my interviewees, I discovered important linkages that people found between past and present. Yet memories—whether oral or written—are like the bones of a dinosaur, a tantalizing but always incomplete record of the past. Oral memories are particularly difficult to deal with because their orality allows for constant change, and the past, now gone forever, cannot be fluid, even though our vision of it may be. Scholars such as myself who use oral sources to learn about the past embrace memory as much as we are frustrated by it. Memory is what we seek, yet memory is changeable, chameleon-like, ultimately uncontrollable. We wish to use memory to learn about the past, yet we fear being taken in by inaccuracy, mistake, even deception.

Scholarly debates about the value of oral sources often fasten on the inherent instability of memory, the primary terrain of the oral artifact. To its critics, oral testimony is, at best, a methodology of scholarly necessity; where no written records exist, scholars must fall back on oral sources. Other scholars have suggested that the tension between spoken memory and written history may be oral testimony's greatest contribution as well as its most troubling problem. Alessandro Portelli has demonstrated that important information may lie in the discrepancies between the historical record and the narrated memory, and concludes: "What is really important is that memory is not a passive depository of facts, but an active process of creation of meanings. Thus, the specific utility of oral sources for the historian lies, not so much in their ability to preserve the past, as in the very changes wrought by memory. These changes reveal the narrators' effort to make sense of the past and to give a form to their lives, and set the interview and the narrative in their historical context" (1991, 52). Thus, memory is not a window to the past or a wrapper within which the past is contained. Instead, memory is an analytical tool by which the past is interpreted in the light of the present.

The privileging of the written over the oral, and the concomitant denigration of memory, is a relatively recent phenomenon, as Walter J. Ong points out (1982, 96–97). Yet such privileging is deeply embedded in contemporary academic discourse; as such, written documents are often simply assumed to be more correct than oral ones. A person's memory often is judged by how well it coincides with the written historical record; where discrepancies exist, memory is generally deemed to be at fault. Faced with an abundance of written documents, historians of wartime Britain often treat memory as an unnecessary distraction, even a distortion, a kind of blinkered false consciousness to which most of Britain has succumbed. Angus Calder's 1969 magnum opus *The People's War* is a magnificent book and remains probably the standard social history of wartime Britain, but it gives very short shrift to oral sources. Tom Harrisson, in *Living through the Blitz*, explains that he is not opposed to oral testimony recorded "on the spot," but he has no faith in long-term memory; in justification for his view, he cites examples of people who described events quite differently in 1940 and in 1970.

Paul Fussell, writing about American and British conceptions of World War II, treats memory as an idiot and a liar and argues, "For the past fifty years the Allied war has been sanitized and romanticized almost beyond recognition by the sentimental, the loony patriotic, the ignorant, and the bloodthirsty" (1989, ix). Indeed, it has become common for scholars to consider the "popular" image of wartime Britain as a kind of smokescreen that one must penetrate before arriving at the truth. Though popular conceptions of the "finest hour" have been debunked and derided, there has been little research done on the extent to which people actually accepted and held these so-called "popular ideas." Popular ideas are often assumed to be equivalent to the representations created by popular culture, governmental directives, and wartime propaganda. Thus the battle lines are drawn between a reified popular memory and an increasingly specialized historical scholarship that either ignores oral and memory-based sources or treats them with a contemptuous and somewhat shrill dismissal.

In crude fashion, the opposing camps are as follows. On one side are the popular oral histories, the memoirs, the films, the television dramas, the whole nostalgia machinery. On this side is the story of a brave and united people standing alone against Hitler, never giving up until victory was theirs. The artifacts of nostalgia all have at their center a bittersweetness, bravery and kindness mixed with hardship and suffering. These artifacts have lost none of their resonance in the half century since wartime. In the early 1990s, while I interviewed survivors and pored through archives, nostalgic representations of wartime blossomed. In 1992 the Winston Churchill Britain at War Theme Museum opened in London, complete with bomb shelters, wartime fashions, and a simulated air raid. At the Imperial War Museum's World War II exhibit, wartime songs (such as "Run, Rabbit, Run") played continuously, while rows of glass cases exhibited gas masks, ration cards, and posters bearing the legend "Careless Talk Costs Lives." In the main gallery of the Imperial War Museum stood an enormous V2; during the war, an instrument of mass destruction inferior only to the atom bomb and the gas chambers. The artifacts of nostalgia do not ignore the suffering and hardship of war, but treat them as the necessary backdrop for the tale of ultimate victory. If the journey was long and dangerous, then its end was so much sweeter.

On the opposing side, the side where historical scholarship usually pitches its tent, is little sweetness and more bitterness. Historical scholarship does not negate the story of a brave people standing alone against Hitler, for the facts seem to bear it out; instead, history objects to the simplification of this story and to the stressing of certain facts at the expense of others. Historians such as A.J.P. Taylor, Angus Calder, Arthur Marwick, and Clive Ponting suggest—with reason, justification, and mortality statistics—that an era filled with privation and siege has a problematic claim as its nation's "finest hour." Their works are more inclusive and less individualistic than the artifacts of nostalgia; thus they have less use for personal memories. Angus Calder, referring to the work of Patrick Wright, who in turn draws from the theories of Agnes Heller, puts this point of view well: "Everyday life is full of stories. These are concerned with 'being-in-the-world' rather than with abstractly defined truth. Such stories have to be plausible, but their 'authenticity,' which is a vital ingredient, does not depend on true knowledge. When authenticity collides with 'factual' truth, people in everyday life, even historians trying to work outside it, will often stubbornly resist the latter" (1991, 9).

In pressing the discrepancies between fact and story, Calder implies that historians can indeed "work outside" the narratives of everyday life. He also implies, with Wright and Heller, that abstract truth is readily recognizable once one takes off the blinders imposed by the vicissitudes of everyday life. This assumption is somewhat dubious even when applied to demonstrable facts, but it is still more problematic when applied to such vague and ambiguous qualities as "morale" or "unity," to name two entities that haunt what Calder terms "the myth of the Blitz." In citing incidents in which the myth does not coincide with actual behavior, he provides an important scholarly analysis, but he furthers the reification of the myth itself by tacitly assuming its obvious character and homogeneous interpretation.

Calder's analysis of the blitz as a myth, a text, is bold and original. He cogently explains his use of the much-abused term "myth": "The account of that event, or series of events, which was current by the end of the war has assumed a 'traditional' character, involves heroes, suggests the victory of a good God over satanic evil, and has been used to explain a fact: the defeat of Nazism" (1991, 2). Yet texts, even sacred texts that we term myths, are not read in the same way by all people. The current, often fierce, debates about the blitz show the abundance of multiple interpretations of this well-known story. The battle that now rages is for the memory of the battles that were fought and won fifty years ago. In the current war of ideas, there is little sign of retreat from either side. Neither the "finest hour" nor the ardent debunkers will go away.

Memory, like any other historical source, should be treated with circumspection. One should not expect it to be a window to the past and then be outraged when it is not. Memory is not a transparent screen through which we step, like Alice through the looking glass, into a strange and distant world. Memory is an analytical tool similar to a microscope, focusing first on one part of the past, then on another, highlighting threads that were perhaps not visible when the business of living the events in question took all of one's concentration. There is, in the work of scholars such as Tom Harrisson and Paul Fussell, a sense that the feelings evoked by memories of past events should correspond exactly to the feelings that were present in those events; and that when these two emotional states do not match up perfectly, distortion or even deception has occurred.

Yet, for most people there is a clear and conscious acknowledgement that memory does change the perception of the past; and this shift in perception, far from being a loss or a lie, is a means of understanding or of healing, of coming to terms with the past. Events that were embarrassing or uncomfortable at the time become humorous in the retelling; events of great pain or hardship may convey wisdom or insight when they are considered in retrospect. We have all heard people say, and we have all said, "I'm sure I'll laugh at this someday" or "I know I'll feel differently tomorrow"—a very real, everyday recognition that memory does alter consciousness in beneficial as well as deceptive ways. My interviewees were well aware of the elusive properties of memory and told me, again and again, that they could not be certain they were remembering things correctly, that it was, after all, fifty years ago. Memory did not consist of dipping one's hand into an easy continuum of experience and bringing up a bit of the past. Instead, memory remained packaged and boxed away, placed in another part of one's life, to be brought out and examined on certain occasions, such as interviews with American graduate students. Ettie Gontarsky told me that answering my questions was like looking at "another life on another planet" (personal interview, 4 April 1993).

Scholarly criticisms of memory-based sources often depend on a commonsense definition of memory, not one that has been carefully examined. At the same time, such arguments usually display an uncritical acceptance of written sources from the era in question. Tom Harrisson concludes that "the only valid information for this *sort* of social history of war is that recorded at the time on the spot" (1990, 327; emphasis in original). He depends for his facts on the archives of Mass-Observation, an organization that he helped found in 1937 and which he ran during the war. During wartime, Mass-Observers went to blitzed towns and areas and wrote down observations of residents' behavior and conversation; these descriptions were then used by the government as a key to the morale of the populace.

The archive, currently at the University of Sussex, is an excellent resource, but it should not be used quite so uncritically: people who have just endured bombing are not at their most lucid or typical, as the following report from wartime Home Intelligence makes clear: "Immediately after the raid, people are dazed and in a condition of mild shock. They are surprised and thankful to be alive. They feel *important* and are inclined to exaggerate the experiences through which they have passed. Those who have suffered loss are feeling sad and depressed. A few feel hopeless. All are tired. There is a considerable degree of isolation, both physical and psychological. There is a craving for attention, sympathy and encouragement" (INF 1, 174A, B.123; emphasis in original). Neither are outside observers always correct in their judgments. Psychological research has shown that eyewitness accounts are notoriously unreliable (Munsterberg 1909; Stern 1982; Loftus and Palmer 1982; U.S. Supreme Court 1982; Buckhout 1982). Mass-Observers were not recording machines; they were human beings who often suffered the same trauma that their subjects did. If these conditions rendered people less capable of sober judgment, such an effect would be true for Mass-Observers as well as for those they observed.

My intention here is not to denigrate the work of Mass-Observation but simply to point out that all methodologies have their problems. Psychological research has shown that memory of even a few hours lag can be highly malleable and subject to outside influence such as an interviewer's question (Stern 1982, Loftus and Palmer 1982, U.S. Supreme Court 1982). Similarly, the very act of perception is selective; one may observe something and not be sure what he or she is observing. The brain fills in cognitive gaps on the spot just as it does in memory. Robert Buckhout writes:

> Human perception and memory function effectively by being selective and constructive. . . . Perception and memory are decision-making processes affected by the totality of a person's abilities, background, attitudes, motives and beliefs, by the environment and by the way his recollection is eventually tested. The observer is an active rather than a passive perceiver and recorder; he reaches conclusions on what he has seen by evaluating fragments of information and reconstructing them. He is motivated by a desire to be accurate as he imposes meaning on the over-abundance of information that impinges on his senses, but also by a desire to live up to the expectations of other people and to stay in their good graces. The eye, the ear, and other sense organs are therefore social organs as well as physical ones. [1982, 117]

Again, I am not suggesting that either memory or eyewitness accounts are useless because they may not always be completely accurate. It is the scholar's job to determine the accuracy of any source used. Eyewitness accounts and narrated memories are invaluable sources of information for the scholar, so long as we are aware of the problems inherent in both—indeed, in all—methodologies.

Though stress and trauma may hamper some forms of perception and memory, they may actually increase others. There has long been an intuitive feeling that this is so, that events of great importance are more firmly etched on the brain than are more ordinary ones. In 1899 F. W. Colegrove published an article in the *American Journal of Psychology* about people's memories of Abraham Lincoln's assassination; in 1977 Roger Brown and James Kulik wrote a similar article about memories of John F. Kennedy's assassination. Brown and Kulik term such memories "flashbulb memories" and cite Robert Livingston's theory that a "Now Print!" mechanism in the brain seals memory more firmly during unusual or unexpected events. Though Livingston's theory was entirely speculative, and Brown and Kulik's use of it was admittedly intuitive, recent work in the neurosciences lends it some credence. The work of Larry Cahill et al. indicates that emotional and traumatic memory may be more deeply fixed into consciousness because of the activation of ß-adrenergic stress hormone systems (1994). Cahill and his colleagues found that when these hormones were blocked, subjects had trouble remembering stories of traumatic or emotional content, but not stories of ordinary events. They concluded that these hormone systems played some part in the maintaining of emotionally charged memories, a phenomenon already observed in studies of animal behavior. Thus memories of the trauma and intensity of wartime may in fact be more accurate than fifty-year-old memories of more ordinary events.

Of course, such a complex phenomenon as human memory cannot be completely explained by the activation of hormone systems. Ulric Neisser, writing before Cahill's suggestive discoveries, postulates that so-called "flashbulb memories" are actually created after the fact: "Memories become flashbulbs primarily through the significance that is attached to them *afterwards*: later that day, the next day, and in subsequent months and years. . . . Moments like these are sure to be pondered, discussed, and redescribed on subsequent occasions: why shouldn't we suppose that their persistence is due to the frequent reconsideration they receive?" (1982, 45, emphasis in original). Neisser also suggests that the formation of these memories into stories is an important factor in their continued existence. If these moments are considered important by the world as well as by ourselves, such valuation is an additional reason for their maintenance as memories: "The notion of narrative structure does more than explain the canonical form of flashbulb memories; it accounts for their very existence. The flashbulb recalls an occasion when two narratives that we ordinarily keep separate—the course of history and the course of our own life—were momentarily put into alignment" (47).

As Neisser points out, memory is not only a biological or psychological phenomenon; it is a profoundly social one. We use the memories of others to check and fill in the gaps in our own memories. Maurice Halbwachs reminds us that memory is the recollection of past events for a social purpose, a purpose that always exists at the time of the remembering rather than at the time of the event remembered. Since we cannot remember everything (the weather of every day of our lives, for example, or all the meals that we have eaten), we choose to remember events that are most salient for present purposes. Memory is a discourse that comments upon and refers to the past but does so in and for the present. Thus, while memory may give us information about the past, it also gives us information about the present, for it indicates which past concerns are considered present ones.

Though we use the memories of others to validate, even create, our own memories, we also experience the opposite phenomenon: incidents in which our memories clash with those of others. When these memories are of events of national importance, the discrepancies become public arenas in which the past is debated for opposing present-day interests. Maurice Halbwachs writes: "Men who have been brought close together—for example, by a shared task, mutual devotion, common ancestry, or artistic endeavor—may disperse afterwards into various groups. Each new group is too restricted to retain everything that concerned the thoughts of the original party, literary coterie, or religious congregation. So each fastens onto one facet of its thought and remembers only part of its activities. Several pictures of that common past are thus generated, none being really accurate or coinciding with any other" (1980, 32).

This process is precisely what has happened to memories of wartime London. The famed wartime unity, the working together for a common goal, created a large group with a deeply felt collective memory. But wartime unity did not survive the postwar era; thus it is not surprising that wartime memory should have dispersed as well. The debates about wartime London are, in many cases, debates about postwar British politics, about the welfare state, the loss of the empire, current economic difficulties, and Britain's place in the world. My interviewees used images of wartime to contrast and criticize contemporary social ills such as crime, unemployment, ethnic divisiveness, a gutted industrial base, and a rapidly fading system of social services. The past provided both warning and example: stories of the past could be cautionary tales or models for the future.

Marx wrote, "The tradition of all the dead generations weighs like a nightmare on the brain of the living" (1959, 320). With this monkey on our backs, we try to avoid the failures of our predecessors. Yet memory can work in a different and more beneficial way: rather than being a nightmare from which we run or to which we cling as an excuse for violence, memory can be a haven to which we turn. As Halbwachs notes, memory allows us to conjure the past at will and to roam in it as we choose. Past people cannot harm us, nor can past events surprise us. We can control our vision of the past—remembering what we choose to remember, highlighting what we choose to highlight—in ways that we cannot control the present. Whether the past is a nightmare or a haven, it is always a point of contrast to the present. Only the assumption that the past is not like the present makes historically based studies valuable and necessary.

Walter Benjamin wrote, "Every image of the past that is not recognized by the present as one of its own concerns threatens to disappear irretrievably" (1968, 255). This danger applies equally to the interviewee and the scholar, the television producer and the storyteller in the pub; for each must decide which information is relevant, which worth repeating. Often, the debates about wartime London are not so much about facts as about meaning. The facts are too easily checked, and in a way it does not matter if a raid took place on 12 May or 16 May, or if an interviewee confuses a Morrison shelter with an Anderson shelter. What is at stake here is the atmosphere, the feelings, and the spirit of wartime London, and what this spirit is called upon to represent. It is a spirit that has been evoked so many times and for so many purposes that it seems to take on a life of its own. Yet this very reification of wartime London is part of the problem. It did not have a life of its own; it had, instead, many lives.

Memories of Wartime

Memory has proven bewildering to scholars of wartime Britain: too many people remember too many different and contradictory things. Tom Harrisson writes: "For most surviving citizens the major effect has been (as often) in two opposite directions, both processes in 'reality obliteration': either to be unable to remember anything much (with no wish to do so), or, more usually, to see those nights as glorious" (1990, 321). To Harrisson, both the absence of memory and the imputation of glory are equally fallacious. Yet he has aptly pinpointed two common visions of wartime Britain: there are those who remember the period with horror and have no wish to speak of it, and those who remember the period as glorious and wish to speak of it with nostalgia.

"Nostalgia," writes David Lowenthal, "is memory with the pain removed" (1985, 8). In the case of wartime London, pain is remembered but no longer felt. Those who speak of wartime London know that the war is over, Britain has won, and they have survived; the bombs have stopped falling and can do no more harm. Pain is remembered because pain and danger give the era its poignancy, just as the romantic hero needs quests to perform or dragons to slay. In this, as in many other cases, nostalgia is the province of the elderly and is, in part, simply the longing of the elderly for the days of their youth. Things were better then if only because one was younger and stronger and saw life as limitless possibility. Nostalgia allows us to do in imagination what we can never do in reality—to relive the days of our youth with the certain knowledge that we will grow old. Youth assumes the promise of age but is never certain if this promise will be fulfilled; old age is the fulfillment of the promise, but without the possibilities of youth. During the war, young people did not know if they would live to see old age or, indeed, the next morning. Nostalgia allows them to relive a time of youth and danger from the vantage point of knowing they have survived it.

Nostalgia for wartime was, interestingly enough, begun during the war. At the same time that wartime rhetoric stressed looking toward the future, it laid in place the seeds for a future nostalgia. Consider how these seeds were sown in the radio broadcasts of J.B. Priestley. Compassionate, beautifully worded, filled with zeal for social reform, these broadcasts reflect Priestley's concerns for social change and his romantic attachment to the "little England" he loved (see also Samuel 1989, xxiii). Priestley's broadcast immediately after Dunkirk praises the "little pleasure steamers" and their effort "so absurd and yet so grand and gallant that you hardly know whether to laugh or to cry when you read about them" (NSA ref. nos. 2562 and LP2560b5). After discussing this event of the immediate past, he switches to the future—but the future is cast as a time of remembering the past: "And our great-grandchildren, when they learn how we began this war by snatching glory out of defeat and then swept on to victory may also learn how the little holiday steamers made an excursion to hell and came back glorious." Thus the present is filled with hope and expectation for a future in which there will be a vigorous remembrance of things past.

Churchill's "finest hour" speech was also a powerful force in wartime memory: it laid in place the idea that wartime would be remembered as a time of splendor. People who know little about World War II and were born long after its end are able to quote, "If the British Empire and its Commonwealth last for a thousand years, men will still say, 'This was their finest hour.'" It is not the sexism and imperialism of Churchill's rhetoric that are remembered, but the idea that this moment of effort, courage, and defiance to Nazism was Britain's finest hour. Like the defeat of the Spanish Armada, the defeat of the Luftwaffe became a key symbol for all that was best in British culture. It is important to remember that the defeat of the Luftwaffe had not actually happened when Churchill made this famous speech; both Churchill and Priestley spoke of remembering a victory that was yet to be.

There is a seamlessness in wartime nostalgia that stretches from Priestley's Dunkirk broadcast and Churchill's "finest hour" speech down to the present day, for the idea of remembering victory began before there was a victory to remember. Churchill and Priestley spoke of a Britain that had to be made before it could be remembered, but it was, in a sense, made to be remembered. If Britain had lost the war, it is likely that Churchill's "finest hour" speech would be forgotten—or perhaps remembered with derision, as Lloyd George's "land fit for heroes" speech was remembered in 1939. Since Britain won the war, was not occupied by enemy troops, and held out during the dreadful days of 1940, a brave David against an iron-heeled Goliath, the memory of the war as Britain's finest hour remains steadfast and potent.

Yet herein lies a problem for present-day Britain. If Britain's finest hour occurred in 1940, then the present must by definition be inferior, a paradise lost, a fall from grace. Britain (and specifically London) in wartime has come to represent a golden age that, like all golden ages, exists in the past and in whose shadow the present appears paler, rougher, less understandable, and less desirable. Jonathan Croall, in the introduction to his popular oral history *Don't You Know There's a War On?*, writes:

> The second world war has been described as the last time we were all happy. As an historical statement this is manifestly nonsense, a sick joke even. . . . Yet if the notion of linking happiness with the war years is ostensibly an absurd one, its emotional validity for many people cannot so easily be denied. . . . Many see the period as one in which their own lives had far greater meaning than they did at other times, before or since. Those years of living dangerously they remember as bringing fulfilment, a sense of adventure, even exhilaration. Because life was more precious it was felt more keenly, and lived more intensely. Somehow the common danger inherent in the threat to the nation gave a shape and purpose to their existence that they have been unable to recapture in peace time. [1988, 1]

The notion of the past as a golden age is remarkably supple and prevalent worldwide. In the *Motif-Index of Folk Literature*, Stith Thompson notes that the motif of a golden age as a former age of perfection (A1101.1) or a reign of peace and justice (A1101.1.1) appears in tales from Irish, Lappish, Hindu, Persian, Chinese, and Aztec cultures, to name a few (1955, 194). At first blush, this idea seems inherently conservative, even reactionary, and indeed it is Conservative politicians who have most stridently invoked "the Dunkirk spirit" and other wartime symbols in recent years. Yet Labour has also invoked wartime as an era to be admired: a time of full employment, class leveling, antifascism, and the vigorous implementation of social welfare programs. "The finest hour" affords a multiplicity of interpretations; the journey from the garden of Anthony Eden to the minor talents of John Major can be viewed in many different ways.

Paradoxically, one of the things that made this past so golden was its sense of hope for the future. Many of my interviewees, in common with Priestley and the Ministry of Information, saw the changes wrought by wartime as a pathway to the twin goals of defeating Hitler abroad and forging a more just society at home. Once the former had been accomplished, the latter should logically follow. R.J.B. Bosworth writes: "Planned while the conflict continued, largely legislated by the

Labour Government (1945–51), and imitated by many other European and non-European societies, the Welfare State, for more than a generation, offered many ordinary people much of the time their reward for defeating fascism. The Welfare State was deemed the essential product of 'the People's war that never ended'" (1993, 33).

Ettie Gontarsky recalls the 1945 elections as a turning point, when the Labour Party (led by Clement Attlee) won handily over the Conservative Party (led by Winston Churchill). For Ettie, as for many others, the Labour government was supposed to fulfill the ideals for which the war had been fought. The memory of the first postwar Labour government provides a telling contrast to the Conservative government of the 1980s and early 1990s. Ettie remarks:

> I think at the time the soldiers, sailors, airmen returning to Britain after the war, I think that had a great impact. They weren't having any more of the officer class, if you like. I think one could say that without any fear of being completely in the wrong there. I think there was this great turn of the tide. That the lads, the boys of the troops, the forces, all the forces, they thought, "Right, we're going to have our own government." . . . And then came the Beveridge Report, the National Health was built, though it's being killed now by the Tory government, of course—I'll get that little bit in for you. But that was the birth of the National Health, and a lot more equality was on the agenda. There was a great levelling of the class system. . . . I feel that the ordinary serving soldier, sailor, airman felt, "Well, it's our turn now. We're going to have something to say. We fought for our country; we're going to have something to say about it." Now, those are my words, but I think this could sum up the feeling of a lot of people at the time. Because there was a Labour government returned. No question about it. When there'll be another one, who can tell, but that's another story" [personal interview, 19 April 1993][1]

In looking back to the hope and solidarity of wartime, one may also look back to the time when these hopes were fulfilled in the form of the welfare state. From the vantage point of 1993, when the welfare state was being gutted and destroyed, the dangerous 1940s and bleak 1950s might look golden indeed.

Ettie was not the only person I met who contrasted the implementation of wartime and postwar social services with the Thatcherite policy of dismantling these services. Anne Lubin was born in the East End of London and was a teenager at the start of the war. She worked in war factories in London and Birmingham, then worked in the Navy, Army, and Air Force Institutes (NAAFI), a canteen for the forces. Anne believed that the war was fought "for a more just society. And of course we were absolutely delighted when there was a land-slide, and a Labour government came in, and we thought this was the beginning of El Dorado" (personal interview, 13 March 1993). Yet El Dorado lasted for a perilously short time, and

Anne saw the beginning of the end in the Conservative victory of 1979. The issue of nutrition is one example that she cited. During wartime the government faced its malnourished population and began nutritional supplements for children, such as free orange juice and free milk for those who could not pay. Anne remarked that it was Margaret Thatcher who "stopped the milk in schools. You ever heard anybody say, 'Margaret Thatcher, milk snatcher'? . . . And that was a very sad thing" (personal interview, 13 March 1993).[2]

George Wagner supplies a trenchant political analysis of Margaret Thatcher's lack of sympathy for the welfare state, based in part on the fact that she is too young to have been involved in politics during World War II. During wartime, the political tenor among Conservative politicians was informed by what George terms a "collective bad conscience" based on the slaughter of World War I and the failures of the 1920s and 1930s: unemployment, the appeasement of Hitler, and the failure to build "a land fit for heroes." In order to atone for past sins—and to convince the fighters and workers of World War II that things would be different this time—it was necessary to establish a series of social programs that would ameliorate the lot of the majority of the population. Margaret Thatcher, a teenager for most of the war, felt no such duty. George explains:

> For all the internal squabbles, the difference between Labour and Conservative governments in Britain until about 1970 or '75 has not been all that great, because the tone in the government was set by the older people. . . . The bad conscience went out of circulation and effectiveness really only in the seventies with Thatcher. And the Lloyd George thing about the "homeland worthy of the returning hero" was of course used as a jibe in all propaganda, and in a way, I think it made the Tories be far more friendly towards innovation, the welfare state, education, the National Health scheme and so on than they would normally be. Many of them probably with clenched teeth, but . . . when they are all moral, you can't go round singing bawdy songs, can you? [personal interview, 23 April 1993]

Of course, not everyone in Britain holds such a critical view of Thatcher or Thatcherism, and the Conservatives ("Tories") were in power from 1979 to 1997. But Conservatives, even when they held the reins of power, were vehement in their belief that Britain was going to the dogs—and had been since World War II. Sir Keith Joseph (Thatcher's political mentor and one of her staunchest allies) admits that (in accord with George Wagner's thesis), "At the end of the Second World War, structural change in Britain was long overdue, much of it from before the First World War" (1978, 101). However, the change that actually came about was not what Sir Keith had in mind: "Our troubles stem, I believe, from two world wars and the mood they produced. . . . Wars create great expectations and the belief that government can do almost anything, yet simultaneously they leave the country very much poorer. . . . The triumph of the Second World War coupled with socialist delusions and the determination not to return to the 1930s left a mood of naive utopianism, coupled with . . . debilitating compassion" (100). Here, the Second World War was a triumph, but not the start of a golden age. To the contrary, its triumphant optimism is seen as the cause of present troubles. Wartime was superior to the present, since things have gone downhill ever since, but wartime was the first step down the slippery slope.

Finally, there are those who believe that the notion of wartime as a golden age is a piece of retrospective nonsense, simple nostalgia on the part of the elderly for the "good old days" or a reckless and obscene cover-up of the hardship and tragedy of war. Most vitriolic of these critics is Paul Fussell who, although American, attempts to debunk both American and British wartime ideology in *Wartime: Understanding and Behavior in the Second World War.* Though he makes the valid point that wartime nostalgia tends to downplay the suffering and death of soldiers, he seems equally outraged by wartime's effect on literature and its restriction of Continental holidays. For Fussell, World War II was a pointless and senseless destruction of human life: "The war seemed so devoid of ideological content that little could be said about its positive purposes that made political or intellectual sense, especially after the Soviet Union joined the great crusade against what until then had been stigmatized as totalitarianism" (1989, 136).

Fussell uses his authority as an officer in World War II and his rage and clever writing style to mask a rather suspect methodology: he uses novels that he likes as transparent historical documents and diaries that he does not like as examples of people being duped. Those who disagree with his interpretation are either ignored or derided; their opinions do not count. One wonders what he would make of the comments of E.P. Thompson, who was also an officer in World War II. Like Fussell, Thompson writes about the past, but for the present:

> I hold the now-unfashionable view that the last war was, for the Allied armies and the Resistance, an anti-Fascist war, not only in rhetoric but also in the intentions of the dead.
>
> So long as Europe remains divided, so long as hostile militarisms occupy both halves, those intentions are being violated. It is not their past credulity but our present inaction which reduces those intentions to futility. My fellow soldiers . . . were not ardent politicians. But they were democrats and anti-Fascists. They knew what they fought for, and it was not for the division of Europe, nor was it for the domination of our continent by two arrogant superpowers. [1985, 200]

The unity that wartime engendered was skillfully wrought from many opposing and contradictory camps: patriotism, internationalism, feminism, domesticity, imperialism, and antifascism. It is inevitable that these contradictions should surface after the war and that the battle for wartime memory should be fought along these lines. The potency of this wartime image makes the ownership of its memory so important, while its many components make it so highly contested.

For Better and For Worse

No one doubts that the Second World War profoundly changed British society. Yet there is enormous debate about what these changes actually were and whether they were for the better or for the worse. One of the fiercest debates is about the extent to which women's wartime roles changed the lives of British women, both during wartime and in the postwar era. The wartime entry of large numbers of women into paid employment—in the United States as well as in Britain—is now a historical cliché, but it is a cliché firmly grounded in wartime fact. Wartime propaganda emphasized the importance of women's contributions to the war effort: in the factories, in the armed services, in the hospitals, in the home, and on the land. Songs praised the industrial female worker, from the American "Rosie the Riveter" to the English "Girl Who Makes the Thingummybob." Posters celebrating women's work are legion—from the British "Women of Britain—Come into the Factories" (done in socialist-realist style) to the less politically charged American portrait of a young woman with her sleeves rolled up and her muscles bulging, declaring "We Can Do It!" The 1942 radio broadcast "Women of Britain" describes an American journalist walking the streets of London, amazed by the variety of women's work and the skill of women workers, impressed that there is "not a giggle in the gaggle" (NSA ref. nos. 5661-5 and T5661). A book entitled *The British People at War* also shows delighted surprise at women's competence: "Women have always played their part in war, but hitherto, among civilized peoples at any rate, their work has been limited to ministries of succour and healing. . . . In our time, war had become total. . . . It made such stringent demands on the nation's man-power that the women had to share its burdens, both of responsibility and danger, to an extent hitherto unknown. . . . And how magnificently they responded! In industry they tackled successfully work that previously everyone had supposed to require both the strength and skill of men" (219).

Yet women were depicted as dangerous as well. In many of the "Careless Talk Costs Lives" posters, a woman is shown as the source of leaking information. An anti–venereal disease poster declares, "The 'easy' girl-friend spreads Syphilis and Gonorrhoea"—with no mention of the fact that the "easy boyfriend" could do so just as well. At the same time that they were depicted as sources of danger, women were also seen as less strong and competent than men. An enormous amount of advertising was aimed at women, urging products to ease the life of the female war-worker and to cater to her uniquely feminine needs; these products ranged from tinned food to dungarees to tampons ("War work won't wait . . . a man's job doesn't allow for feminine disabilities"). In these advertisements, as in many posters urging women to do war work, women's contributions are considered important partly because they free men to do the really crucial work. (A poster for the Women's Royal Naval Service [WRNS], pronounced "Wrens," urged women to "Join the Wrens and Free a Man for the Fleet.") Thus, the notions of women as essential to the war effort and as secondary to it are constantly intertwined.

Feminist analyses of wartime have underscored the sexist and patriarchal assumptions that lurked in even the most progressive rhetoric and policy. Di Parkin reminds us that even though women were incorporated into all branches of the armed services, they were never allowed to bear arms (1989). Denise Riley remarks that women's war work was always considered temporary, "for the duration only," and that "married women employed in industry were never taken seriously as real workers, and by 1945 the dominant rhetoric described the figures of woman as mother and woman as worker as diametrically opposed and refused to consider the possibility of their combination" (1987, 260). Susan Gubar traces misogynist and patriarchal tendencies in wartime literature and posters and concludes that the war's heightened emphasis on masculinity resulted in denigration of and violence against women (1987).

Analyses of general patterns are immensely useful; yet, as I discovered in my interviews, they do not tell the whole story, for they ignore the realm of personal experience. Telling as these general criticisms are, it is inadequate to judge policy only as it deviates from some prescribed ideal; it is also important to determine how it differed from previous policy and how it affected the lives of those it controlled. Here again, memory can play a key role. When I asked my interviewees about the changes that wartime had wrought for women, they told me not only about the war but about gender relations in the prewar years and in the present. Both women and men had much to say about the ways that wartime changed sexual expectations and behavior.

G.H.R. is an extremely thoughtful and articulate man, a retired teacher, who considered my questions carefully and answered them in great detail. Both he and his wife were from left-wing, working-class families (they met at a youth organization of the Labour Party); he had worked in a factory and she in a post office prior to the war. Like Riley, he discusses the fact that women's jobs often lasted only "for the duration" and comments:

> I don't really believe women gained anything from the wartime experiences in the long run. It certainly suited authority to let it be thought that women were now recognised for what they were worth but it was rather a case of necessity. . . .

There are roughly two sorts of jobs. On one hand there are the interesting ones like doctors, teachers, editors of fashion magazines and there
are the other sort which consist of the unpleasant characteristics of work—
boredom, monotony, drudgery and dirt. Discussing women's work people
tend to dwell on the first sort—the few—rather than the second sort—
the millions. [personal letter]

G.H.R. is correct in pointing out that many discussions of women's emancipation have focused on the upper and middle classes and have ignored the experiences of working-class women. Being fair-minded, he discussed the matter with
his wife and reported that she agreed with his analysis that "between the wars girls
saw marriage as an escape from the boring humdrum life which most girls experienced at work" (personal letter). And lest the word "girl" be seen as a simple
example of an unreflective sexism, I should point out that before the war, most
working-class children left school and began work at the age of fourteen.

On the other hand, not all women married, not all marriages were happy, and
not all men returned from the war. Working-class women chose to take boring
and unfulfilling jobs for the same reasons that working-class men did. Many
women, married and single, wished to remain in paid employment after the war.
Jean McCulloch, from a working-class family in central London, responded to my
question as follows: "Of course the war offered new opportunities for women, wars
always do. Being widowed in 1937, the only jobs available to my mother before
the war were charring or, possibly, some kind of home needlework. We were able
to let a room in the flat (allowed for widows but nobody else) which helped. When
we returned in 1942 mother was able to get a reasonably good job as a cashier in
Selfridges, and in fact she retained this until she retired, well after the end of the
war" (personal letter, 13 January 1993).

Though some skilled work was available to working-class women before the
war, often it required more training than a housewife would have had time to
acquire. As Jean McCulloch mentions, the needle trades were among the few places
in which women could find work. A widow with children faced the additional
problem of finding child care, thus home needlework was a reasonable option. Kitty
Brinks's mother supported her four children in precisely this way. Kitty also became a garment worker and continued in this trade until her retirement. When I
asked her about the changes that wartime had made in women's lives, she responded:

Well, a person like me worked anyway. It didn't give me another opportunity. The only thing was that after the war, there was a shortage of
various crafts, which made it easier to get into a different kind of work.
. . . I had other commitments, so I stayed in what I was doing. But some
of them did. Some of them in my trade, they got jobs in offices where
they wouldn't have got it before the war because they didn't have a degree

in English. They got jobs in post offices because the men weren't there. In food offices, they needed girls because of the ration books. . . . So there was a lot more opportunities for the younger women. And the older ones just went out to work instead of where they used to have to do cleaning, they did more skilled jobs. [personal interview, 25 January 1993]

Anne Lubin credits wartime with giving her the opportunity to leave home, support herself with factory work, meet new people, and learn about trade unionism. In response to my question about how wartime changed women's lives, she replied:

I think it made a tremendous amount of difference to women. A lot of it for the better. First, because their labour was needed, nurseries were set up, and there were 24 hour a day nurseries. So that whatever shift you were working on, if you had young children, they were safe. You knew they were okay.[3] And the children, of course, were fed. . . . Working-class people in particular were never better fed than during that war. They had to fight still to get equal pay with the men, doing the same jobs. . . . I've no doubt it broke up a lot of homes when women realized that it didn't have to be as it used to be. Holding your hand out if you wanted to buy a lipstick or a pair of stockings, which is what a lot of women did. . . . Certainly, for a lot of women, it must have been a very liberating experience. [personal interview, 13 March 1993]

Conversely, Retta Read, who spent her childhood on the vaudeville circuit with her parents, believes that wartime destroyed a valuable part of relationships between the sexes: "I don't believe in women's lib. I liked it when men opened the doors. I liked it when a man drew the chair out whenever you sat down. I liked it when a man said 'Will you go first?' I don't want to be his equal; I liked the old ways. I don't like this, I don't know what you want to call it, this liberation. You know, it's not my scene. I think you've lost a lot. The romance is gone; the value of life has gone" (personal interview, 30 April 1993).

Sylvia Gordon, an office worker in London prior to the war, has mixed feelings about the ways that war changed women's lives:

They took on the men's jobs; they did the men's jobs. And they did them very well. . . . And, well, life was different for a woman. And on top of that, they were earning the money that the men earned, whereas before the war women used to earn a pittance compared with the men. I used to work in an office with men; the men would do exactly the same work as us but they'd get twice as much as us. So, but when the war came along the women were earning the same money as the men.[4] And as far as the money was concerned, that made the women too independent. I think it's gone a bit too far now. It's gone too far over the edge now;

women are not women any more. You know what I mean? They're almost men. [personal interview, 18 June 1993]

Albert Fredericks also sees the changes in women's roles as immense. Interestingly, his comments are highly approving, suggesting that women remained women even though they worked as hard as men—and perhaps even harder: "They proved they were capable of doing any job that the men did. And with a woman's way of doing it. I think that was definitely the biggest change that came over this country as a result of the war—the part that women played. And that's when we first realized what it meant for a woman to bring up a family and do a full-time job as well. I couldn't see most men coping with that" (personal interview, 6 May 1993). Ettie Gontarsky recalls that women participated in many aspects of war work, but that "woman as helper" was still the dominant mode: "I still feel somehow that it was women supporting men. The great feminist movement that we've now seen and has gone on for a long time wasn't yet started in that sense. There was no great sense of women being liberated" (personal interview, 19 April 1993). These comments tell as much about the speakers' present political beliefs as they do about the experience of wartime, which is not to suggest that the speakers are lying or even remembering improperly. They are simply interpreting the past in the light of the present, as all of us must do.

In the above remarks of Anne Lubin, Jean McCulloch, Kitty Brinks, and G.H.R., we can see their own working-class backgrounds reflected in their comments about the way life changed for working-class women. Class played a central, though not necessarily definitive, part in many discussions about whether Britain improved or declined after the war. Creina Musson, an army officer's daughter who spent several years with her parents in Gibraltar and India, comments on Britain's decline as an imperial power and economic giant: "Well, the whole country has changed; the country has got very poor. I mean, we were quite a rich country before. I mean, they say we're one of the richer countries now but—well, we lost the empire to begin with. I mean, that all went. So the services were very much cut. Well, everything has changed, you know. But it's not only because of the war, I mean, it's got worse and worse and worse. I mean, this country is dreadful now! Then, probably so is every other one. [laughs]" (personal interview, 28 July 1993).

Many of my working-class interviewees, by contrast, expressed a general belief that life had improved for the working classes since wartime, with greater opportunities for education and career and with services such as health care provided by the government. The loss of empire and the loss of Britain's status as a "great power" were of less importance to them than the implementation of the welfare state. Ettie Gontarsky, in discussing the postwar change to a Labour government, remarks:

One does take sides in one's own interest. Let's be realistic. And my interests are with what I call the ordinary working people. I've never been money-mad; I've never had loads of money; I've never been property owning; I've never been a business person, and that's where I see my loyalties. I want to see more equality and justice for *more* people, not less. I don't want to see a rich elite and a massive poor and near-poor working class. . . . After the war, the British electorate elected a Labour government. And though I truly can't say I remember clearly how this tremendous change came about, come about it did. So there must have been some kind of change, sea-change, in people's feelings. Must have been a sense of disillusionment, obviously. [personal interview, 19 April 1993]

Since many of my interviewees were Jewish, and many of them the children of immigrants, the issues of anti-Semitism and the treatment of ethnic minorities also figured in their analyses of wartime and postwar life. Anne Lubin's earlier comments about the roles of women during wartime reflect her own experience as a woman, a Jew, and a child of the working class. Like virtually all of my Jewish interviewees, Anne was strongly supportive of the Second World War. (Even the Ministry of Information had no qualms about the patriotism of British Jews. In a secret document of 1939, the ministry decided that propaganda for its Jewish population would be unnecessary, because British Jews "for reasons which require no elaboration are already strongly anti-Nazi" [INF 1/770].) Anne's feelings at the start of the war show that appeasement could not be an option for her:

I mean being Jewish, for one thing, it was a frightening prospect to think that Hitler might win a war. That really was frightening. I can tell you, I can still sometimes feel the tension that there was. When Germany invaded Russia and we held our breath until Churchill announced that we would be an ally of the Soviet Union. Because there was always that feeling—there had been before that—this feeling that we should let those two fight it out between them, and then Britain would be okay. And it really was quite a frightening thought that this might have happened, and it didn't, so there was a great relief when that happened. Oh yes. That was one of the reasons why I volunteered to go and work in a factory instead of waiting until I was called up. [personal interview, 13 March 1993]

Similarly, her personal experiences of being on the receiving end of prejudice strengthened her resolve to fight prejudice in the postwar era. She recalls the 1936 march of the British Union of Fascists through a then largely Jewish section of the East End and compares it with similar racist and anti-immigrant actions today: "They are now marching through the East End again, being deliberately provocative in an area which is mainly Asian. . . . And there are so many racist incidents

going on there. . . . Once again, you see, I was confirmed in my beliefs. You have
to fight this thing. So, we'd fought it—I mean, not me personally, obviously, but
a war had been fought on that issue—and we weren't going to let it, at least I wasn't
going, if there was anything I could do in any way, I wasn't going to let it slip
through" (personal interview, 13 March 1993).

Yet despite the optimistic promises of wartime, many of my working-class
interviewees also saw evidence of decline as the camaraderie of the "finest hour"
dissipated after the war. The wartime caring and concern for others, which was
precipitated by a common danger, was inessential once the danger had gone. One
of my interviewees put this point of view well:

> The one good thing which the war created was the friendly, sympathetic
> and cooperative spirit which existed everywhere. Gone were the class
> barriers. Everyone spoke to everyone and it almost seemed to bind us
> into one huge family.
>
> What a pity that spirit died when the war was over. [private papers]

Many saw the postwar world neither as continuous progress nor as unmiti-
gated decline but as a combination of the two. Betty, I.E.W., and Shirley Ann,
three friends who currently live in suburban London, are working-class women
whose lives were profoundly and irrevocably changed by the Second World War.
Like Creina Musson, they commented on Britain's economic decline. Like Anne
Lubin, they cited the similarities between the prewar Blackshirts and the present-
day National Front. The continuity is not comforting; the postwar world has not
lived up to its expectations:

> *Betty*: With the way things are now you wonder if it was worth going
>   through sometimes.
> *JF*: What do you mean?
> *Betty*: Well, our country, you know, things seem to be slipping down-
>   hill fast, I think. Not only economically, but morally and, you
>   know, there's not—there's no integrity really. You keep hearing all
>   these frauds and that, like that Guinness affair and that sort of
>   thing. And then the crimes.
> *Shirley Ann*: There doesn't seem to be any honesty any more. I mean,
>   you could leave your door open.
> *Betty*: I mean, people were poor before the war, weren't they?
> *Shirley Ann*: Yes.
> *Betty*: But I mean, they didn't go round making a living out of
>   burglary. And with Dad, when he was in the police, I mean, he
>   went in in 1922. My mother never worried about him like the
>   wives must now; the policemen's wives must be worried sick every
>   time their husbands go on duty. The only time I can remember her

being worried was when he had to go up to the Mosley League, the Blackshirts before the war.

JF: Can you tell me about that? Do you remember that?

Betty: Well, yes, I can remember my dad going there. Sometimes he went with the uniform policemen and sometimes he went as a plainclothes, sort of undercover. And these Mosley people, they were Nazis really. Blackshirts they were called. And they used to meet up in the East End, I think it was, which was predominantly a Jewish area. And, you know, they'd have to draft in extra men from the outside boroughs in case there was any flare ups, you see.

JF: Was he ever there when there was any trouble?

Betty: No, I think it was contained quite well really. Yes, I don't think they would have got away with it really, you know. Not like perhaps the National Front—

I.E.W.: I was telling Jean about the fact that we had that awful business down in Lewisham that time with the National Front. [mentions several other National Front incidents]

JF: Was there any trouble? Was there any violence?

I.E.W.: Yes!

Betty: That's what I mean, before the war there wouldn't have been. It would have been absolutely—

I.E.W.: The police could deal with it

Betty: If they were there that stopped it. But it doesn't now. They just get the knives out—

Shirley Ann: There's no respect any more. No respect for oneself or anybody else. [personal interview, 18 February 1993]

Many of my interviewees cited crime as a manifestation of this growing lack of fellow feeling and concern for others. Crime increased during the war, in part because activities such as "careless talk" were suddenly classed as crimes, in part because stringent government regulation and the blackout created golden opportunities. Yet by present-day standards, the wartime rate of serious crime was inconsequential; for example, there were only ninety-five murders in England and Wales in 1944 (Smithies 1982, 152). Several of my interviewees told me that despite the blackout and the air raids, they walked unafraid through the streets of London, "not like now." Anne Lubin, discussing a late-night walk through the blackout, said, "One wasn't afraid of being knocked on the head then." Of course, Anne realized the danger of going around "with the shrapnel falling, like a bloody fool" and realized that part of her bravado depended on her being "young enough not to be frightened" (personal interview, 21 January 1993). Though no one suggested that wartime danger was better than peacetime crime, and all realized that the blitz was far more dangerous than present-day London, there was a general agreement that danger is somehow more acceptable if it comes from the recognizable and supposedly temporary enemies of wartime than from one's own neighbors and compatriots. There is, after all, a difference between a soldier and a criminal.

Discussions of postwar Britain are filled with references to the war and to the ways that society has changed since then, for better and for worse. Though not all changes were directly due to the war itself, many were the continuations and logical extensions of wartime policy. Many of my interviewees celebrated the postwar initiatives that loosened the class system and ameliorated the lot of much of the population. Others lamented the loss of a certain everyday civility, a lifestyle in which courtesy and safety could be taken for granted. In recent years, some have raised their voices in anger and sorrow about Britain's changing status as a nation, a change they attribute to the Second World War.

What's Wrong with the New Jerusalem?

Though the image of the "finest hour" remains potent, particularly to the age group that experienced it, the image has also come under a good deal of attack. In the 1960s these attacks came largely from the left: scholars such as A.J.P. Taylor and Angus Calder attacked the complacency and self-congratulatory sentiments that had abandoned the search for a New Jerusalem (or considered it done), while leaving many social and economic inequities intact. They also attacked the false piety of those who had once promoted the appeasement of Hitler and the dismemberment of Czechoslovakia. R.J.B. Bosworth, in a spirited defense of A.J.P. Taylor's widely misunderstood book *The Origins of the Second World War,* writes: "It [*Origins*] suggested that the endless reciting of the 'lessons of the 1930s' was no longer enough in a modern and still changing world. . . . It hinted that the promises made about genuine democracy in the People's war had not always been achieved or defended, and ought to be renewed" (1993, 43).

In the late 1970s and particularly in the 1980s and 1990s, coeval with the rise of Thatcherism, attacks on the "finest hour" have often come from the New Right, from those who believe that a New Jerusalem was the wrong goal to begin with. These are the "declinists," who believe that Britain's greatness was diminished by World War I and finished by World War II. In attacking the welfare state, the New Right critics are simultaneously attacking the most sacred of British ideas: the belief that the Second World War was right and just, that Winston Churchill was a great leader, and that the defeat of Nazism was worth the sacrifices that Britain made. To these critics, the "finest hour" was, in fact, the "hour of national decline." In 1978, a gloomy little book entitled *What's Wrong with Britain?* tried to determine the root causes of national malaise and lack of economic growth (Hutber 1978). Fifteen commentators, including academics, politicians, businessmen, and one anti-Communist trade unionist, responded to the question. Most of the commentators were drawn from the right; J.B. Priestley was a cranky and disillusioned exception. The reasons given for Britain's poor performance included insufficient scientific training, moral decay, poor industrial management, insufficient capital expenditures, and an overweening dependence on the powers of government. They were, of course, writing when the Labour government was still in power. But after years of Conservative rule, malaise has only deepened and economic problems continue, while the diminishment of social programs has increased personal suffering and overall discontent. A better explanation of British decline was needed, and it was found in the Second World War.

One of the most influential attacks on the "finest hour" came from the military historian Correlli Barnett, whose *The Audit of War: The Illusion and Reality of Britain as a Great Nation* appeared in 1986. Barnett audited wartime and postwar Britain and found them wanting. His thesis, baldly stated on the final page of the book, is that Britain took the wrong path in the wake of the Second World War and is paying for this mistake now:

> The wartime coalition government therefore failed across the whole field of industrial and educational policy to evolve coherent medium-or long-term strategies capable of transforming Britain's obsolete industrial culture, and thereby working a British economic miracle. Instead all the boldness of vision, all the radical planning, all the lavishing of resources, had gone towards working the *social* miracle of New Jerusalem.
>
> But New Jerusalem was not the only wartime fantasy to beguile the British from a cold, clear vision of their true postwar priorities. Their political leaders and the governing Establishment, conditioned as they had been from their Edwardian childhoods to take it for granted that Britain stood in the first rank of nation states, simply could not accept that British power had vanished amid the stupendous events of the Second World War, and that the era of imperial greatness that had begun with Marlborough's victories had now ineluctably closed. [304]

For Barnett, Britain's "true postwar priorities" were ensuring that Britain remained a world power and an industrial giant, rather than ameliorating or eliminating human suffering, a project he terms a "fantasy." Of course, no one doubts that a sound economy is necessary for a nation's prosperity, and Barnett's criticisms of Britain's out-of-date industrial infrastructure are neither new nor surprising. But are his conclusions correct? David Edgerton, in his trenchant analysis of *The Audit of War*, supplies a convincing critique of Barnett's theory of decline: "Rates of economic growth, not to mention levels of output, were higher in the era of 'decline' than the era of 'progress'. . . . The explanations of the 'declinists' too often turn out to be explanations not of relatively slow *growth* but of an imagined stagnation or even absolute decline" (1991, 366; emphasis in original). Nor can the welfare state be blamed for sucking the Exchequer dry, for other industrialized nations, some of which Barnett praises for their economic prosperity, were implementing social welfare programs as well. Even as he praises American industrial prowess, he does not seem to realize that the New Deal served as an inspiration to many European welfare states. Peter Hennessy writes: "If you look at the proportion of GDP going to welfare in the advanced western countries in the first ten years after the Second World War, we are not the odd nation out by any means. It is a common factor, by and large, with one or two exceptions" (1993, 11).

As Hennessy points out, maintaining status as a "great power" takes a great deal of money as well. In direct contrast to Barnett's thesis, Hennessy writes: "If I were in the business of scapegoating, which I am not, . . . I would not round up the usual suspects in the National Insurance Offices, and the National Health Service Boards and the housing departments of the local authorities, or inside the allegedly bleeding hearts of that guilt-ridden generation of public schoolboys in high places. If I was rounding up suspects the one I would put in the dock is the great power fixation. . . . Our likely overseas deficit in the first post-war years would almost entirely match that of our overseas commitments" (1993, 12–13). It is that "guilt-ridden generation of public schoolboys in high places" that Barnett holds responsible for Britain's secondary place in the postwar world. It is they he holds responsible for decline because they listened to cries of the heart rather than coolly and sensibly taking marching orders from the head. David Edgerton writes:

> According to Barnett, the same factor led both to poor industrial performance during the war and to the creation of the welfare state: a British elite which from the nineteenth century was composed of do-gooding liberals rather than modern technocrats who understood the military and economic cruel-real-world. His central argument is that the British elite went wrong when it took to heart liberal arguments, by Herbert Spencer and others, that militant societies would give way to peaceful, free-trading, internationalist, industrial societies. For Barnett modern societies are both industrial and militant; but Britain was neither. Furthermore, its liberalism became romantic, idealistic, moralizing, chivalrous, and aristocratic. *Noblesse oblige* was taken so far that it undermined the British economy and nearly led to the destruction of the state in war through failure to understand the German threat. [1986, 361]

Although the Liberal Party virtually disappeared during the war and in the postwar period (resurfacing in the 1980s with its marriage of convenience to the Social Democrats), welfare state capitalism emerged as a kind of liberal compromise between charity and entitlement. Just as wartime policy stood on a remarkably broad political base, so too did the formation and implementation of the welfare state; it managed to combine ideas of Victorian charity and Christian good works with militant trade unionism, liberal reformism, and orthodox Marxism. Barnett looks at this motley brew with horror; this is no way to run a country. In his view, the effete, impractical, and softheaded British elite have allowed a misguided compassion to destroy the economy and benefit no one, much like a person who gives away a fortune penny by penny. But did it benefit no one? To take only one example, the rate of poverty declined enormously. As Peter Hennessy points out, the number of working-class households in York living in poverty was 31.1 percent in 1936 and only 2.77 percent in 1950. But for the wartime and postwar interventions that Barnett decries, the rate of poverty would have fallen only to 22.18 percent (Hennessy 1993, 11). As Keith Middlemas points out, "What the Attlee government did was to give the better life of the 1930s to everyone. . . . For those in work the 1930s was a very good period indeed" (1993, 18). And to many this goal seemed more important and reasonable than maintaining some romantic vision of Britain as a "great power."

Even though Barnett eschews party politics and claims to be speaking only in the pure pursuit of the facts, there is a deeply political (and highly subjective) subtext to his criticisms. Although he insists that he is in favor of economic planning and good management and even praises instances when such strategy is controlled by the state, when planning comes about by left-wing measures, he damns it as "artificial." Barnett's use of natural metaphors is quite telling; though all economies are artificial, he uses this term as a criticism: "For the truth is that Britain's war economy was in its fundamental nature artificial: as dependent on American strength as a patient on a life-support machine" (1986, 145). His choice of medical metaphor is extremely interesting; he does not compare American aid to antibiotics or lifesaving surgery but instead picks on the easy target of medical last resort. When he speaks of economic initiatives designed to improve the economy in the "depressed areas" (urban areas of high unemployment), he suggests that there is a "natural course of events" in economics, and that New Jerusalemites, blinded by tears of pity, are foolishly attempting to thwart nature: "Given the evidence, the depressed areas must be accounted an outmoded industrial-cum-social species on the way to extinction. . . . The alternative first proffered by the Barlow Report and thereafter by New Jerusalemers like Dalton was for the state artificially to perpetuate the endangered species in the industrial equivalents of zoos or wild-life reserves" (251). He even refers to the Great Depression as a "hurricane" (259), suggesting that it is simply a natural force we can do nothing about, not an unnecessary event brought about by human greed and lack of foresight.

Barnett's politics are further revealed in his loathing for trade unions and his utter contempt for the working class. The following passage, though especially vicious, is by no means atypical:

Whether Britain in the postwar era was to prove, in Conrad's phrase, "stronger than the storms" did not depend on natural bounty like coal and iron-ore, or on the once heaped-up and now dissipated wealth of the past, or even on the present conditions of her industries, but on the intelligence, energy, zeal and adaptability of the mass of her industrial population. Unfortunately, this mass lacked such qualities in marked degree. Of all the grievous long-term handicaps bequeathed to modern Britain by her experience in the first industrial revolution from 1780 to 1850, one of the most pervasive and the most intractable was that of a workforce too largely composed of coolies, with the psychology and primitive culture to be expected of coolies. (1986, 187)

He then goes on to detail the deficiencies of this "class of coolies," using suspect methodologies such as 1930s intelligence tests (see Gould 1981) and expressing well-bred horror at descriptions of Glasgow slums as "dirty and untidy" (without seeming to realize that cleanliness requires money and time, neither of which was in great supply in the Gorbals). When the working classes, whom he condemns as lacking zeal and energy, take matters into their own hands, he recoils in disgust. In discussing workers' grievances that resulted in wartime strikes, he dismisses them all as "trivial and parochial," and in one of his few references to women workers, he calls them "females," a term more often used in regard to animals than people (154–55). One wonders if he considers such a hopeless mass capable of self-government.

In discussing policy formation in 1941, Barnett writes, "In education, as with other aspects of New Jerusalem, Whitehall found itself frogmarched by progressive public opinion faster and further than it might have wished" (1986, 277). He seems to be decrying an unfortunate case of a government, shanghaied by democracy, into bowing to the wishes of the governed. One also grows uneasy with his constant praise of German accomplishments during the Nazi period. In comparing German and British wartime production, he writes: "In making comparisons it has to be recalled that Germany fought her war from first to last out of her own national resources or the resources of countries her army could occupy: the German machine-tool industry equipped German factories; German factories designed and manufactured the Wehrmacht's excellent equipment; and the Wehrmacht never ran short of munitions until the very end of the war. Britain, however, critically depended on the United States, not only as a basic economic lifeline, but also for huge supplies of equipment both for factories and for the armed forces" (61). Surely Barnett is not suggesting that it is superior policy to occupy foreign countries, loot their riches, and employ slave labor than to depend on foreign aid? Surely not. Yet he manages to write a book dealing extensively with wartime Germany without ever once mentioning the Holocaust or even seeming aware that it happened. Indeed, he writes of Nazi policy as "muddled" and "vacillating," seemingly unaware of its evil purpose. Though Barnett avows no political loyalties, he is riding the crest of a wave; he is the soul mate of a group of New Right critics who combine a hatred of all things liberal with a fervent devotion to liberalism's most enduring contributions: nationalism and industrial capitalism. This combination is, of course, the same one that breeds fascism.

The limits of historical memory appear to be two generations. People avoid the mistakes of their parents and go on to make the mistakes of their grandparents. In the 1990s in Europe and the United States, we are awash with the rhetoric of the 1930s: isolationism, blaming immigrants for unemployment, seeing fascism as an acceptable alternative, treating palliative social programs as the opening wedge for the specter of communism. The British are justifiably proud that fascism never entered British politics as more than a strand of the lunatic fringe. But partial approval of fascist methods and turning a blind eye to fascist policy is something else again. Sir Oswald Mosley's aristocratic background made him, in some ways, an odd choice for the leader of a party with a lower middle-class base. On the other hand, Mosley's class did contain people who had a sneaking—and sometimes not so sneaking—admiration for rough-and-tumble political movements that kept Jews and workers in their place.

The British New Right are not fascists, of course; they are Conservatives, at least in name. But their conservatism is not the genteel variety of Lady Bountiful or the political (if shamefaced) pragmatism that produced the wartime coalition. Old-fashioned conservatism values all the things that New Rightists disdain: honor, duty, breeding, manners, great literature, liberal education, individualism, a well-run empire, and kindness to servants. To the New Right, this old-fashioned conservatism is just the sort of softheaded pap that is ruining the country. Ian Buruma, in a chilling analysis of several New Right texts, writes: "Even though the so-called new right came onto the scene in the 1970s to launch an attack on left-wing orthodoxies, the worst vitriol was reserved for patricians in the Tory Party, 'wets' with bleeding hearts, who were supposedly letting the country go to the dogs. Thinkers of the new right, of whom few were born into the upper class, had contempt for upper-class liberals—politicians such as Sir Ian Gilmour, the former owner of *The Spectator*. They were seen as members of a ruling class that refused to rule" (1994, 67).

The prototype of these bleeding-heart Tories, the archvillain who pushed Britain down the slippery slope, was Churchill. It was this warmongering, imperial-minded, upper-class former Liberal who sacrificed British interests for a bunch of foreigners. In *Churchill: The End of Glory*, John Charmley writes, "Churchill's leadership was inspiring, but at the end it was barren, it led nowhere, and there were no heirs of the tradition" (1993, 3). Many of the New Right lament the fact that Churchill did not continue Chamberlain's policy of appeasement and avoid war with the Nazis in any way possible. In 1989 Maurice Cowling wrote in the *Sunday Telegraph*: "It is wrong to assume that a dominant Germany would have been more intolerable to Britain than the Soviet Union was to become, or that British politicians had a duty to risk British lives to prevent Hitler from behaving intolerably against Germans and others" (quoted in Buruma 1994, 68). This is approximately the same argument that Lord Haw-Haw made in his final broadcast on 30 April 1945. Even more bloodcurdling is Alan Clark, whose recently published diaries have become the toast of the New Right. Clark, a former cabinet minister in the Thatcher government, has his own thoughts on the 1940s: "The Third Reich got people back to work. And they really didn't need all that horsing around with the Wehrmacht and the SS. *The Holocaust was completely unnecessary*" (quoted in Buruma 1994, 69; emphasis added). After reading Clark, one is inclined to believe that there is, indeed, something rotten in Denmark.

The "finest hour," once an unassailable source of national consensus, has become a political football. It was once attacked for promoting complacent imagery instead of substantive change; now it is attacked for sowing the seeds of hope in the first place. Kitty Brinks, one of my interviewees, quotes her mother as saying, "Somebody that's had a good meal doesn't believe that there are any hungry people about" (personal interview, 25 January 1993). The New Right shows that there are also members of the well-fed who simply do not care.

Conclusion

It is hard to imagine an affliction more terrible than the loss of memory. Memory is the very stuff of identity, the keeper of the past, the recorder of consciousness, the essence of personality. Without memories, we have no way of knowing if we have even lived. Nations too need memories to define themselves, a past that legitimates the present and helps to determine the future. For many years, a major part of Britain's identity rested on its experience of World War II, its memory of that era as the nation's finest hour. Yet nations are made up of many individuals, each of whom has personal memories that may not coincide with national self-presentation. To attack the "finest hour" is, for some, to bring personal memories to the forefront. It is to attack the personal memories of others. World War II was probably the most influential event of the twentieth century, and those who experienced it have memories that have shaped the rest of their lives. That these memories are widely divergent and lovingly defended is only to be expected. To attack such memories is to attack one's very being.

Memory focuses on the past but cannot affect it. It does, however, affect the present and future, and this gives it additional importance as an object of study. The ways in which we remember the past affect what we will do in the present and future: the causes we support, the people we see as allies or as enemies, the techniques that we choose to employ. Memory, like history, tries to make sense of the past in ways that enable us to live in the present. Few have expressed this idea more eloquently than Walter Benjamin, who was destroyed by an enemy he so clearly recognized: "To articulate the past historically does not mean to recognize it 'the way it really was' (Ranke). It means to seize hold of a memory as it flashes up at a moment of danger. . . . Only that historian will have the gift of fanning the spark of hope in the past who is firmly convinced that *even the dead* will not be safe from the enemy if he wins. And this enemy has not ceased to be victorious" (1968, 255; emphasis in original). Keeping faith with the dead is a way of not betraying the living. But the lessons of the past are neither simple nor clear-cut. The narratives of nationhood may claim one interpretation, while the voices of individuals may whisper many others.

The dialectic between history and memory will not resolve and go away, nor should it, for it is in the interstices between them that scholars may find their most fruitful work. History takes account of the structural, the political, the overarching epochal narratives. Memory deals with the personal, the individual, the narratives of self. Both memory and history are essential, and each is insufficient without the other. History is the voice of the group; memory the voice of the individual. The tension between the individual and the group is the fundamental problem of scholarship; it is also the fundamental problem of democracy. It is a tension often resolved by an invocation of the past, and this, among other reasons, is why the past matters.

Notes

1. Introduction

1. This line is taken from "London Pride," a celebrated wartime song written by Noël Coward.

2. Paul Fussell's *Wartime: Understanding and Behavior in the Second World War*, Clive Ponting's *1940: Myth and Reality*, and Tom Harrisson's *Living through the Blitz* are examples of scholarly works that condemn memory as a barrier to the truth. These works will be treated in more depth in subsequent chapters.

3. The National Sound Archive and the Imperial War Museum have large collections of tapes and transcripts of oral history interviews about the war years. The London Museum of Jewish Life has a smaller collection of oral history tapes and transcripts that deal specifically with London's Jewish population. In my own interviews, I found people willing, even eager, to talk: to tell their own stories and to fill in the gaps they felt existed in the official histories.

4. Some of them are quite valuable as primary sources, however. Examples include Jonathan Croall's *Don't You Know There's a War On?*, Ben Wicks's *Waiting for the All Clear*, and the many publications of the Age Exchange.

5. See, for example, Luisa Passerini's *Fascism in Popular Memory* and *Memory and Totalitarianism*.

6. There are several books describing wartime cultural activities, such as Guy Morgan's *Red Roses Every Night*; there are books of songs such as W. Ray Stephens's *Memories and Melodies of World War II*; and there are memoirs that highlight cultural artifacts, such as Vera Lynn's *We'll Meet Again*.

7. How to refer to the people with whom one works is another vexed problem. I prefer not to use the anthropological term "informant," which sounds unpleasantly similar to "informer." "Respondent," a term found in oral history and sociology, implies too passive a role for people who usually do much more than simply "respond" to the interviewer's questions. I have chosen to use the more neutral word "interviewee."

8. The issue of class in Great Britain has been the subject of numerous studies, and it is beyond the scope of this book to summarize them here. In the United States, class has also been of great interest to scholars, but in popular discussion it means little more than "income." In Great Britain, "class" refers not only (and sometimes not primarily)

to income or profession but also to a host of customs and traditions, ranging from speech patterns to clothing styles to food preferences. In referring to the class origins of my interviewees, I have based my definition of class largely on profession. The children of artisans, manual workers, and servants are considered "working class"; the children of business people and professionals are considered "middle class." "Upper class" is an even more vexed term; in Great Britain, the term can refer to those in power (making it synonymous with "ruling class"), to those who hold hereditary titles, or to those who are free from earning a living, among other definitions. Nancy Mitford, in her brilliant satire of her own (upper) class, takes language as the definitive class marker and defends her argument with the scholarship of linguist Alan Ross: "The Professor, pointing out that it is solely by their language that the upper classes nowadays are distinguished (since they are neither cleaner, richer, nor better-educated than anybody else), has invented a useful formula: U (for upper class)-speaker versus non-U-speaker" (1956, 325).

9. None of my interviewees were from the upper classes, though one (an army officer's daughter) came close. Instead, I made liberal use of the many written sources that describe upper-class experiences of the war.

10. There is some information about the wartime experience of Jews in the archives of the London Museum of Jewish Life. There are also scattered references in other archives, though the Ministry of Information files on anti-Semitism were closed for seventy-five years and hence will not be available for decades. Possibly because of the inaccessibility of certain archival documents, Kushner's book is one of the few scholarly studies of wartime Britain to use oral sources.

11. Virtually all young men were called up for military service, except for those in essential occupations and those for whom health problems rendered military service impossible. Though military service did not necessarily mean leaving London, many men spent at least part of their military service overseas or in other parts of Britain. Women were also called up for military service, though there were more exemptions than for men, such as those for mothers whose children had not been evacuated. Many women were given the option to perform wartime service in factories, hospitals, or on the land instead of in the armed forces. Women's wartime service could usually be performed without leaving Britain and often without leaving London. Only a relatively small number of women volunteers served overseas. Children were encouraged to leave London and other large cities; a massive evacuation of children from London took place before war had even been declared.

2. London Can Take It

1. Though the entirety of the United Kingdom was at war, I shall be concentrating only on the war as it was experienced in Great Britain, with special emphasis on London.

2. Mass-Observation was founded in 1937 in order to observe and document British behavior. Tom Harrisson, one of its founders, describes its purpose: "to supply accurate observation of everyday life and *real* (not just published) public moods, an

anthropology and a mass-documentation for a vast sector of normal life which did not, at that time, seem to be adequately considered by the media, the arts, the social scientists, even by political leaders" (1990,13; emphasis in original). During the war, it remained an independent organization, with Harrisson at the helm, but it worked closely with governmental bodies and provided vast amounts of information useful to governmental efforts. Wartime Social Survey was set up in 1940 to determine the effectiveness of governmental policies and propaganda. According to a Home Intelligence memorandum, "The Wartime Social Survey is an independent body controlled by, but not part of, the Ministry of Information" (INF 1/273). Wartime Social Survey fieldworkers, most of whom were women, used techniques of direct observation combined with interviews of a random sample of the population. In addition to the Ministry of Information, the Wartime Social Survey conducted studies for the Ministry of Food, the Ministry of Health, and the Board of Trade, among others.

3. For an excellent analysis of Hitler's rhetoric, see Kenneth Burke's essay "The Rhetoric of Hitler's 'Battle'" in *The Philosophy of Literary Form*.

3. Careless Talk Costs Lives

1. Aristotle defined rhetoric as "the faculty of discovering the possible means of persuasion in reference to any subject whatever" (1975, 15). More than two thousand years later, the *International Encyclopedia of Communications* defined rhetoric in much the same way: "The study and teaching of practical, usually persuasive, communication" (Arnold 1989, 461).

2. The identification of evil with physical deformity has long precedent in British folk culture. In the ballad "The Dæmon Lover" (Child 243), the faithless wife discovered her lover's true identity when "she espied his cloven foot / And she wept right bitterlie." During the war, some people apparently believed that all Germans, whatever their politics, had hairy wrists: while on holiday in Scotland, George and Irene Wagner, who were refugees from Nazi Germany, met an innkeeper who would not believe they were Germans because they did not have hairy wrists.

3. As a broadcaster for the BBC, Orwell was subject to the ministry's extensive and often erratic censorship. W.J. West (1985) suggests that the ministry served as the model for the Ministry of Truth in *1984*, and one feels a shock of recognition upon reading Minister of Information Brendan Bracken's memoranda signed "B.B."

4. A guinea was worth one pound and one shilling in the monetary system used prior to 1969. In 1940 the sum of fifteen guineas was more than many working-class people earned in a month.

5. According to Charles J. Rolo, Americans were treated to a similar experience by Fred Kaltenbach, a German-American Nazi broadcasting from Germany under the name "Lord Hee-Haw" (1942, 96).

6. English was the lingua franca of the United Kingdom, but Welsh, Gaelic, Scots, and a variety of dialects were very much alive.

7. Great Britain comprises England, Scotland, and Wales, while the United Kingdom includes Great Britain and Northern Ireland. The British Isles include Great Britain and the entirety of Ireland. In practice, many people outside of Scotland, Wales, and Northern Ireland incorrectly use "England" to mean Britain, as people incorrectly use "Holland" to mean the Netherlands.

8. In similar fashion, the Germans during World War II were nicknamed "Jerry."

9. During the first three years of the war, enemy action killed more British civilians than soldiers. Over the total course of the war, 60,000 British civilians and 264,000 members of the British armed forces died as a result of the war (Calder 1969, 226).

10. Admiration for the Russians abounds in wartime sources, among people of all political stripes. Interestingly, it seems to be remembered only by those on the left.

11. A wartime poster shows a young boy in shorts and a tin helmet, his gas mask slung on his back, trying to lift a sandbag that is too heavy for him. A man, also with gas mask and tin helmet, leans over him and points an admonishing finger. The legend reads: "Leave this to us Sonny—*You* ought to be out of London."

12. Of course, even such harsh and specific criticism of the government could be turned into propaganda in its favor. The government did not stifle criticism or freedom of speech even during its darkest days; though Britain may have been imperfect, it was still a democracy.

4. Time Long Past

1. Hayden White's seminal work *Metahistory* has informed much of my argument in this chapter.

2. Brecht's poem "Fragen eines lesenden Arbeiters" ("Questions of a Worker Who Reads") is a series of questions asked by a worker who has been reading history books and is puzzled by the fact that only kings, generals, and wealthy men are mentioned therein. The worker wonders who really built the gates of Thebes, since it is unlikely that the king listed as the builder hauled the stones himself. The worker wants to know about the masons and builders who built the Great Wall of China, and the soldiers who brought about the victories attributed to Caesar, Alexander the Great, and others. The English lines quoted in the text are my translation of Brecht's original: "Cäsar schlug die Gallier. Hatte er nicht weingstens einen Koch bei sich?"

3. Strictly speaking, the term "near miss" is incorrect; more properly, such incidents should be called "near hits." However, near miss is common in everyday speech and is the term used by my interviewees; hence I have chosen to retain it here.

4. She could have been smelling airplane fuel, the ash from fires, the residue of bombs, or some combination thereof, and using her experience of air raids to estimate the length. However, there is no indication of any such rational or scientific explanation in Marjorie Newton's letter. It is clear that her mother employed sensory, rather than analytic, skills, using what Anthony Giddens (1979) calls "practical consciousness" as opposed to "discursive consciousness."

5. The Stoke Newington shelter also housed British Jews, such as Vera and her family.

6. Several Ministry of Information reports remark that Jews did not engage in the kind of hysterical behavior attributed to them, and the ministry tried to publicize this fact by producing a small amount of philo-Semitic propaganda. Interestingly, in the report quoted above, "Cockney" is used as an ethnic category that excludes Jews, in the fashion discussed by Gareth Stedman Jones, rather than in the more inclusive usage of the term employed by Harry Geduld.

7. In recent years, a small right-wing contingent has seriously attacked the overall wartime narrative. The commentary of this group is discussed in the final chapter of this book.

5. London Pride

1. In this discussion I will analyze music as it exists in what is loosely termed "Western culture," more precisely in the culture of the United States and Great Britain. In other cultures, the word "music" may have no precise translation, and the art no exact equivalent. I make no claims to universality, nor am I troubled by this lack, for I do not believe that an entity's power need be diminished by the fact of its being culturally bound.

2. "Deutschland, erwache!" ("Germany, Awake!") and the Horst Wessel song were well-known Nazi songs.

3. One of the World War I songs, "Keep the Home Fires Burning," in retrospect strikes one as ironic in a city about to suffer massive firebombing.

4. Several people told me that the pop singer Petula Clark got her start by singing in wartime shelters.

5. According to ministry reports, films about "dangerous gossip" made a great impression. Another film, which encouraged women to seek work in munitions factories, infuriated women who had been looking for such work but had been unable to find it (INF 1/264, 24 and 26 July 1940).

6. The musical preferences of *servicewomen* received virtually no attention.

7. Irregularities are, of course, in the eye and ear of the beholder. The famed "Scots snap," a short note followed by a sustained note, sounds irregular if one is expecting a Sousa march. To one reared on Scots music, it is probably the Sousa marches that are full of irregularities.

8. The one exception to this trend is Wales, where the number of classes in music appreciation actually went down slightly. This is a puzzling development, since Wales is generally reckoned the most musical part of Great Britain. It is difficult to obtain census data for the war years (no official census was taken in Britain between 1931 and 1951), but a possible explanation could be a decline in population in Wales, with jobs being readily available in the armed forces and in the factories of England. Since interest in music was already high before the war, the decline in classes could simply reflect the decline in population.

9. The internment of German and Austrian refugees, along with their pro-Nazi compatriots, remains an embarrassment of British wartime policy. A.J.P. Taylor's insistence that German Jewish refugees were "warmly welcomed" (1965, 419) does not apply for internees who were held without decent food, housing, or medical care, were separated from their families, and were denied books and letters. Italians who had resided in Britain for less than twenty years were given the same treatment. After the *Arandora Star*, a ship carrying fifteen hundred German and Italian internees to Canada, was torpedoed and sunk by the Germans on 2 July 1940, the internment policy lost some of its ferocity. Nonetheless, many internment camps were filled with musicians and intellectuals escaping from the Third Reich. Martin Goldenberg, an Austrian Jewish refugee who came to England as a child in March 1939, was interned as an enemy alien the following year. He remembers the camp orchestra filled with former members of the Berlin and Vienna Philharmonic Orchestras (quoted in Croall 1988, 134).

10. According to Noël Coward, the tunes of both "London Pride" and "Deutschland über alles" are based on a traditional lavender-seller's song, "Won't you buy my sweet blooming lavender / there are sixteen blue bunches one penny." Coward says: "This age-old melody was appropriated by the Germans and used as a foundation for 'Deutschland über alles,' and I considered that the time had come for us to have it back in London where it belonged" (1953, 191).

11. A Cockney is conventionally defined as someone born within the sound of Bow bells.

12. In the film *Judgment at Nuremberg*, people sing "Lili Marlene" as Marlene Dietrich walks the ravaged streets with Spencer Tracy. Dietrich points out that the original German words are much sadder than their English translations.

13. Lale Andersen writes that she became so identified with the song that people asked her to sign autographs not with her own name but with that of Lili Marleen (1972, 221).

14. According to Professor Harry Geduld, Lale Andersen's nationality is ambiguous. She was born in Bremerhaven, Germany, but may not have held German citizenship. Some sources list her as being Swedish, others as Danish.

15. I am indebted to Harry Geduld (personal communication) for calling to my attention a French version of "The Siegfried Line." Written by P. Misraki, the French version is entitled "On Ira Prendre Ligne sur la Siegfried." Professor Geduld has also unearthed a remarkable parody entitled "I'm Sending You the Siegfried Line" that was performed by the Nazi band Charlie and His Orchestra. Though the musicians were German, this band played American-inspired swing music with lyrics in English. Many of the lyrics are quite savage, but the music is tame and insipid, for jazz was strictly forbidden by the Nazi regime. Their version of "The Siegfried Line" shares nothing with the British song except the pun; it does, however, play on several British songs from World War I. A reissuing from Harlequin of their "German Propaganda Swing" also includes a sentimental English version of "Lili Marlene," a viciously anti-Semitic parody of "Onward, Christian Soldiers," and a sneering takeoff of "Bye, Bye, Blackbird" that says, "Bye, Bye, Empire" (*German Propaganda Swing 1939–1944, Volume Three*).

16. As previously noted, the BBC "and the rest" did increase their performances and broadcasts of British music, precisely in order to celebrate British culture. Yet the feeling of musical inferiority remained, as is apparent in Hughes's comments. His ignorance of Japanese music and the blazing musical ethnocentrism it represents were probably not uncommon in his day.

17. Another interesting case of the capturing and inverting of cultural symbols was the use of the two-finger gesture during the Vietnam War, when it was used to signify "peace" rather than "victory."

6. Present Tense

1. In 1997, a Labour government was returned under the leadership of Tony Blair, who excised the socialist clauses from Labour's platform and dubbed his party "New Labour." Many of my interviewees were outraged by what they considered Blair's betrayal of Labour's principles. It is perhaps significant that Blair is a relatively young man, born after the end of the Second World War, and hence has no memory of life before the welfare state.

2. Margaret Thatcher earned the epithet "milk-snatcher" when she was education minister in the early 1970s. As a cost-cutting maneuver, Thatcher ended children's automatic right to free milk in school.

3. Though the government did set up day nurseries for the children of war workers, the demand was always greater than the supply. Most women had to make their own arrangements for child care. See Summerfield 1988: 105-6.

4. Many women fought for pay equity during the war, but this goal was never achieved. The gap between men's and women's wages narrowed by only a small amount. See Summerfield 1988.

References

Printed Sources

Andersen, Lale. 1972. *Leben mit einem Lied.* Stuttgart: Deutsche Verlags-Anstalt BmgH.

Aristotle. 1975. *The "Art" of Rhetoric.* Trans. John Henry Freese. Cambridge, Mass.: Harvard Univ. Press; London: William Heinemann.

Arnold, Carroll C. 1989. "Rhetoric." In *International Encyclopedia of Communications,* ed. Erik Barnouw, George Gerbner, Wilbur Schramm, Tobia L. Worth, and Larry Gross. Vol. 3. New York: Oxford Univ. Press. Published jointly with the Annenberg School of Communications, University of Pennsylvania.

Bakhtin, M.M. 1981. *The Dialogic Imagination.* Trans. Caryl Emerson and Michael Holquist. Austin: Univ. of Texas Press.

Banning, Margaret Culkin. 1943. *Letters from England.* New York: Harper and Brothers.

Barnett, Correlli. 1986. *The Audit of War: The Illusion and Reality of Britain as a Great Nation.* London: Macmillan.

Bauman, Richard. 1986. *Story, Performance, and Event.* Cambridge: Cambridge Univ. Press.

Bauman, Richard, and Joel Sherzer. 1989. "Introduction to the Second Edition." In *Explorations in the Ethnography of Speaking,* ed. Richard Bauman and Joel Sherzer, pp. ix–xxvii. Cambridge: Cambridge Univ. Press.

Benjamin, Walter. 1968. *Illuminations.* Trans. Harry Zohn. New York: Schocken Books.

Blacking, John. 1973. *How Musical Is Man?* Seattle: Univ. of Washington Press.

Boni, Margaret Bradford, ed. 1947. *The Fireside Book of Folk Songs.* New York: Simon and Schuster.

Bosworth, R.J.B. 1993. *Explaining Auschwitz and Hiroshima: History Writing and the Second World War 1945–1990.* London: Routledge.

Brecht, Bertolt. 1961. *Gedichte 1934–1941.* Frankfurt am Main: Suhrkamp Verlag.

Briggs, Susan. 1975. *The Home Front: War Years in Britain 1939–1945.* London: George Weidenfeld and Nicolson.

The British People at War. 1944. London: Odhams Press.

Brown, Roger, and James Kulik. 1982 (1977). "Flashbulb Memories." In *Memory Observed: Remembering in Natural Contexts,* ed. Ulric Neisser, pp. 23–40. San Francisco: W.H. Freeman.

Brown, W.J. 1941. *What Have I to Lose?* London: George Allen and Unwin.

Buckhout, Robert. 1982 (1974). "Eyewitness Testimony." In *Memory Observed: Remembering in Natural Contexts*, ed. Ulric Neisser, pp. 116–25. San Francisco: W.H. Freeman.

Burke, Kenneth. 1962. *A Grammar of Motives and a Rhetoric of Motives*. Cleveland: World Publishing.

————. 1967. *The Philosophy of Literary Form*. Baton Rouge: Louisiana State Univ. Press.

————. 1967. "The Rhetoric of Hitler's 'Battle.'" In *The Philosophy of Literary Form*, pp. 191–220. Baton Rouge: Louisiana State Univ. Press.

Burke, Peter. 1987. "Introduction." In *The Social History of Language*, ed. Peter Burke and Roy Porter. Cambridge: Cambridge Univ. Press.

Buruma, Ian. 1994. "Action Anglaise." *New York Review of Books* 41(17): 66–71.

Cahill, Larry, Bruce Prins, Michael Weber, and James L. McGaugh. 1994. "ß-Adrenergic Activation and Memory for Emotional Events." *Nature* 371:702–4.

Calder, Angus. 1969. *The People's War: Britain 1939–1945*. London: Pimlico.

————. 1991. *The Myth of the Blitz*. London: Pimlico.

Calder, Ritchie. 1941. *Carry On, London*. London: English Universities Press.

Callinicos, Alex. 1988. *Making History*. Ithaca, N.Y.: Cornell Univ. Press.

Cantwell, John D. 1989. *Images of War: British Posters 1939–45*. London: Her Majesty's Stationery Office.

Carr, E.H. 1961. *What Is History?* New York: Alfred A. Knopf.

Child, Francis James. 1882. *The English and Scottish Popular Ballads*. Boston: Houghton-Mifflin.

Charmley, John. 1993. *Churchill: The End of Glory*. London: Hodder and Stoughton.

Christie, Agatha. 1982. *The Mousetrap*. New York: Samuel French.

Cole, J.A. 1964. *Lord Haw-Haw and William Joyce: The Full Story*. New York: Farrar, Straus and Giroux.

Colegrove, F.W. 1982 (1899). "The Day They Heard about Lincoln." In *Memory Observed: Remembering in Natural Contexts*, ed. Ulric Neisser, pp. 41–42. San Francisco: W.H. Freeman.

Cooper, Tim. 1992. "Revealed: The Forgotten 164 Killed by One Bomb." *Evening Standard*, 21 October, p. 20.

Coward, Noël. 1953. *The Noël Coward Song Book*. New York: Simon and Schuster.

Croall, Jonathan. 1988. *Don't You Know There's a War On? The People's Voice 1939–45*. London: Hutchinson.

Crook, Gladys. 1946. "New Audiences." In *Hinrichsen's Musical Year Book 1945–46*, ed. Ralph Hill and Max Hinrichsen. London: Hinrichsen Editions.

Eade, Charles, comp. 1951. *The War Speeches of the Rt. Hon. Winston S. Churchill*. Vol. 1. London: Cassell.

Edgerton, David. 1991. "The Prophet Militant and Industrial: The Peculiarities of Correlli Barnett." In *Twentieth Century British History* 2(3): 360–79.

Fawkes, Richard. 1978. *Fighting for a Laugh: Entertaining the British and American Armed Forces 1939–1946*. London: MacDonald and Jane's.

Fussell, Paul. 1989. *Wartime: Understanding and Behavior in the Second World War.* New York: Oxford Univ. Press.

Fyfe, Hamilton. n.d. *But for Britain . . .* London: MacDonald.

Gardner, John Hargrave Wells. 1940. *Words Win Wars.* London: Darton.

Geduld, Harry. 1995. "Yes, Virginia, I Really Did See the Battle of Britain: A Kid's-Eye View of World War II." In *Contemporary Authors Autobiography Series,* vol. 1, pp. 45–59. Gale Research.

German Propaganda Swing 1939–1944, Volume Three. 1988. Crawley, West Sussex: Harlequin.

Giddens, Anthony. 1979. *Central Problems in Social Theory.* Berkeley: Univ. of California Press.

Ginzburg, Carlo. 1980. *The Cheese and the Worms.* Trans. John and Anne Tedeschi. New York: Penguin Books.

Gould, Stephen Jay. 1981. *The Mismeasure of Man.* New York: W.W. Norton.

Gramsci, Antonio. 1981. "Antonio Gramsci." In *Culture, Ideology and Social Process,* ed. Tony Bennett, Graham Martin, Colin Mercer, and Janet Woollacott. London: Batsford Academic and Educational Ltd. in association with Open Univ. Press.

Gubar, Susan. 1987. "'This Is My Rifle, This Is My Gun': World War II and the Blitz on Women." In *Behind the Lines: Gender and the Two World Wars,* ed. Margaret Randolph Higonnet, Jane Jenson, Sonya Michel, and Margaret Collins Weitz, pp. 227–59. New Haven, Conn.: Yale Univ. Press.

Halbwachs, Maurice. 1980. *The Collective Memory.* Trans. Francis J. Ditter Jr. and Vida Yazdi Ditter. New York: Harper and Row.

———. 1992. *On Collective Memory.* Ed. and trans. Lewis A. Coser. Chicago: Univ. of Chicago Press.

Harrisson, Tom. 1990. *Living through the Blitz.* London: Penguin Books.

Havighurst, Alfred F. 1985. *Britain in Transition: The Twentieth Century.* Chicago: Univ. of Chicago Press.

Hennessy, Peter. 1993. "Never Again." In *What Difference Did the War Make?* ed. Brian Brivati and Harriet Jones, pp. 3–19 Leicester: Leicester Univ. Press.

Huggett, Frank E. 1979. *Goodnight Sweetheart: Songs and Memories of the Second World War.* London: W.H. Allen.

Hughes, Spike. 1945. "Popular Taste in Music." In *Pilot Papers: Social Essays and Documents,* ed. Charles Madge. No. 1. London: Pilot Press.

Hutber, Patrick, ed. 1978. *What's Wrong with Britain?* London: Sphere Books.

Joad, C.E.M. 1941. *What Is at Stake, and Why Not Say So?* London: Victor Gollancz.

Jones, Gareth Stedman. 1989. "The 'Cockney' and the Nation, 1780–1988." In *Metropolis London: Histories and Representations Since 1800,* ed. David Feldman and Gareth Stedman Jones, pp. 272–324. London: Routledge.

Joseph, Sir Keith. 1978. "Proclaim the Message: Keynes Is Dead!" In *What's Wrong with Britain?* ed. Patrick Hutber, pp. 99–106. London: Sphere Books.

Kendall, Doreen. 1992. "The Bethnal Green Tube Disaster." *East London Record* 15:27–35.

Kushner, Tony. 1989. *The Persistence of Prejudice: Antisemitism in British Society during the Second World War.* Manchester: Manchester Univ. Press.

—. 1992. *The Heymishe Front: Jews in War-time Britain.* London: London Museum of Jewish Life.

Labov, William, and Joshua Waletzky. 1967. "Narrative Analysis: Oral Versions of Personal Experience." In *Essays on the Verbal and Visual Arts*, ed. June Helm, pp. 12–44. Seattle: American Ethnological Society.

Lambert, Richard S. 1940. *Home Front.* Toronto: Ryerson Press.

Legge, Walter. 1946. "A Report on E.N.S.A. Music Division's Work, September 1943 to July 1944." In *Hinrichsen's Musical Year Book 1945–46*, ed. Ralph Hill and Max Hinrichsen, pp. 308–12. London: Hinrichsen Editions.

Loftus, Elizabeth F., and John C. Palmer. 1982 (1974). "Reconstruction of Automobile Destruction." In *Memory Observed: Remembering in Natural Contexts*, ed. Ulric Neisser, pp. 109–15. San Francisco: W.H. Freeman.

Lowenthal, David. 1985. *The Past Is a Foreign Country.* Cambridge: Cambridge Univ. Press.

Lynn, Vera. 1975. *Vocal Refrain.* London: W.H. Allen.

Lynn, Vera, with Robin Cross and Jenny de Gex. 1989. *We'll Meet Again: A Personal and Social Memory of World War II.* London: Sidgwick and Jackson.

Mack, Joanna, and Steve Humphries. 1985. *The Making of Modern London 1939–1945: London at War.* London: Sidgwick and Jackson.

Marwick, Arthur. 1976. *The Home Front: The British and the Second World War.* London: Thames and Hudson.

Marx, Karl. 1959. "Excerpts from *The Eighteenth Brumaire of Louis Bonaparte.*" In *Basic Writings on Politics and Philosophy*, ed. Lewis S. Feuer, pp. 318–48. Garden City, N.J.: Anchor Books.

McKenna, Marian C. 1976. *Myra Hess: A Portrait.* London: Hamish Hamilton.

McLaine, Ian. 1979. *Ministry of Morale: Home Front Morale and the Ministry of Information in World War II.* London: George Allen and Unwin.

Middlemas, Keith. 1993. "Commentary." In *What Difference Did the War Make?*, ed. Brian Brivati and Harriet Jones, pp. 16–18. Leicester: Leicester Univ. Press.

Minns, Raynes. 1980. *Bombers and Mash: The Domestic Front 1939–45.* London: Virago.

Mitford, Nancy. 1956. "The English Aristocracy." In *Noblesse Oblige*, ed. Nancy Mitford. New York: Harper and Brothers.

Morgan, Guy. 1948. *Red Roses Every Night: An Account of London Cinemas Under Fire.* London: Quality Press.

Mouffe, Chantal. 1981. "Hegemony and Ideology in Gramsci." In *Culture, Ideology and Social Process*, ed. Tony Bennett, Graham Martin, Colin Mercer, and Janet Woollacott, pp. 219–34. London: Batsford Academic and Educational Ltd. in association with Open Univ. Press.

Munsterberg, H. 1909. *On the Witness Stand.* New York: Doubleday.

Murdoch, Brian. 1990. *Fighting Songs and Warring Words: Popular Lyrics of Two World Wars.* London: Routledge.

Myers, Rollo H. 1948. "Music since 1939." In *Since 1939: Ballet, Films, Music, Painting*, by Arnold L. Haskell, Dilys Powell, Rollo Myers, and Robin Ironside, pp. 97–144. London: Readers Union by arrangement with the British Council.

Neisser, Ulric. 1982. "Snapshots or Benchmarks?" In *Memory Observed: Remembering in Natural Contexts*, ed. Ulric Neisser, pp. 43–48. San Francisco: W.H. Freeman.

Nevins, Allan. 1984. "Oral History: How and Why It Was Born, the Uses of Oral History." In *Oral History: An Interdisciplinary Anthology*, ed. David K. Dunaway and Willa K. Baum, pp. 27–36. Nashville, Tenn.: American Association for State and Local History in cooperation with the Oral History Association.

Nicolson, Harold. 1939. *Why Britain Is at War*. Harmondsworth, Middlesex: Penguin Books.

Ong, Walter J. 1982. *Orality and Literacy: The Technologizing of the Word*. London: Methuen.

Orwell, George. 1949. *1984*. New York: New American Library.

Page, Martin, ed. 1973. *Kiss Me Goodnight, Sergeant Major: The Songs and Ballads of World War II*. London: Hart-Davis, MacGibbon.

Parkin, Di. 1989. "Women in the Armed Services, 1940–5." In *Patriotism: The Making and Unmaking of British National Identity, Vol. II: Minorities and Outsiders*, ed. Raphael Samuel, pp. 158–70. London: Routledge.

Passerini, Luisa. 1987. *Fascism in Popular Memory: The Cultural Experience of the Turin Working Class*. Cambridge: Cambridge Univ. Press.

———. 1992. *Memory and Totalitarianism*. Oxford: Oxford Univ. Press.

Ponting, Clive. 1990. *1940: Myth and Reality*. Chicago: Ivan R. Dee.

Portelli, Alessandro. 1991. *The Death of Luigi Trastulli and Other Stories: Form and Meaning in Oral History*. Albany: State Univ. of New York Press.

Ricoeur, Paul. 1984a. *Time and Narrative*. Trans. Kathleen McLaughlin and David Pellauer. Vol. 1. Chicago: Univ. of Chicago Press.

———. 1984b. *The Reality of the Historical Past*. Milwaukee, Wis.: Marquette Univ. Press.

———. 1986. *Lectures on Ideology and Utopia*. New York: Columbia Univ. Press.

Riley, Denise. 1987. "Some Peculiarities of Social Policy Concerning Women in Wartime and Postwar Britain." In *Behind the Lines: Gender and the Two World Wars*, ed. Margaret Randolph Higonnet, Jane Jenson, Sonya Michel, and Margaret Collins Weitz, pp. 260–71. New Haven, Conn.: Yale Univ. Press.

Rolo, Charles J. 1942. *Radio Goes to War: The "Fourth Front."* New York: G.P. Putnam's Sons.

Ross, A.S.C. 1954. "Linguistic Class-Indicators in Present-Day English." *Neuphilologische Mitteilungen* 55:20–56.

Saltzman, Rachelle Hope. 1988. *The 1926 General Strike and the Volunteers: Upper-Class British Play Genres and the Maintenance of Social Class*. Ph.D. diss., University of Texas at Austin.

Samuel, Raphael. 1989. "Introduction: Exciting to Be English." In *Patriotism: The Making and Unmaking of British National Identity, Vol. I: History and Politics*, ed. Raphael Samuel, pp. xviii–lxvii. London: Routledge.

Schutz, Alfred. 1971. "Making Music Together: A Study in Social Relationships." In *Collected Papers II: Studies in Social Theory*. The Hague: Martinus Nijhoff.

Silvey, Robert J.E. 1944. "Radio Audience Research in Great Britain." In *Radio Research 1942–1943*, ed. Paul F. Lazarsfeld and Frank N. Stanton, pp. 151–77. New York: Essential Books.

———. 1946. "The Public for Broadcast Music." In *Hinrichsen's Musical Year Book 1945–46*, ed. Ralph Hill and Max Hinrichsen, pp. 170–175. London: Hinrichsen Editions.

Smithies, Edward. 1982. *Crime in Wartime: A Social History of Crime in World War II*. London: George Allen and Unwin.

Stephens, W. Ray. 1987. *Memories and Melodies of World War II*. Erin, Ontario: Boston Mills Press.

Stern, William. 1982 (1904). "Realistic Experiments." In *Memory Observed: Remembering in Natural Contexts*, ed. Ulric Neisser, pp. 95–108. San Francisco: W.H. Freeman.

Struther, Jan. 1940. *Mrs. Miniver*. New York: Harcourt, Brace.

Summerfield, Penny. 1988. "Women, War and Social Change: Women in Britain in World War II." In *Total War and Social Change*, ed. Arthur Marwick, pp. 95–118. New York: St. Martin's Press.

Taylor, A.J.P. 1963. *The Origins of the Second World War*. Harmondsworth, Middlesex: Penguin Books.

———. 1965. *English History 1914–1945*. New York: Oxford Univ. Press.

Thompson, E.P. 1985. *The Heavy Dancers*. New York: Pantheon Books.

Thompson, John B. 1984. *Studies in the Theory of Ideology*. Berkeley: Univ. of California Press.

Thompson, Paul. 1988. *The Voice of the Past: Oral History*. Oxford: Oxford Univ. Press.

Thompson, Stith. 1955. *Motif-Index of Folk Literature*. Vol. 1. Bloomington: Indiana Univ. Press.

U.S. Supreme Court. 1982 (1968). "Photographs and Personal Identification: A Legal View." In *Memory Observed: Remembering in Natural Contexts*, ed. Ulric Neisser, pp. 126–29. San Francisco: W.H. Freeman.

Vološinov, V.N. 1973. *Marxism and the Philosophy of Language*. Trans. Ladislav Matejka and I.R. Titunik. Cambridge, Mass.: Harvard Univ. Press.

West, W.J., ed. 1985. *Orwell: The War Broadcasts*. London: Duckworth/British Broadcasting Corporation.

White, Hayden. 1973. *Metahistory: The Historical Imagination in Nineteenth-Century Europe*. Baltimore: Johns Hopkins Univ. Press.

Wicks, Ben. 1990. *Waiting for the All Clear*. London: Bloomsbury.

Williams, Raymond. 1966. *Communications*. London: Chatto and Windus.

———. 1977. *Marxism and Literature*. Oxford: Oxford Univ. Press.

Woon, Basil. 1941. *Hell Came to London*. London: Peter Davies.

Workers' Educational Association. 1946. "The Workers' Educational Association and

Music Appreciation." In *Hinrichsen's Musical Year Book 1945–46*, ed. Ralph Hill and Max Hinrichsen, pp. 240–42. London: Hinrichsen Editions.

Worsley, Francis. 1946. "Anatomy of Itma." In *Pilot Papers: Social Essays and Documents*, ed. Charles Madge. Vol. 1, no. 1, January 1946. London: Pilot Press.

Wright, Lawrence. n.d. *War-Time Songs*. London: Lawrence Wright Music Company.

Wright, Patrick. 1985. *On Living in an Old Country: The National Past in Contemporary Britain*. London: Verso.

Archival Sources

Documents from the Imperial War Museum, Department of Documents

The Papers of George and Helena Britton
The Papers of Oswald Edwards
The Papers of Vere Hodgson
The Papers of Josephine Oakman
The Papers of William Bernard Regan and Violet Ivy Regan
The Papers of Len Waller
Document 88/21/1

Sound Documents, National Sound Archive (NSA)

All sound documents were originally broadcast by the British Broadcasting Corporation and are listed chronologically by date of broadcast.

"Postscript to the News: The Epic of Dunkirk" by J.B. Priestley, NSA ref. nos 2562 and LP2560b5, broadcast 5 June 1940.

"Address at Welsh National Eisteddfod" by David Lloyd George, NSA ref. nos. 2619-20 and LP26122b6, broadcast 7 August 1940.

"Marching to Victory: War Songs from the Dominions," NSA ref. nos. 2577-9 and MT2577, broadcast 11 August 1940.

"Surface Air Raid Shelter," NSA ref. nos. 2951 and LP2943f7, broadcast 5 October 1940.

"Below Ground," NSA ref. nos. 2730-2 and LP2716b1, broadcast 1 November 1940.

"Christmas under Fire," King George VI's Christmas message, NSA ref. nos. 2831-2 and LP2812f2, broadcast 25 December 1940.

"Tonight's Talk: What Have I to Gain?" by W.J. Brown, NSA ref. nos. 6348-9 and LP6348, broadcast 14 February 1941.

"The Air Bombardment of Great Britain" by Winston Churchill, NSA ref. nos. 3843-5 and T3843b1, broadcast 14 July 1941.

"Music for 'Lift Up Your Hearts,'" NSA ref. nos. 3324-6 and MT3324, broadcast 19 September 1941.

"ITMA," NSA ref. nos. F41/102 and T28071b1, broadcast 26 September 1941.

"Introduction to 'Worker's Playtime'" by John Watt, NSA ref. nos. 4125 and LP4125b1, broadcast 26 October 1941.

"Introduction to 'Worker's Playtime'" by Ernest Bevin, NSA ref. nos. 3411 and LP3404f7, broadcast 25 and 28 October 1941.

"ITMA," NSA ref. nos. 2684-R, F42/3, and T28071b2, broadcast 9 January 1942.

"Symphony in V," NSA ref. nos. 4000 and T3999b2, broadcast 27 February 1942.

"Living Opinion: What Shall We Do with Our Future?" NSA ref. nos. 4621-3 and T4621b1, broadcast 22 May 1942.

"London's Burning," NSA ref. nos. 4396 and T4395b3-5, broadcast 4 July 1942.

"An American in England: Women of Britain," NSA ref. nos. 5661-5 and T5661, broadcast 5 September 1942.

"Tonight's Talk: New Scheme for Social Security" by Sir William Beveridge, NSA ref. nos. 4936-8 and LP4936f1, broadcast 2 December 1942.

"State Organised Medicine," NSA ref. nos. 5932-4 and T5932b1, broadcast 5 February 1943.

"The Stage Presents," NSA ref. no. LP37454f3, broadcast 16 May 1943.

"Lili Marlene" (Italian version), NSA ref. nos. 7624 and T7599b8, and "Lili Marlene" (Canadian version), NSA ref. nos. 7624 and T7599b7, broadcast 12 September 1943.

"ITMA," NSA ref. nos. 22230-3 and T22226b2, broadcast 28 October 1943.

"ITMA," Navy edition, broadcast 13 January 1944.

"London Calling: Signature Tune," NSA ref. nos. 6586 and T6573b7, broadcast 9 February 1944.

"Godfrey Talbot in Italy," NSA ref. no. LP33654b8, broadcast 27 September 1944.

"As a Great Year Ends," NSA ref. nos. F44/214 and LP24739-40, broadcast 31 December 1944.

"Lili Marlene" (German version), NSA ref. nos. 8306 and T8282b3, broadcast 26 February 1945.

"Journey into Daylight" by J.B. Priestley, NSA ref. nos. 8018-9 and MT8018, broadcast 11 May 1945.

"'V' Signal," NSA ref. no. LP36346b10, broadcast 4 June 1945.

Documents from the Public Record Office, Kew

All documents are from the wartime Ministry of Information and are listed in numeric order by document number.

INF 1/10, A.46/2, "Functions and Organisation of Ministry." Memorandum by E.B. Morgan, 18 September 1939, and comments on memorandum.

INF 1/159, "Regulations for Censorship 1938," subheading "Principles of Censorship," paragraph 8, 15 July 1938.

INF 1, 174A, B.123, "Broadcast Commentaries on Effects of Air-Raids. Criticisms." "Advice on the Preparation of Broadcasts Describing Conditions in Heavily Raided Towns," 31 March 1941.

INF 1/770, "General Policy Regarding Jews: Formation of a Jewish Section." Memorandum of 20 May 1940.

INF 1, 250, H. 1/1, "Planning Committee—Minutes of Occasional Meetings and Reports." "Home Morale Emergency Committee, First Interim Report," paragraphs 5 and 14, 22 May 1940.

INF 1, 250, H. 1/1, "Planning Committee—Minutes of Occasional Meetings and Reports." "Report of Planning Committee on a Home Moral [*sic*] Campaign," section 3, paragraph c, 1940.

INF 1, 250, H. 1/1, "Planning Committee—Minutes of Occasional Meetings and Reports." "Home Morale Emergency Committee Report to Policy Committee," paragraph 3 ("Suspicion"), paragraph 4 ("Class-Feeling"), 4 June 1940.

INF 1, 250, H. 1/1, "Planning Committee—Minutes of Occasional Meetings and Reports." Letter from Sir Wyndham Deedes to Sir Kenneth Clark, 23 July 1940.

INF 1/257, H.7, "Home Morale: Defeatism and Fifth Column Activities." Letter from Gavin Brown.

INF 1/257, H.7, "Home Morale: Defeatism and Fifth Column Activities." Minute Sheet from Mr. C.H. Wilson to Sir Kenneth Clark.

INF 1/257, H.7, "Home Morale: Defeatism and Fifth Column Activities." "The Fifth Column: How It Works."

INF 1/263, H.I. 85, "Wartime Social Survey: Memoranda on Policy and Organization." "Ministry of Information Public Opinion Studies by Wartime Social Survey," subheading "Results," paragraph 5, 15 August 1940.

INF 1/264, 97/15 Home Intelligence, "Morale: Summaries of Daily Reports." 18 May 1940; 19 and 20 May 1940; 21 May 1940; 22 May 1940; 24 May 1940; 25 May 1940; 27 May 1940; 30 May 1940; 31 May 1940; 5 June 1940; 6 June 1940; 7 June 1940; 10 June 1940; 13 June 1940; 28 June 1940; 10 July 1940; 11 July 1940; 12 July 1940; 17 July 1940; 20 July 1940; 22 July 1940; 2 August 1940; 5 August 1940; 6 August 1940; 14 August 1940; 17 August 1940; 26 August 1940; 28 August 1940; 31 August 1940; 5 September 1940; 6 September 1940; 7 September 1940; 9 September 1940; 10 September 1940; 11 September 1940; 12 September 1940

INF 1/265, H.I. 1005/1, Part A, "Rumours. Haw-Haw Legends." May 1940–December 1940.

INF 1/273, H.I. 1008, "War-time Social Survey Policy." Memorandum from Mr. Parker.

INF 1/284, H.I. 1013/3, "Public Morale: Monthly Reports for the Cabinet." "War Cabinet, Report on Home Opinion, Memorandum by the Minister of Information," 9 October 1942.

INF 1/318, H.P. 345, "Uses of Psychology in Propaganda." "Memorandum on the Functions of the Ministry of Information" by Edward Glover.

INF 1/318, H.P. 345, "Uses of Psychology in Propaganda." Letter from Professor Bartlett.

INF 1/862, X140, "Post War Aims." "Social Reconstruction at Home," paragraphs 15 and 17, December 1939–August 1940.

INF 5/76. G.P.O. Film Unit. "Ordinary People: London Carries On."

INF 6/29, C.F.U. 272. "Myra Hess." 1946.

INF 6/328, C.F.U. 201. "London Can Take It." 1940.

INF 6/330, C.F.U. 204. "Ordinary People." 1941.

INF 6/338, C.F.U. 212. "Words for Battle." 1941.

INF 6/339, C.F.U. 213. "Listen to Britain." 1942.

INF 6/360, C.F.U. 241. "The True Story of Lilli Marlene." 1944.

INF 6/471, MI 173. "C.E.M.A." 1945.

INF 6/525, MI 256. "Dangerous Comment." 1939.

INF 6/1810. "Tell Me Where Is Fancy Bread." 1943.

INF 6/1813, MT 292. "Thereby Hangs a Tail." 1945.

Index